TRADE IN BANKING AND INSURANCE SERVICES

TRADE IN BANKING AND INSURANCE SERVICES

By

Dr. Srijanani Devarakonda

Associate Professor

Vignana Jyothi Institute of Management

Hyderabad

DISCOVERY PUBLISHING HOUSE

INDIA

Published by:

DISCOVERY PUBLISHING HOUSE
4383/4B, Ansari Road, Darya Ganj
New Delhi-110 002 (India)
Phone : +91-11-23279245; 23253475; 43596065
E-mail : discoverybooksindia@gmail.com
discoverypublishinghouse@gmail.com
namitwasan9@gmail.com
web : www.discoverypublishinggroup.com

First Edition: **2023**

ISBN: 978-93-94917-05-7

Trade in Banking and Insurance Services

Printed at:
Infinity Imaging Systems
Delhi

Dedicated to my Father
Late Sri Devarakonda Kesava Murthy
who has been my inspiration and a great teacher

Preface

The process of development usually coincides with a growing role of services in the economy alongside a reduced role for agriculture and industry. Trade in services can help create opportunities for countries to expand their outputs of services in sectors where they have a comparative advantage. Services exports can be an important part of a developing countries growth strategy. In addition, imports of services can significantly improve performance by bringing greater competition, international best practice, better skills and technologies and investment capital. The entry of Foreign Service providers resulted in better services for domestic consumers and improved the performance and competitiveness of domestic firms.

Of all the services, financial Services are fundamental to economic growth and development. Banking, savings and investment, insurance, debt, and equity financing help private citizens save money, guard against uncertainty, and build credit, while enabling businesses to start up, expand, increase efficiency, and compete in local and international markets.

The financial services sector is the largest in the world in terms of earnings, comprised of a wide range of businesses including merchant banks, stock brokerages and insurance companies among others. A significant share of innovation is originating outside the traditional financial services sector.

Many countries, both developed and developing, have to a significant extent liberalized and opened up their financial sector to foreign financial providers. Openness to foreign financial service providers often results in greater efficiency, dynamism, and innovation. It stimulates improvements in domestic banking performance and has significant potential benefits for consumers through improved service delivery and for the economy as a whole through a more efficient allocation of capital.

Insurance is a key component for economic development and an important driver for growth. Insurance is therefore an accelerator for economic growth, an economic shock absorber and is intertwined with development and protection of social assets and aspirations.

Given the importance of Banking and Insurance services and their trade, the present study aims at examining the various reforms in banking and insurance, trends in trade in banking and insurance services and the relationship between economic growth and banking and insurance performance.

Special Thanks to my research supervisor Dr. Usha Munipalle, Professor, Department of Commerce, Osmania University, Hyderabad, has been a guiding spirit and a source of inspiration for the conception and completion of the present study. I am indebted to Dr. Ch.S. Durgaprasad, Director, Vignana Jyothi Institute of Management for his motivation. Without his encouragement and support it would not have been possible for me to undertake this work.

I will be failing in my duty if I don't thank my mother, my father, my brother, my sister who have given me great moral support. My heartfelt thanks to my husband, Sandeep, and my son, Sohan, for making my life meaningful and for being silent and constant source of moral and emotional support. I wish to express my heartfelt gratitude to all of them for their help in many ways without which I would not have dared to take up this academic work.

Dr. Srijanani Devarakonda

Contents

Abbreviations

BIPER:	Banking and insurance share as percentage of total services of country
BLUE:	Best Linear Unbiased Estimator
BPM5:	Balance of Payments Manual 5
BPM6:	Balance of Payments Manual 6
CAMEL:	Capital Adequacy, Asset Quality, Management, Earnings and Liquidity
CCIL:	Clearing Corporation of India Limited
CIBIL:	Credit Information Bureau of India Limited
CRR:	Cash Reserve Ratio
CRS:	Constant returns to scale
CV:	Coefficient of Variation
DEA:	Data Envelopment Analysis
DMU:	Decision Making Unit
DOMCREDIT:	Domestic Credit as percentage of Gross Domestic Product of country
EBOPS:	Extended Balance of Payments
EU:	European Union
FDI:	Foreign Direct Investment
FTA:	Free Trade Agreement
GATS:	General Agreement on Trade in Services
GDP:	Gross Domestic Product
GDPP:	Gross domestic Product Per capita of country
GIC:	General Insurance Corporation
GNP:	Gross National Product
HSBC:	Hong Kong Shanghai Banking Corporation
IBEF:	India Brand Equity Foundation

ICICI:	Industrial Credit Investment Corporation of India
IDBI:	Industrial Development Bank Of India
IMF:	International Monetary Fund
IRDA:	Insurance Regulatory Development Authority
ITBS:	International Trade in Banking Service
ITBS:	International trade in banking services
LIC:	Life Insurance Corporation
M2GD:	M2 to Gross Domestic Product of country
MNC:	Multi-National Companies
NBFCs:	Non-Banking Financial Companies
NRI:	Non-resident Indian
NDS:	Negotiated Dealing System
NPA:	Non Performing Asset
OECD:	Organization for Economic Co-operation and Development
PSBs:	Public Sector Banks
RBI:	Reserve Bank of India
ROA:	Return on Assets
RTGS:	Real Time Gross Settlement System
SARFAESI:	Securitization and Reconstruction of Financial Assets and Enforcement of security Interest Act, 2002s
SCB:	Scheduled Commercial Banks
SLR:	Statutory Liquidity Ratio
SME:	Small and Medium Enterprises
SWIFT:	Society for Worldwide Interbank Financial Telecommunication
UAE:	United Arab Emirates
UBI:	United Bank of India
UCB:	United Commercial Bank
ULIPS:	Unit-linked insurance plans
UK:	United Kingdom
UNCTAD:	United Nations Conference on Trade and Development
US:	United States
USD:	United States Dollar
WOS:	Wholly Owned Subsidiaries
WTO:	World Trade Organization

Introduction

BACKGROUND

Services sector is a major contributor to the world's GDP, this phenomenon is also visible in the developing economies. Services share in the world GDP was 65.9 per cent share in the US $ 72.7 Trillion world GDP (at current prices) in 2012.

Historically it has been established that as the economy progresses the impact of services sector has been growing compared to industry and agricultural sectors. India too is following the same trend which is visible from the share of service sector's contribution to GDP. US ranks first in services GDP, with Japan and China a distant second and third, India ranked 10th in terms of overall GDP and 12th in terms of services GDP. India's services sector to GDP is 64.8% (2013)[1]. India has the second largest growing services sector with its compound annual growth rate at 9 percent, just below China's 10.9 per cent, during the last 11 year period from 2001 to 2012 as per the Economic Survey for 2013-14.

The services GDP growth at 6.8 per cent for the sector was above the 4.7 per cent overall GDP growth in 2013-14. The growth was seen in financing, insurance, real estate and business services at 12.9 per cent.

As a natural consequence trade in services took the centre stage. World services export was at 0.1 per cent in 2001 and reached a high of 5.5 per cent in 2013. India's share in world services exports, which increased from 0.6 per cent in 1990 to 1.1 per cent in 2000 and further to 3.3 per cent in 2013, has been increasing faster than its share in world merchandise exports as per the Economic Survey. India's exports of financial services moving in tandem with global exports of financial services recorded a high growth of 34.4 per cent in 2013-14.

The reasons for the growth of this service sector are the urbanization, privatization and more demand for the intermediate and final consumer services. Several factors can be identified for this development. Extensive negotiations to liberalize trade in financial services have taken place, a major achievement in this respect has been the General Agreement on Trade in Services (GATS) under the aegis of the World Trade Organization (WTO).

All branches of economic activity today are fundamentally dependent on access to financial services. A healthy and stable financial system, accompanied by sound macroeconomic management and prudential regulation, is an essential ingredient for sustained growth. Conversely, macroeconomic instability arising from weaknesses in the financial sector can undermine the process of development.

Trade is playing a growing role in the financial services sector in many countries through cross-border transactions, and even more so through foreign direct investment. As economic activities become more globalized through increased trade and investment flows, the need for internationalized intermediation and risk management services has also grown. Significant potential exists for further expansion in financial services trade, as economies continue to be opened and technological developments present new trading opportunities. The continuing globalization of economic activity and the challenge of attracting productive investment in a competitive international environment necessitate the need to maintain a healthy and efficient financial sector.

International cooperation in financial matters is hardly new, but the General Agreement on Trade in Services (GATS), which emerged from the Uruguay Round, represents the first multilateral effort to establish rules governing services trade, including financial services, and to provide a framework for multilateral negotiations on improved market access for foreign services and service suppliers. This effort was a significant step forward in international economic cooperation. It reflected a growing realization of the economic importance of trade in services, as well as the need for closer cooperation among nations in a world of growing interdependence. The GATS negotiations in the financial services sector covered all financial services, including banking, securities, and insurance.

The General Agreement on Trade in Services (GATS) is the first multilateral trade agreement to cover trade in services. It entered into force as a result of the Uruguay Round negotiations, in January 1995. The GATS mandates WTO member governments to progressively liberalize trade in services through successive rounds of negotiations.

GATS Services sector Classification List

1. Business Services

2. Communication Services
3. Construction and Related Engineering services
4. Distribution Services
5. Educational Services
6. Environmental Services
7. Financial Services
    (a) All insurance and insurance related services
    (b) Banking and other financial Services
8. Health Related and Social Services
9. Tourism and Travel Related Services
10. Recreational, Cultural and Sporting Services
11. Transport Services
12. Other Services not included elsewhere

The General Agreement on Trade in Services (GATS) defines a 'financial service' as 'any service of a financial nature offered by a financial service supplier of a Member'. Financial services include two broad categories of services: insurance and insurance-related services and banking and other financial services. These two categories are further broken down into the following:

- **Insurance and insurance-related services**

Insurance and insurance-related services cover life and non-life insurance, reinsurance, insurance intermediation such as brokerage and agency services, and services auxiliary to insurance such as consultancy and actuarial services.

- **Banking and other financial services**

This category includes all banking and other financial services, such as the acceptance of deposits and other repayable funds from the public, lending of all types (e.g. consumer credit, mortgage credit, factoring and financing of commercial transaction), financial leasing, all payment and money transmission services (e.g. credit, charge and debit cards, travellers' cheques and bankers' drafts), guarantees and commitments, securities trading, underwriting, money broking, asset management, settlement and clearing services, provision and transfer of financial information, and advisory, intermediation and other auxiliary financial services.

In any country, the financial services sector is typically made up of banks, trust and loan companies, credit unions, life and health insurance companies, property and casualty insurance companies, securities traders and exchanges, investment fund companies, pension funds, finance and leasing companies, insurance agents and brokers, and a myriad of auxiliary service providers, such as independent financial advisors, actuaries, and intermediaries. Apart from its participation in GDP, the financial services sector is usually a significant contributor to employment.

Cross-border trade in financial services is becoming increasingly important in the international economy. The cross-border provision of financial services to customers – including institutions, other financial services firms, and individuals is slowly getting established and is also continuing to expand. Technological developments have reached a point where the provision of cross-border services to customers is now both possible and commercially feasible. These possibilities are yet to become widely accepted and used by customers and firms.

With this background the present study has been taken up in the area of trade in financial services with special focus on banking and insurance services.

NEED AND IMPORTANCE OF THE STUDY

The development of a country rests on the existence of a robust financial system. Time and again it has been established that a healthy and a stable financial system is undoubtedly an essential ingredient for sustained growth of any economy. Infact all the branches of economic activity are fundamentally dependent on access to financial services. Hence, financial services constitute an important segment of the financial system.

The robust performance of the services sector is attributable to a host of factors, internal and external; the important among them is the liberalisation of the financial sector acted as a catalyst for faster growth of the financial services. The liberalization of trade in financial services is one aspect of the trend toward international economic and financial integration. A close look at the experience of the last two decades shows that the relative importance of the component ' financial and business services' has steadily increased within the services sector.

Trade in financial services is defined as the provision of financial services by a financial firm located in one country to a customer residing in another country without the establishment of a commercial presence, such as a branch or subsidiary, in the country of the customer (the "host country"). In this definition, the country in which the financial firm is "located" could be either the country in which it is headquartered or a third country in which it has a branch or subsidiary.

For the purpose of negotiations, the GATS classify the entire range of services trade into following four 'modes' (United Nations 2002). The GATS covers services supplied.

(a) *Mode 1 – Cross border trade*: from the territory of one Member into the territory of any other Member;

(b) *Mode 2 – Consumption abroad*: in the territory of one Member to the service consumer of any other Member;

(c) *Mode 3 – Commercial presence*: by a service supplier of one Member, through commercial presence, in the territory of any other Member; and

(d) *Mode 4 – Presence of natural persons*: by a service supplier of one Member, through the presence of natural persons of a Member in the territory of any other Member.

An extensive review of literature has been done covering the following areas:

1. Trade in services, trade in services and growth, barriers to trade in services
2. Trade in Financial Services
3. Reforms in the financial services sector
4. Reforms in Insurance services sector
5. Trade in banking services
6. Efficiency of the banks and branches of banks
7. Insurance services and international trade
8. Insurance services and reforms
9. Insurance services and impact on growth
10. Economic growth and banking and insurance performance etc.,

The gap in the research has been identified through survey of literature. The research gap identified is that there is no study on the impact of the entry of foreign banks on the performance of domestic banks. Although there are studies which measure the impact of banking and insurance trade performance on the economic growth of economies, there is no study which studies the impact of economic growth on the banking and insurance performance in low and middle income countries in south Asia.

The present study attempts to fill the gap and the focus would be on trade in banking services of foreign banks in India and on the efficiency of the domestic banks during 2005-2013. It examines if the entry of foreign banks has an impact on the performance and efficiency of the domestic banks. It also studies the impact of Economic growth on the banking and insurance trade performance, and identified the literature gap in study in South Asian countries of the Low and Middle income group.

With this background, the present study has been undertaken with the following objectives.

OBJECTIVES OF THE STUDY:

1. To examine the reforms in the banking and insurance sector in India
2. To study the composition, trends and efficiency in the trade in banking services w.r.t Indian banks abroad and foreign banks in India
3. To study the trends in the trade in insurance services in India w.r.t insurance penetration and insurance density
4. To examine the impact of the economic growth on the performance of trade in banking and insurance services in select Asian countries

PLAN OF THE STUDY

The present research is organized into seven chapters.

Chapter 1 - Introduction

Chapter 2 - Review of Literature

Chapter 3 - Reforms in the Banking and Insurance Sectors

Chapter 4 - Trends in Trade in Banking Services

Chapter 5 - Trends in Trade in Insurance Services

Chapter 6 - Economic Growth and Banking and Insurance Performance

Chapter 7 - Findings, Conclusion and Suggestions

Chapter one is introductory in nature.

It gives a brief background of financial services and the need for the present study. It also spells out the Objectives, scope, period, methodological framework and the limitations of the study.

Chapter two gives the review of literature.

It shows how the gap in the literature is identified after examining the literature under various topics relating to services trade, barriers to trade, international trade in banking services, international trade in insurance services, do foreign banks follow the customers abroad etc.

Chapter three examines the Reforms in the banking and insurance sectors in India.

The reforms of the financial services sector, especially banking and insurance services reforms leading to the growth of trade are discussed. The reforms like reduction in the SLR, CRR, restructuring of public sector banks, allowing new private banks and foreign banks, encouraging competition, reducing NPAs etc., in banking and increasing operational autonomy of insurance providers and review the regulation and supervision of the insurance sector and opening up of the insurance sector.

Chapter four covers the trends in the trade in banking services.

The performance of the Indian banks abroad and the foreign banks in India is examined for the various aspects like number of banks, number of branches, number of employees, business trends, profitability, activity wise business and country wise comparison to give a global picture and India's position. The impact of the entry of foreign banks on the performance of the domestic banks is also studied w.r.t efficiency taking three inputs i.e., number of branches, number of employees and operating expenses and three outputs i.e., profit per employee, interest income and return on assets.

Chapter five discusses in detail the trends in the trade in insurance services.

The international trade in insurance services is studied with respect to insurance penetration and insurance density in India and a global picture is given.

Chapter six examines the relationship between economic growth and the banking and insurance trade performance for select Asian Countries taking BIPER as the independent variable and DOMCREDIT, GDPP and M2toGDP as the dependent variables representing economic growth of the economies.

The study is done for select Asian countries.

Chapter seven gives Findings, Conclusion and Suggestions

The findings, conclusion and suggestions are presented in this chapter.

PERIOD OF THE STUDY

For the present study there are two financial services considered whose data is taken differently for the study. The data of the analysis of trade in banking services is taken for a period of 9 years i.e., 2005 to 2013 as the international trade in banking services data is available from only 2005.

The period of the study for trade in insurance Services is 13 years i.e., from 2001 to 2013.

SCOPE OF THE STUDY

The scope of the study is as follows:

The reforms related to the trade in banking and insurance services only are covered. Of all the services as per the GATS classification in the present study only banking and insurance services trade are covered. The study also examines the impact of the entry of foreign banks on the performance of the domestic banks. The banking and insurance trade performance and its relationship with growth is also examined for select Asian Countries. The countries selected for the analysis are Indonesia, India, Sri Lanka, Maldives, Malaysia, Pakistan, Phillippines and Thailand. These are Low and Middle income countries and are also chosen based on the availability of data.

DATA SOURCES

The information and data for the present study (is) are drawn mainly from standard and authentic secondary sources such as:

1. Reports and publications of the Reserve Bank of India.
2. Survey and Reports of Technical Group on International Trade in Banking Services
3. Annual reports of IRDA
4. SWISS RE reports. [SIGMA reports]
5. Reports and publications of the Department of Financial Services
6. Annual Reports of banks and financial institutions.
7. Reports and publications of World Bank and International Monetary Fund.
8. Publications of the Centre for Monitoring Indian Economy.
9. Other publications relating to financial services.

METHODOLOGICAL FRAMEWORK

1. For analyzing the trade in banking services as stated in the second objective Data Envelopment Analysis, an econometric tool has been used. The relative efficiency of each bank identified has been calculated using Data Envelopment Analysis (DEA).

   Data Envelopment Analysis (DEA) is a mathematical programming approach to assess relative efficiencies with a group of decision making units (DMUs). The name DEA is attributed to Charnes, Cooper and Rhodes (1978). DEA represents a mathematical programming methodology that can be applied to assess the efficiency of a variety of institutions using a variety of data. The objective of DEA is to determine which firms operate on their efficiency frontier and which firms do not. That is, DEA partitions the inputs and outputs of all firms into efficient and inefficient combinations. The efficient input-output combinations yield an implicit production frontier against which each firm's input and output combination is evaluated. If the firm's input- output combination lies on the DEA frontier, the firm might be considered efficient; if the firm's input-output combination lies inside the DEA frontier, the firm is considered inefficient.

   The period of the study is nine years from 2005 to 2013. The study has two aspects : first is to identify the efficient banks and those who are consistently efficient and second is to check if the entry of the foreign banks has affected the efficiency of the domestic banks. This is done by calculating the efficiency of both domestic and foreign banks operating in India. Thus identifying the consistently efficient banks both domestic and foreign and also as the study is done for a period of nine years and choice of the input and output variables is made such that it reflects the efficiency and also the impact of the entry of the foreign banks on the domestic banks. The input variables considered for the study are number of offices, number of employees and operating expenses and output variables taken for analysis are profit per employee, interest income and return on assets.

The ranks and efficiency of the select banks, denoted by è (theta), are calculated. The value of θ obtained will be the efficiency score for the i-th DMU. It will satisfy $\theta \leq 1$, with a value of 1 indicating a point on the frontier and thus a technically efficient DMU is obtained according to the Farrell (1957) definition. The most efficient bank is one that obtains the highest efficiency score.

The consistent performance of these banks across a period of time has based identified based the theta. Then the standard deviation (SD) and coefficient of variation (CV) are calculated for each bank across a period of nine years. The SD (α) signifies the variability and shows the deviation in the efficiency of the bank. The CV is a normalized measure of dispersion of a probability distribution or frequency distribution. It is defined as the ratio of the standard deviation to the mean. The lower the CV the more consistent is the performance. Through this method, out of the domestic banks and foreign banks operating in India, the best and consistent performing banks have been identified.

2. To study the relationship between economic growth and banking and insurance performance as stated in the fourth objective, panel co-integration method has been used.

   For studying the impact of economic growth on the banking and insurance trade performance, four variables have been identified. Gross domestic Product Per capita [GDPP], M2 to Gross Domestic Product [M2toGDP], Domestic Credit as percentage of Gross Domestic Product [DOMCREDIT] are taken are the dependent variables representing economic growth and Banking and insurance share as percentage of total services [BIPER] is taken as an independent variable to represent the banking and insurance trade performance.

   To analyse this objective the following hypothesis have been tested.

Hypotheses

I. H_0: There is no co-integration evidence between BIPER and DomCredit.

$H_{1:}$ There is co-integration evidence between BIPER and DomCredit.

II. H_0: There is no co-integration evidence between BIPER and GDPP.

$H_{1:}$ There is co-integration evidence between BIPER and GDPP.

III. H_0: There is no co-integration evidence between BIPER and M2 to GDP.

H_1: There is co-integration evidence between BIPER and M2 to GDP.

Where,

BIPER = Banking and insurance share as percentage of total services of country ; GDPP = Gross domestic Product Per capita of country;

M2GDP = Ratio of M2 to Gross Domestic Product of country;

DOMCREDIT = Domestic Credit as percentage of Gross Domestic Product of country.

To ascertain the appropriate estimation technique, the variables have been first examined for stationarity in a panel context. Stationarity means Mean and Variance are consistent over a period of time. The data was tested and grouped into panel data thus combining time series and cross section data. For this, the Panel Unit Root test is used. Panel Unit roots facilitate checking whether the series is stationary or not [Series means - each variable data]. Time Series Unit roots do not give Best Linear Unbiased Estimate [BLUE], they give inconsistent and biased estimates. Hence Panel Unit Roots are used.

The variables are found to contain a unit root, and were then examined for possible co-integration. If co-integration exists between the variables, Fully Modified OLS (FMOLS) estimation technique is used to obtain coefficient estimates. Specifically, the panel unit root tests developed by Levin, Lin and Chu and Im, Pesaran and Shin have been employed. Pedroni's method is used to test for panel co-integration.

3. To study which countries have strong relationship between Economic Growth and Banking and insurance performance, fixed effects - a panel regression model of econometrics has been applied.

LIMITATIONS OF THE STUDY

The study takes into consideration only select Asian countries when measuring the relationship between banking and insurance trade performance and growth. Another limitation is that the RBI is maintaining the international trade in banking services details only from the year 2005 hence the study covers a period of eight years from 2005.

Given this background, Review of literature has been covered in the following chapter which provides insights on issues like trade in services, barriers to trade, trade liberalization, impact of financial development on economic growth, financial services, trade in banking services, reforms in banking and insurance services, efficiency of banks, etc.

REFERENCES

1. Government of India," India's Fiscal Budget 2012-13 chapter 10, "February 2014.

Review of Literature

INTRODUCTION

This chapter presents the literature on services trade, services trade liberalization, trade in financial services, reforms in the banking and insurance sectors, trade in banking services, international trade in insurance services, trade in banking and insurance services and its relationship with economic growth and related aspects.

The opening up of financial sector to foreign participation as a part of national financial reforms contributes to international efforts aimed at strengthening the global financial architecture. At the same time international frameworks tend to support national programs of financial services liberalization. The most comprehensive of such framework is General Agreement on Trade in Services (GATS) of the World Trade Organisation (WTO).

While financial reforms are ongoing in the EU and many other countries, little attention is paid to free trade agreements that continue to liberalise financial services as well as restrict regulatory freedom and controls on capital movements. 'Trade in financial services' does not only mean trans-border movements of financial services (e.g. internet banking with foreign customers) but also the establishment of foreign banks or insurance companies, etc. abroad (i.e. foreign direct investment) and movement of high level personnel. GATS and FTA have a special clause that allows countries to take prudential financial measures for the integrity and stability of the financial system and protect investors and consumers.

INTERNATIONAL TRADE IN FINANCIAL SERVICES

The existing literature on the link between services and growth focuses primarily on the financial sector.

Goldsmith (1969), in the seminal work stressed the role of financial services in channeling investment funds to their most productive uses, thereby promoting growth of output and incomes. Goldsmith uses the ratio of the value of financial intermediary assets to GNP to gauge financial performance and enters it in a regression with economic growth as the dependent variable. He finds a "rough parallelism" between economic growth and financial other growth controls in his regressions.

More recently, King and Levine (1993a) postulate that financial services can affect growth through enhanced capital accumulation and/or technical innovation. They systematically control for other factors affecting long run growth and construct additional measures of financial sector development such as the ratio of liabilities of the financial system to GDP and the ratio of gross claims on the private sector to GDP, which they use in growth regressions. They find their measures to be significant and the sizes of their coefficients to imply an economically important relationship. Finally, to counter the endogeneity problem, they study whether the level of financial sector development in 1960 as measured by one of their ratios, predicts the rate of economic growth over the 1960-1990 period. They find indeed that the level of financial sector development in 1960 is a significant predictor of economic growth over the later period.

Levine (1997) adopts a functional approach to the link between financial development and growth. He identifies five major functions that financial systems perform which help in minimizing transactions costs and improving the allocation of real resources. These functions include facilitating the trading of risk, allocating capital to productive uses, monitoring managers, mobilizing savings through the use of innovative financial instruments and lastly, easing the exchange of goods and services. However, the author admits that research in this area does not sufficiently account for the role of international trade in financial services. Moreover, the paper is silent on the role of policy.

Francois and Schuknecht (1999) study the growth of per capita real GDP on a measure of the general degree of openness in trade, on certain macroeconomic variables and the concentration ratio for the financial sector. They find a strong positive relationship between growth and financial sector competition. However, the concentration ratio is an outcome based variable, and, moreover, a misleading indicator of the level of competition in the banking system because a concentrated market for banking services can still be contestable. A large number of developed countries such as Canada and many European countries have banking systems characterized by a small number of banks, but still produce competitive outcomes.

Goldstein (1999) Although the liberalization of controls on capital movements and trade in financial services helps integrate international financial markets, it does not necessarily alter patterns of international capital flows. As financial markets become more integrated, the role of capital flows in restoring market equilibrium through arbitrage might actually diminish.

Tamirisa *et al.*, (2000) studied the trade in financial services is closely linked to capital movements (). Establishing a commercial presence in local markets through entry or equity participation requires foreign direct investment. The cross-border supply of some financial services involves portfolio and other capital flows, for example, lending. However, the provision of some other financial services, such as advisory services, does not require capital transfers.

Apostolos Gkoutzinis (2004) in his article reviews the progress achieved in the liberalization of international trade in banking services as part of the General Agreement on Trade in Services (GATS). In particular, it examines the existing legally binding commitments and discusses the progress in the negotiations at the Doha Round.

REFORMS IN FINANCIAL SERVICES – BANKING AND INSURANCE SERVICES

The regulatory framework for banks known as "**Prudential Regulation**" in the literature consists of broadly of capital adequacy norms, restrictions on the lines of activities that banks can participate in, restrictions on entry and deposit insurance (Sen & Vaidya, 1997).

Rajan and Zingales (1998) argued that the banking sector liberalization has particularly favorable effects on those sectors that rely relatively heavily on external finance for their investment and growth.

Structural reform approaches seek to shield deposits and payments functions of banks from the risks that are generated in the investment banking activities which are linked to volatilities in the financial market. Calomiris (1998) and Fisher (1998 & 1999) In the global policy context, the liberalization of financial services trade is closely linked to the reforms of the institutions architecture underlying the international financial system.

Manoj (2007) in his work assessed the banking sector reforms in India. It has been more than 20 years of the start of the economic reform in India and the financial sector reform was one of the important parts of the process. The study listed the major reforms of the Indian baking sector and found out the impacts of these reform and the future prospects. The study confined itself to the impacts of reforms upon credit delivery, share of market of banks, profitability and prudential regulations.

Vyas and Zhaveri (2007) in their work studied the performance of the Banking Sector in India. They also did a critical review of the performance as well as impact of Banking Sector Reforms in India. The study examined the role and measures initiated by the Reserve Bank in India [RBI] in order to implement the Banking Sector Reforms in India.

Radha (2002) critically evaluate the impact of Banking Sector Reforms on the performance of Commercial Banks in India. In her study, she analysis the magnitude of deposits and borrowings, and trends in branch expansion, advances and 48 investments, trends income and expenditure and also studied the magnitude of achievements in priority sector advances, capital adequacy, CD ratio, staff position in different bank groups and individual banks within the group.

Schnabl, (2008) they felt that the benefits of financial liberalization must be weighed against the costs of increased financial fragility. They have argued that some degree of financial regulatory reforms is still inevitable and in fact preferable to premature liberalization in developing countries.

Kalpana (2008) presented financial sector reforms in India identified the emerging issues and explored the prospects for further reform. The first part is devoted to a brief background financial sector reforms. The second part is devoted to the institutional aspects of the reform but banking sector will be analyzed in the paper. Issues relating to ownership, competition and regulation in the financial sector as a whole are discussed. The third part relating to legal policy framework focuses on monetary policy and credit delivery.

Prasad and Rajan (2008) discuss the deep linkages among different reforms, including broader reforms to monetary and fiscal policies, and recognizing these linkages is essential to achieve real progress. They also feel that the Indian government has taken a number of steps to improve the banking system. Banking reforms, which started nearly two decades ago, have increased the efficiency of the banking system, and the ratio of nonperforming loans to deposits is about 1 percent—a remarkably low level. They felt that principles-based regulation will be more conducive to rapidly evolving financial markets and is also more adaptable.

Seelanatha & Wikremasinghe (2009) in their study on the financial sector reforms in Srilanka and its influence on banking industry, found that the depth of the banking industry has improved significantly as a result of the reforms.

FTI Consulting in a paper said that the financial sector faces legislation that is intended to amend existing market structures and business models. The paper critically discussed the different elements of the Volcker, Vickers and Liikanen proposals, analyzed the implied costs and benefits and shed light on elements that will require further work.

TRADE IN BANKING SERVICES

Grubel (1977) gave the most cited explanation has been the "follow-the – customer" hypothesis; banks go multinational to better serve the foreign operations of domestic corporate entities. Intuitively if the home country has extensive trade links with a foreign nation, then the demand for a variety of trade-related intermediary services (eg. Provision of documentary credits, foreign exchange credits, insurance etc.,) will typically be high.

Goldberg, & Saunders (1981) In their study showed that rapid growth of foreign banking activity in the United States has led to major changes in the regulation of foreign banks. This paper seeks to determine the factors causing this growth of foreign banks. Goldberg and Saunders (1981), Hultman and McGee (1989), Khoury (1980) and others have also presented evidence that support this view. Sabi (1988) found no significant relationship between foreign bank participation and size of import – export activity with the country.

Germanidi, (1982) found that the basic motive for the achievement of cross-border banking activities is the redistribution of international fluidity and international capital between the various countries. In relation to the above approach, the profit from the internationalization work of banking is the increase of the so called surplus of the consumer, that is to say the difference between the initial sum that the consumer has to pay for a banking service and the final sum that he finally pays.

Vastrup (1983) points out that there is a substantial fixed cost element in credit rating activities; thus banks can lend more cheaply to existing clients than can competitors. It has also been suggested that failure to follow the customer may make the way for others to come in and even encroach on existing domestic business with the parent company.

Glover (1986) said the industry was transformed in the 1970s. Until then most banks concentrated on their home markets, considering themselves as domestic institutions that handled foreign business. With the rapid expansion of international networks, the talk is of global banks.

Tschoegl (1987) presents evidence that banks sometimes go multinational to serve the banking needs of a few specific communities abroad. He attributes the worldwide spread of Indian banks, and the operations of Finish banks in Sweden for this reason.

Neu (1988) in his work on international trade in banking services identified the obstacles in trade in banking services and the issues in the trade in banking services. He identified that developments in telecommunications and computers may result in some banking services which are currently undertaken by local subsidiaries and branches being transferred to the bank's headquarters, involving the movement of activities.

Walter (1988) suggests that banks may actually be leading their customers. Well established banks in a country abroad can often provide 'useful information, contacts, advice and financial services to foreign firms considering entering the foreign market'.

Robert Grosse & Lawrence Goldberg (1991) In their work have shown the presence of foreign banks in the United States has grown dramatically in recent years. In particular, Japanese bank activity has grown rapidly and has raised concern from domestic bankers who have felt competitive pressure. This paper assesses the extent of the foreign bank presence in the United States and indicates its distribution by country of origin.

Henkel and Levi (1992) studied foreign banking in the USA to examine the choice of form of representation by foreign banks – branches, agencies, represenatatives or subsidiaries – on the basis of the following country – specific factor: exports to the US; claims against the specific country held by US customers; and the size of the capital market of the bank exporting country.

Swary and Top (1992) concluded that the loss of a comparative advantage by commercial banks as providers of credit to large borrowers, competition from non-bank financial firms, and increased competition from foreign banks have created the impetus for adoption of universal banking.

Wengel (1995) investigates which of the theories of international trade best explains trade in international banking in its various forms: branches, subsidiaries and representatives. Strong evidence is found to support the newer economies of scale theories and it is proposed that the foreign exchange and capital markets exhibit declining costs to production. It is also discovered that the relaxation of exchange and capital controls by potential host countries diminishes the incentives of banks to seek direct representation.

Seth (1996) in his study investigates the lending patterns of US – BASED banks from Japan, Canada, France, Germany, the Netherlands, and the U.K., countries which account for the vast majority of foreign – owned bank activity in the U.S. Simultaneously, they looked at the borrowing patterns of U.S nonbank affiliates of firms from those countries. They found that banks from four of the six countries (Japan, Canada, the Netherlands and the U.K.) allocated a majority of their loans to non-home country borrowers, for some or all of the 1981 -1992 period. That result suggest that "follow the customer" hypothesis may have a more limited applicability than previously supposed.

Maesterrs, Hasan ,Lensink and Koetter in their work say that the positive relation between financial development and economic growth seems to have weakened in recent years and when analyzing only developed countries. They suggest that banks' relative ability to intermediate funds cost-efficiently is a quality-based measure of financial development that complements conventional quantity-based measures.

The benefits and costs of foreign bank entry are investigated extensively in the literature. The World Bank (2002) summarizes the benefits as follows

1. Foreign bank entry increases the efficiency of the domestic banking sector. Increased competition tends to reduce costs and to increase profits (World Bank, 2001; Claessens, Kunt, and Huizinga, 1998).
2. The allocation of credits to the private sector may be improved since it is expected the evaluation and pricing of credit risks to be more sophisticated (Clarke, Cull, and Soledad Martinez Peria, 2001; Barth, Caprio, and Levine, 2001). This may help foster higher growth (Levine, 1996).
3. The presence of foreign banks helps build a domestic banking supervisory and legal framework, and enhance the overall transparency.
4. It is expected foreign banks to provide more stable sources of credit since they may refer to their parents for additional funding and they have easier access to international markets. Thus, domestic financial markets will be less vulnerable to domestic shocks.
5. Foreign banks may reduce the costs associated with recapitalizing and restructuring banks in the post-crisis period.

The costs of foreign bank entry are specified as follows:

1. If the franchise value of domestic banks decreases with foreign bank entry, they may have an incentive to take on greater risks (Hellmann, Murdock, and Stiglitz, 2000).
2. With more advanced services and products, foreign banks attract the most profitable portion of domestic markets. Thus, riskier sectors will be served by domestic banks.
3. With increased foreign bank presence, access to credit may be impaired for some sectors of the economy.
4. Foreign banks may increase financial instability by pulling out of host countries or by contagion from problems in the home country.
5. Since foreign banks have different priorities and business focus, their lending pattern tends to ignore domestic priorities.

Claessens, Demirguc-Kunt, and Huizinga (1998) examine the effects of foreign bank entry on the domestic banking sector. They show that in developing countries foreign banks tend to have greater profits, higher interest margins, and higher tax payments compared to domestic banks. But the opposite is true in developed countries. Another interesting conclusion is that both profitability and overhead expenses of domestic banks fall with foreign bank entry. In this study, we apply their empirical technique to a different data set. While their data cover 80 countries and the period of 1988-95, our data set includes 29 countries and covers the period of 1995-2002. Thus, our study will be helpful to confirm their results.

Demirguc-Kunt, Levine, and Min (1998) show that foreign bank participation lowers the possibility that a country will experience a banking crisis. They indicate that the presence of foreign banks lowers overhead costs and profits of domestic banks. Foreign banks also increase overall economic growth by raising the efficiency of domestic banks.

Hernes and Lensink (1998) in their research work analyse the relationship between foreign bank presence and the performance of the domestic banking sector and takes into account the role of the level of development of the financial sector of the recipient country. They used the bank level data of 982 banks in 48 countries for the period 1990-1996. The results support the hypothesis that financial development does matter.

Demirguc-Kunt and Huizinga (1999) show that foreign banks have generally higher profits and margins compared to domestic banks in developing countries, while the opposite is true in industrial countries.

Agenor (2001) is pointed out cost of foreign bank entry. Since foreign investors may not be familiar with the emerging markets, they tend to retreat promptly and massively at the first encounter of difficulty. This may lead to deeper crises in domestic financial markets.

Padwal S.M. (2002) in his paper made an attempt to assess the impact of liberalization on Indian Banking. Padwal came to a conclusion that high cost of branch expansion, growing percentage of credit portfolio to low yielding assets; increasing operating and establishment expenses have adversely affected banks' profitability. He in this paper strongly felt that deregulation in the banking sector is expected to help to widen credit market, enhance saving mobilization and stimulate competition but there is a need to prepare the banking industry to face the consequence of liberalization.

Lensink and Hermes (2003) in their work investigated the short-term effects of foreign bank entry on the behaviour of the domestic banking sector. They hypothesized that these effects are dependent on the level of economic development of the host country. They found that at lower levels of economic development foreign bank entry is generally associated with higher costs and margins for domestic banks. At higher levels of economic development the effects appear to be less clear: foreign bank entry is either associated with a fall of costs, profits and margins of domestic banks, or is not associated with changes in these domestic bank variables.

Focarelli, D., Pozzolo, A.F.,(2005) in their paper investigate the patterns of banks Foreign investment. They used a unique database of 260 large banks from OECD countries and their branches or subsidiaries in each of the other OECD countries. They also considered the role of institutional and regulatory constraints and a wide set of variables that can influence the pattern of bank internationalization. They found that high degree of integration between home and destination countries has an effect on location choice of multinational banks. Profit opportunities resulting from high expected economic growth and the prospect of competing with relatively less efficient banks is a key factor affecting expansion abroad.

Vasiliadis, (2009) is concerned with two different aspects of internationalization. The first aspect refers to the exchange in terms of import and export of banking services and transactions in foreign currency. The second aspect, however, is related to the strategy of banks when internationalizing.

Goetz Von Peter (2012) in his paper on 'After the financial crisis: from international to multinational banking ?' says the financial crisis has led to a reconsideration of banks' global business models. Using a dataset derived from the BIS banking statistics, this paper studies the geography of global banking. It distinguishes between "international" and "multinational" banks, their respective funding models and the associated degree of centralization in their operations. As a result of post-crisis regulatory reform, the long-term trend toward local banking is likely to accelerate, especially if liquidity regulations are applied locally.

Niepmann (2013) in his paper on banking across borders says that the international linkages between banks play a crucial role in today's global economy. Existing models explain these links on the basis of portfolio theory, in which banks diversify lending. These models have found only limited empirical support and do not speak to many relevant dimensions of the data. They do not address heterogeneity in the degree to which banking sectors fund their foreign operations locally in foreign markets. He in his paper proposes an alternative theory to explain banking across borders that is based on elements of international trade theory. In the model, banking across borders arises because countries differ in their relative factor endowments and in the efficiency of their banking sectors. Based on these differences, the pattern of foreign bank asset and liability holdings emerges endogenously.

EFFICIENCY OF BANKS

There are numerous studies on measuring the efficiency of financial institutions.

Charnes, Cooper and Rhodes (1978) developed measures of 'decision making efficiency' with special reference to possible use in evaluating public programs. Their measure is intended to evaluate the accomplishments, or resource conservation possibilities, for every DMU with the resources assigned to it. They have provided a variety of ways of assessing the efficiency of DMU's in public programs in order to improve the planning and control of these activities. They have proposed measure of the efficiency of any DMU is obtained as the maximum of a ratio of weighted outputs to weighted inputs subject to the condition that the similar ratios for every DMU be less than or equal to unity.

Seiford and Thrall (1990) found that mathematical programming procedure used by DEA for efficient frontier estimation is comparatively robust.

Berger and Humphrey (1997) reviewed 130 studies that applied frontier efficiency analysis to financial in 21 countries. They observed that various efficiency measures do not necessarily yield consistent results and suggested some ways to make it consistent.

Bhattacharyya *et al.* (1997) examined the productive efficiency of 70 Indian commercial banks during early stages (1986-1991) prior to liberalization. They used DEA to calculate radial technical efficiency scores.

Resti (1997) analyzes the cost efficiency of 270 Italian banks over the period 1988-1992. He compares the parametric and non-parametric efficiency scores and finds that econometric and linear programming results do not differ substantially. He reports higher efficiency scores between 81% and 92% for SFA as opposed to DEA scores between 60% and 78%. Rank correlation between SFA and DEA is statistically significant at the 1% level and ranges from 44% to 58%. The rank ordering of firm specific inefficiency is strongly correlated over time, although it is more persistent with DEA than with SFA.

The Bauer *et al.* (1998) study is among all the most significant, given the application of four approaches SFA, DEA, Thick Frontier Analysis (TFA) and Distribution Free Analysis (DFA) on a data set of 683 US banks over the period 1977-1988. They suggest six consistency conditions to analyze the robustness of frontier efficiency measures. They compare the efficiency distributions, the rank order correlation of the efficiency distributions, the correspondence of best-practice and worst-practice banks across techniques, the stability of measured efficiency over time, the consistency of efficiency with market competitive conditions and the consistency with standard non-frontier performance measures. conclude that there is no single correct approach to specify an efficient frontier. Instead, both measures seem to react to varying degrees to particularities of the data.

Jackson and Fethi (2000) study on Turkish banks found that the profitable banks are more likely to operate at higher levels of technical efficiency.

Yang, Ma, Koike (2000) in their work point out the defect of the first DEA model CCR (Charnes, Cooper and Rhodes, 1978) in measuring the efficiencies of the production system with k independent subsystems and propose a new model YMK (Yang, Ma and Koike) by improving CCR model. Some properties and the relationship between CCR and YMK models are also discussed. It is concluded that the overall efficiency (YMK) of each DMU has a great deal to do with the efficiencies of its subsystems under CCR model. In fact, the overall efficiency value (YMK) of each DMU is equal to the maximum among the efficiency values of all its subsystems under CCR model. The examples given demonstrate the effectiveness of YMK model in measuring efficiencies of the production system with k independent subsystems.

Maudos and Pastor (2003) analyzed cost and profit efficiencies of Spanish banks using DEA and observed that there is a positive rank correlation coefficient between cost efficiency and profit efficiency of Spanish banks. Further, if banks are more cost efficient, they are also more profit efficient.

Sathye (2003) measured the productive efficiency of banks in India using DEA. The study shows that the mean efficiency score of Indian banks compares well with the world mean efficiency score.

Das *et al.* (2005) analyzed the cost, revenue and profit efficiency of Indian banks for 1997-2003 using DEA. The study observes that Performance Evaluation of Banks in India – A Shannon- DEA Approach results of input-oriented, output-oriented and cost efficiency measures are more or less similar, but the results in respect of revenue and profit efficiencies differ sharply during this period. They found that the bank's size, ownership, listed in stock exchange had a positive impact on the profit efficiency and to some extent revenue efficiency.

Hermann, Leipig, Todter (2006) investigate the consistency of efficiency scores derived with two competing frontier methods in the financial economics literature: Stochastic Frontier and Data Envelopment Analysis. A sample 34,192 observations for all German universal banks and analyze whether efficiency measures yield consistent results according to five criteria between 1993 and 2004: levels, rankings, identification of extreme performers, stability over time and correlation to standard accounting-based measures of performance. Furthermore, their results show that accounting for systematic differences among commercial, cooperative and savings banks is important to avoid misinterpretation about the status of efficiency of the total banking sector. Finally, despite ongoing fundamental changes in Europe's largest banking system, efficiency rank stability is very high in the short run. However, they also found that annually estimated efficiency scores are markedly less stable over a period of twelve years, in particular for parametric methods.

Uppal and Kaur (2007) concludes that the efficiency of all the bank groups has increased in the second post banking sector reforms period but these banking sector reforms are more beneficial for new private sector banks and foreign banks. This paper also suggests some measures for the improvement of efficiency of Indian nationalized banks. The sample of the study in Indian banking industry which comprises five different ownership groups and the ratio method is used to calculate the efficiency of different bank groups. New private sector banks are compelling with foreign banks for continuous improvement in their performance.

Sufian (2007) has employed the DEA method to investigate the effects of mergers and acquisitions on the efficiency of Malaysian banks. DEA has become increasingly popular in measuring efficiency in different national banking institutes.

Kumar and Gulati (2008) in their study measured the extent of technical, pure technical, and scale efficiencies in 27 public sector banks (PSBs) operating in India in the year 2004/05. The empirical findings reveal that PSBs operate at 88.5 percent level of overall technical efficiency i.e., inputs could be reduced by 11.5 percent without sacrificing output if all banks were efficient as 7 benchmark banks identified by DEA. Further, the contribution of scale inefficiency in overall technical inefficiency has been observed to be smaller than what been observed due to managerial inefficiency (i.e., pure technical inefficiency). The findings pertaining to returns-to- scale in Indian public sector banking industry highlight that the predominant form of scale inefficiency is decreasing returns-to scale.

Soleimani-damaneh and Zarepisheh (2009) observed that existing super-efficiencybased ranking methods in the DEA literature (Adler *et al.*, 2002; Andersen and Petersen, 1993) has a desirable feature of differentiating between some of the efficient DMUs that have identical efficiency scores equal to one in the basic DEA models. Soleimani-damaneh and Zarepisheh (2009) proposed combining of efficiency scores of various DEA models using Shannon's entropy method to provide a more balance ranking of DMU.

Mohd Tahir (2009) examined whether the domestic and foreign banks are drawn from the same environment by performing a series of parametric and non-parametric tests. The results from the parametric and non-parametric tests suggest that for the years 2000-2004, both domestic and foreign banks possessed the same technology whereas results for 2005 and 2006 suggest otherwise. This implies that banks in recent years have had access to different and more efficient technology.

Ray and Das (2010) studied the cost and profit efficiency of Indian banks using DEA during the post reforms period and observed that public sector banks are more efficient compared to private sector banks and small banks (with assets up to Rs.50 billion) are operating below the efficiency frontier. Also,there is a strong evidence of ownership explaining the efficiency differentials of the banks.

Kaur and Kaur (2010) examined the impact of mergers on the cost efficiency of Indian commercial banks using DEA. They observed that the merger has led to higher level of cost efficiency of merged banks, while the merger between distressed and stronger banks did not yield any significant efficiency gains. Further, they opined that the stronger banks should not merge with the weaker banks, as the weaker banks will have adverse effect upon the asset quality of the stronger banks.

Dwivedi and Charyulu (2011) seek to determine the impact of various market and regulatory initiatives on efficiency improvements of Indian banks.

Das and Kumhakar (2012) studied the productivity and efficiency of Indian banks using hedonic aggregator function and observed that efficiency of public sector banks surpassed the efficiency of private sector banks during the post reform period 1996-2005.

Anastasios D. Varias and Stella Sofianopoulou (2012) in their study evaluate the efficiency of the biggest commercial banks that operated in Greece at the financial year 2009. The method used is Data Envelopment Analysis. Each bank was modelled as a linear system with multiple inputs and outputs. The data used was derived from the balance sheets, income statements and the annual report of each commercial bank. These data include the interest expenses, fixed assets, deposits etc. The results indicate several inefficiencies that have no direct relation to the profitability of such institutions.

Hoque and Reyhan (2012) analysed twenty four different banks in Bangladesh. Data Envelopment Analysis is mainly of two types – constant returns to scale and variable returns to scale. Since this study attempts to maximize output, so the output oriented Data Envelopment Analysis is used. The study found that CRS-DEA consists of 3 efficient banks and the range of the efficiency scores is too large whereas VRS-DEA consists of 12 efficient banks and the range of efficiency scores is smaller than CRS-DEA.

Jayaraman and Srinivasan (2014) in their study evaluate the performance of the banks in India using cost, revenue and profit models of DEA and come out with a comprehensive efficiency index for banks, by combing the efficiency scores of various DEA models, using the Shannon entropy. The banks included in this study are sound in terms of total assets, manpower, branch network etc., and they have been ranked based on their performance, which depends on optimal utilization of select variables. In order to measure the degree of agreement between rankings of banks based on three different models, namely cost, revenue and profit model, Kendall's coefficient of concordance has been used. The study observes that Shannon-DEA approach provides a comprehensive efficiency index for banks and a reasonable way of ranking.

INSURANCE SERVICES: INTERNATIONAL TRADE AND GROWTH

There is a growing empirical literature seeking to assess the relationship between macroeconomic performance of the insurance sector and economic growth which contributes to increase the international trade among countries. Insurance sector is a central element of the trade and development matrix and is considered as one of the key pillars of the financial services.

A sound national insurance sector represents an essential feature of a proper economic system, contributing to economic growth and fostering high employment (UNCTAD, 1964). As both, an infrastructural and commercial service, a well-functioning insurance sector plays a crucial r ole in economic development not just at a macro-economic level but also in terms of the activities of individuals and businesses (UNCTAD, 2007). From an infrastructural perspective it promotes financial and social stability which mobilizes and channel savings, supports trade, commerce and entrepreneurial activity and improves the quality of the lives of individuals (Puri 2007).

Liberalization and privatization helps bring substantial financial strength, technological and industry know how. At the same time, good risk management and asset liability management skills are required especially in the context of developing countries (Puri 2007). He mentioned the following areas of concerns in the insurance sector which is needs to be consider on priority basis: security and stability of the insurance sector; the importance of building supply side capacity; the role of regulation frameworks; current negotiations on insurance services within the GATS; the role of the Government as a provider of insurance services and the extent of its role as a provider of insurance services.

"The development of the life insurance market has a positive effect on economic growth." Chen, Lee, Chang, Feng has taken the conditional variables of middle-income countries which are savings, the real interest rate, social security, the stock market turnover ratio, and the young dependency ratio to show the positive impacts of the development of the life insurance market on growth. According to their study, a country with a well-developed financial system does not necessarily enhance (and maybe lessens) the positive effects of the development of the life insurance market on economic growth.

"Improved access to insurance services, given their importance to global growth and development would be tangible way to underpin the recovery of the global economy."

Recently many developing countries such as India have taken initiatives to promote their state and private sector insurance providers to bolster regional trade. This will also help enhance the growth of their economies. Arkell (2011) explained that these initiatives involve restrictions to the opportunities for abroad based insurers which would affect their potential benefit. Further, the new limitations affect both national insurers and affiliates in which investment has been made from abroad, which might even reduce the market access accorded to foreign insurers under GATS commitment of the WTO on trade in services. Moreover, insurance can increase saving rate, create deeper financial markets which lead to greater working capital; where capital markets are not well developed they might benefit from the long term investment (Arkell 2011).

Venkatesh (2013) in his study concluded that Indian insurance sector is having increasing growth rate. From the above trend analysis we can observe that trend percentages are increasing, so we can conclude it is improving year to year and it is so sad to say that still India has less density percentage in the world wide when compared, it might be the reasons we discuss above. Now India is also improving it density percentages year to year. So let us hope better that India can also improve in insurance sector.

Puri (2007) mentioned the following areas of concerns in the insurance sector which is needs to be consider on priority basis: security and stability of the insurance sector; the importance of building supply side capacity; the role of regulation frameworks; current negotiations on insurance services within the GATS; the role of the Government as a provider of insurance services and the extent of its role as a provider of insurance services.

Chen, Lee, Chang, Feng has taken the conditional variables of middle-income countries which are savings, the real interest rate, social security, the stock market turnover ratio, and the young dependency ratio to show the positive impacts of the development of the life insurance market on growth. According to their study, a country with a well-developed financial system does not necessarily enhance the positive effects of the development of the life insurance market on economic growth.

"Improved access to insurance services, given their importance to global growth and development would be tangible way to underpin the recovery of the global economy." [1]Recently many developing countries such as India have taken initiatives to promote their state and private sector insurance providers to bolster regional trade. This will also help enhance the growth of their economies. Arkell (2011) explained that these initiatives involve restrictions to the opportunities for abroad based insurers which would affect their potential benefit

The study of Sinha *et al* (2012) identified the per capita number of agents and the per capita number of insurance offices (both are supply driven), as two other influencing factors, apart from per capita GDP, which explained together large section of data appropriately.

There are several studies [Carter and Dickinson (1992), Enz (2000), Zheng *et al* (2008), Sastry (2011), Sinha *et al* (2012), Kamiya (2012) etc.], which have attempted to examine the nature of inter-relationship between the insurance penetration and the percapita GDP. These studies have revealed that a positive relationship holds between insurance penetration and per capita GDP. Insurance penetration normally increases with the increase in the per capita GDP. The relationship between the two could be linear or non-linear (curvilinear).

The studies of Carter and Dickinson (1992) and Enz (2000) indicated that the relationship between the insurance penetration and per capita GDP can be explained with an S-curve (a non-linear form). They demonstrated that the insurance penetration cannot go on increasing with the same pace forever with income per capita. The study of Enz (2000) proposed a logistic curve, which tracks an S-curve appropriately. Enz (2000) analyzed the insurance penetration by plotting it with the per capita GDP for select countries both for the life and non-life segments, separately.

RELATIONSHIP BETWEEN ECONOMIC GROWTH AND BANKING AND INSURANCE PERFORMANCE

Goldsmith (1969) was the first to show empirically the existence of a positive relationship between financial development and economic growth, and provides the earliest evidence that development of financing accelerates economic growth. According to the Goldsmith's (1969) work, the evolution of domestic financial markets leads to a high level of capital accumulation efficiency, and the positive correlation between financial development and growth is mainly due to the efficient use of capital stock.

Hicks (1969) also noticed that financial institutions might facilitate growth. Though he focused on capital formation. From this perspective capital formation can be influenced by financial institutions through altering the savings rate or by reallocating savings among different capital producing technologies. Liquidity is crucial here. The high-return projects involve a long-run commitment of capital and savers are generally reluctant to lose control of their savings for a long time. The task of financial institutions is to enhance the liquidity of long-term investments so that more investment is expected in the high-return projects.

Adams, Andersson and Landermark in their study found that the development of insurance fosters demand for banking services but only in times of economic growth. For the entire period of our analysis, we find that banking is the predominant influence on both economic growth and the demand for insurance.

McKinnon (1973) and Shaw (1973) demonstrate the importance of financial liberalisation in promoting savings and investment, and admit the significance of financial development in promoting economic growth through high capital productivity.

Greenwood and Jovanovic (1990) model the dynamic interactions between financial sector development andeconomic growth and tested the causality between them. They find that an expanded system of financial intermediation is able to allocate more capital to efficient investments and promote economic growth.

King and Levine (1993), studying a sample of 70 countries, introduced new measures of financial development and examined the impact of financial development on economic growth, capital accumulation pace and economic factors' productivity. The obtained results show an empirical link between financial development indicators and growth. Worth noting is that the regressions indicate that level of financial development offers an accurate prediction of economic growth rates and economic efficiency improvement in the future.

Hermes (1994) argues and financial liberalization theory and the new growth theories basically assume that financial development leads to economic growth.

Murinde and Eng (1994) and Luintel and Khan (1999) argue that a number of growth models show a two-way relationship between financial development and economic growth.

Rajan and Zingales (1996) analyzed the correlation between the performance and the growth of firms and the financial market developments, while Demirguç-Kunt and Maksimovic (1996) argued that the firms accessing developed stock-markets are characterized by high growth rates.

Demetriades and Hussein (1996) examined 16 countries and showed that finance is a leading sector in the process of economic development. They also find bidirectional causality between financial development and economic growth, mainly in developing countries. Odedokun (1996) analysed 71 developing countries and showed that financial intermediation promote economic growth, in the majority of those countries.

According to Hicks the industrial revolution in England was mainly caused by the capital market improvements that moderated liquidity risk (Levine, 1997).

Levine (1997), after reviewing many studies on the relationship between financial development and economic growth for individual or broad cross-country level concluded that the functioning of financial markets is important for economic growth. According to the survey results provided by Levine, countries with larger banks and more active stock markets grow faster. Furthermore, the consolidation of the banking and insurance markets provide a stimulus for developing other industries and firms further.

Accordingly, Levine and Zevros (1998) reach the conclusion that financial development is an accurate indicator of economic growth. However, these studies did not mention the causality thesis, pointing out that levels of bank development and incoming liquidity are significantly and positively correlated with economic growth and productivity future rates.

Roussau and Watchell (2000) applied time series tests on the variables financial development and economic growth in 5 countries. Using measures of financial development which include banking and non-banking assets, Rousseau and Watchell (2000) find out that the most dominant causality direction is financial development towards economic growth. The VAR approach allows the identification of long-term effects of financial development on growth and considers the dynamic interactions between the explanatory variables.

Ward and Zurbruegg (2000) examined the relationship between GDP and insurance growth. With, the data set of 9-OECD countries, and these countries were Australia, Austria, Canada, France, Italy, Japan, Switzerland, UK and US. It was found that insurance premium was Granger Cause of GDP in some countries but for some countries it was not true.

Koivu (2002) find that the efficiency of the banking sector accelerates economic growth in the transition economies. Drakos (2002) examined also the relation between financial sector and economic development in 21 transition economies and showed that imperfect competition in banking sectors lowers economic growth and deepen business cycles.

Calderon and Liu (2003) studied a large sample of 109 developing and industrial countries and found that:

1. financial development leads to economic growth in all countries;
2. financial deepening stimulates economic growth and, simultaneously, economic growth propels financial development;
3. financial deepening contributes more to the causal relationships in the developing countries than in the industrial countries, which implies that the developing countries have more roomfor financial and economic improvement; and
4. the longer the sampling interval, the larger the effect of financial development on economic growth, which suggests that it takes time for financial deepening to impact the real economy.

Muthusamy and Meera (2008) demonstrated the important role of Indian life insurance sector in economic development. Parekh and Banerjee (2010) reviewed that in India insurance sector has had significant impact on the economic development. This sector is gradually increasing and its contribution in GDP is also increasing.

Han, *et al.* (2010) investigated the relationship between insurance development and economic growth, using the data set of 77 countries. It was found that insurance density impact plays very important role in developing countries rather than developed ones. Ching, *et al.* (2011) analyzed the existence of causal relationship between total assets of general insurance sector and GDP in Malaysia. It was found that the long-run relationship exists between the total assets of general insurance and GDP. And in the short-run causal relationship was absent (in both directions).

Michael, Ojo (2012) examined the short and long run relationships between GDP and insurance sector growth of Nigeria. It was found that insurance sector growth positively and significantly affect the GDP. The long run relationship between the insurance growth and GDP was also confirmed.

Hou, *et al.* (2012) investigated the impact of financial institutions and GDP in 12 Euro-countries. Two major conclusions were found: first it was from cross-country evidences that life insurance penetration and banking development do not have any significant impact on GDP. Secondly, the life insurance and banking development are significant predictors of GDP.

Horng, *et al.* (2012) examined the relationship among the insurance demand, financial development and The Relationship between Life Insurance and Economic Growth: Evidence GDP of Taiwan. It was found that there was an equilibrium relationship between the insurance demand, financial development and GDP. The study found that in short run, GDP was Granger cause of insurance demand and financial development was Granger cause of GDP. It was finally concluded that financial development promotes GDP and GDP further promotes the insurance demand.

Lee, *et al.* (2013) analyzed the long term and short term relationship between the GDP and real life insurance premium of 41 countries. It was found that in the long term one unit increment in the real life premium will raise the GDP by 0.06 units. The life insurance markets development determines the economic growth in the long-run and in the short term, bidirectional causalities were found between them.

Chang, *et al.* (2013) investigated the causal relationship between the insurance activities and GDP, using a data set of 10 OECD countries. It was found that there was a significant and positive relationship between the overall insurance growth and economic growth for 5 countries out of 10 OECD countries.

Habibullah and Eng (2006) using the GMM technique developed by Arellano & Bover (1995) and Blundell & Bond (1998) conducted causality testing analysis on 13 Asian developing countries. The result is in agreement with other causality studies by Calderon & Liu (2003); Fase & Abma (2003) and Christopoulos & Tsionas (2004). They found that financial development promotes growth, thus supporting the old Schumpeterian hypothesis.

Eatzaz and Malik (2009) analyses the role of financial sector development in economic growth, their studies reported that domestic credit to private sector is instrumental in increasing per worker output and hence promoting economic growth in the long-run.

Keeping in view India's growing integration with global financial markets, external-sector vulnerabilities have an increasingly large impact on India through the trade and capital account channels. It is therefore important that the development of an efficient and healthy financial market should also be accompanied by an effective regulatory mechanism that keeps track of external vulnerabilities[2].

The survey of the above literature reveals that there is a gap and to address this gap the present study is undertaken. There is no study covering the period 2005 to 2013 and also taking the low and middle income group countries in Asia. The next chapter discusses the reforms in the banking and insurance sectors in India.

REFERENCES

1 Julian Arkell (December 2011), "The Essential Role of Insurance Services for Trade Growth and Development," *The Geneva Association, Risk and Insurance Economics, https://www.genevaassociation.org/media/99321/ga2011- the_ essential_role_of_ insurance_services.pdf (accessed on 10/10/2013)*

2 op.cit., Economic Survey 2012-2013, p. 105.

Reforms in Banking and Insurance Sectors

This chapter outlines the important aspects of financial sector reforms in India. It covers the reforms in the banking sector as well as insurance sector. The importance of the reforms in the banking sector in improving the competition and efficiency among the domestic and foreign banks in India is discussed. The insurance sector reforms and importance in improving the performance of the sector is also covered in this chapter. The chapter is divided into two parts. Part A covers the Banking Sector Reforms and part B covers the Insurance Sector Reforms.

FINANCIAL SECTOR REFORMS

India's path of reforms has been different from most other emerging market economies: it has been a measured, gradual, cautious, and steady process. The main objective of the financial sector reforms in India initiated in the early 1990s was to create an efficient, competitive and stable financial sector that could then contribute in greater measure to stimulate growth. The financial system was characterised by extensive regulations such as administered interest rates, directed credit programmes, weak banking structure, lack of proper accounting and risk management systems and lack of transparency in operations of major financial market participants (Mohan, 2004b). Such a system hindered efficient allocation of resources. Financial sector reforms initiated in the early 1990s has attempted to overcome these weaknesses in order to enhance efficiency of resource allocation in the economy.

The financial sector reforms since the early 1990s could be analytically classified into two phases. The first phase - or the first generation of reforms – was aimed at creating an efficient, productive and profitable financial sector which would function in an environment of operational flexibility and functional autonomy. In the second phase, or the second generation reforms, which started in the mid-1990s, the emphasis of reforms has been on strengthening the financial system and introducing structural improvements.

PART A

BANKING SECTOR REFORMS IN INDIA

The main objective of banking sector reforms was to promote a diversified, efficient and competitive financial system with the ultimate goal of improving the allocative efficiency of resources through operational flexibility, improved financial viability and institutional strengthening. The reforms have focused on removing financial repression through reductions in statutory pre- emptions, while stepping up prudential regulations at the same time. Furthermore, interest rates on both deposits and lending of banks have been progressively deregulated.

As the Indian banking system had become predominantly government owned by the early 1990s, banking sector reforms essentially took a two pronged approach. First, the level of competition was gradually increased within the banking system while simultaneously introducing international best practices in prudential regulation and supervision tailored to Indian requirements. In particular, special emphasis was placed on building up the risk management capabilities of Indian banks while measures were initiated to ensure flexibility, operational autonomy and competition in the banking sector. Second, active steps were taken to improve the institutional arrangements including the legal framework and technological system.

The major reforms in Banking Sector are summarized as below:

A. Competition Enhancing Measures

1. Granting of operational autonomy to public sector banks, reduction of public ownership in public sector banks by allowing them to raise capital from equity market up to 49 per cent of paid-up capital.
2. Transparent norms for entry of Indian private sector, foreign and joint-venture banks and insurance companies, permission for foreign investment in the financial sector in the form of Foreign Direct Investment (FDI) as well as portfolio investment, permission to banks to diversify product portfolio and business activities.
3. Roadmap for presence of foreign banks and guidelines for mergers and amalgamation of private sector banks and banks and NBFCs.
4. Guidelines on ownership and governance in private sector banks.

B. Measures Enhancing Role of Market Forces

1. Sharp reduction in pre-emption through reserve requirement, market determined pricing for government securities, disbanding of administered interest rates with a few exceptions and enhanced transparency and disclosure norms to facilitate market discipline.
2. Introduction of pure inter-bank call money market, auction-based repos-reverse repos for short-term liquidity management, facilitation of improved payments and settlement mechanism.
3. Significant advancement in dematerialization and markets for securitized assets are being developed.

C. Prudential Measures

1. Introduction and phased implementation of international best practices and norms on risk- weighted capital adequacy requirement, accounting, income recognition, provisioning and exposure.
2. Measures to strengthen risk management through recognition of different components of risk, assignment of risk-weights to various asset classes, norms on connected
3. Lending, risk concentration, application of marked-to-market principle for investment portfolio and limits on deployment of fund in sensitive activities.
4. 'Know Your Customer' and 'Anti Money Laundering' guidelines, roadmap for Basel II, introduction of capital charge for market risk, higher graded provisioning for NPAs, guidelines for ownership and governance, securitization and debt restructuring mechanisms norms, etc.

D. Institutional and Legal Measures

1. Setting up of Lok Adalats (people's courts), debt recovery tribunals, asset reconstruction companies, settlement advisory committees, corporate debt restructuring mechanism, etc. for quicker recovery/ restructuring.
2. Promulgation of Securitization and Reconstruction of Financial Assets and Enforcement of Securities Interest (SARFAESI) Act, 2002 and its subsequent amendment to ensure creditor rights.
3. Setting up of Credit Information Bureau of India Limited (CIBIL) for information sharing on defaulters as also other borrowers.
4. Setting up of Clearing Corporation of India Limited (CCIL) to act as central counter party for facilitating payments and settlement system relating to fixed income securities and money market instruments.

E. Supervisory Measures

1. Establishment of the Board, for Financial Supervision as the apex supervisory authority for commercial banks, financial institutions and non-banking financial companies.
2. Introduction of CAMELS supervisory rating system, move towards risk-based supervision, consolidated supervision of financial conglomerates, strengthening of off- site surveillance through control returns.
3. Recasting of the role of statutory auditors, increased internal control through strengthening of internal audit.
4. Strengthening corporate governance, enhanced due diligence on important shareholders, fit and proper tests for directors.

F. Technology Related Measures

1. Setting up of INFINET as the communication backbone for the financial sector.
2. Introduction of Negotiated Dealing System (NDS) for screen-based trading in government securities and Real Time Gross Settlement (RTGS) System.

ASSESSMENT AND IMPACT OF BANKING SECTOR REFORMS

An assessment of the banking sector shows that banks have experienced strong balance sheet growth in the post-reform period in an environment of operational flexibility. Improvement in the financial health of banks, reflected in significant improvement in capital adequacy and improved asset quality, is distinctly visible.

It is noteworthy that this progress has been achieved despite the adoption of international best practices in prudential norms. Competitiveness and productivity gains have also been enabled by proactive technological deepening and flexible human resource management.

Spread of Banking

The banking system's wide reach, judged in terms of expansion of branches and the growth of credit and deposits indicate continued financial deepening. In the Post-reform period, banks have consistently maintained high rates of growth in their assets and liabilities.

Since the beginning of reforms, a set of micro-prudential measures have been stipulated aimed at imparting strength to the banking system as well as ensuring safety.

Competition and Efficiency

In consonance with the objective of enhancing efficiency and productivity of banks through greater competition - from new private sector banks and entry and expansion of several foreign banks - there has been a consistent decline in the share of public sector banks in total assets of commercial banks. Notwithstanding such transformation, the public sector banks still account for nearly three-fourths of assets and income. Public sector banks have also responded to the new challenges of competition, as reflected in their increased share in the overall profit of the banking sector. This suggests that, with operational flexibility, public sector banks are competing relatively effectively with private sector and foreign banks. Public sector bank managements are now probably more attuned to the market consequences of their activities.

The public sector banks have shown the declining trend in share of Total assets, share in net profit and also the share in gross profit during this period of financial reforms. This is because the private sector banks and foreign banks have entered in the market in very aggressive way and shown tremendous performance. The public sector banks have improved their business performance as well as service quality during the last 10 years and now they are at comfortable position.

BANKING SECTOR REFORMS – RECOMMENDATIONS OF VARIOUS COMMITTEES

Following the nationalization, the banking system underwent a lot of favourable changes despite the fact that banks were progressing; the excessive control enforced on them by the government resulted in certain rigidities and inefficiencies in the banking system. This also eroded the profitability of banks. By 1991, the country had erected an unprofitable, inefficient and financially unsound banking sector.[1]

Because of these shortcomings, banking sector was regarded as priority area by the P.V. Narasimha Rao government which initiated reforms in 1991.

Since the formal announcement of the first initiative of financial sector reforms in the form of Committee on Financial system (Narasimham Committee I) in 1991-92 to the Committee on Banking Sector Reforms in 1998 (Narasimham Committee II), a considerable ground has been covered putting in place the financial system which can meet the requirement of a more competitive and open economy.

Chakravarthy Committee (1985)

Formed by the government to review the monetary system. They suggested that government borrowing should move progressively towards market determined rates of interest. As a result the lending rates were rationalized with initially freeing of ceiling on commercial lending.

Narasimham Committee I (1991)

The major recommendations of the Narasimham Committee I were

1. Reduction of the SLR from maximum of 38.5 per cent to 25 per cent of the net owned demand and time liabilities in the next five years;
2. Reduction of CRR should be progressively between 3 per cent and five per cent;
3. Priority sector lending should be restricted for some time to small and marginal farmers, the tiny sector, small businesses, transport operators, village and cottage industries, rural artisans and other weaker sections;
4. The public sector banks should be restructured through mergers and acquisitions encouraging competition through setting up of new private banks and encouraging joint ventures between foreign and Indian banks;
5. Allowing foreign players to upgrade technology;
6. Improving organizational methods and procedures through freedom and autonomy.

Narasimham Committee II (1998)

The Government of India appointed one more committee on Banking sector reforms under the chairmanship of Mr. M. Narasimham to review the progress of banking sector reforms to date and chart a programme of financial sector reforms to strengthen the Indian financial system and make it internationally competitive.

The report submitted by the committee in 1998, covered an entire gamut of the issues ranging from capital adequacy, bank mergers, setting up of global-sized banks, recasting bank boards and revamping banking legislation.

The major recommendations of the committee were

1. Merger of strong banks (three or four banks) must be of international character;
2. Suggestion to adopt of narrow banking , due to high volume of NPAs;
3. Suggestion of setting up of small local banks to serve local trade, small industry and agriculture within a given state or a cluster of districts;
4. Raising capital adequacy norms of banks; setting up of asset reconstruction fund for taking over the bad debts of the banks;
5. Suggestion for greater autonomy to the boards, such that RBI should not interfere in the day-to-day management of banks;
6. The committee urged the need to review and amend the provisions of the RBI Act, Banking Regulation Act, State Bank of India Act, and Bank Nationalisation Act so as to bring them in line with the needs of the banking industry.

Verma Committee (1998)

This is the third in the banking reforms. The committee recommended a strategy for rescuing and restructuring the three weakest banks in the public sector viz., Indian Bank, United Commercial Bank (UCB) and United Bank of India (UBI). The committee recommended that restructuring as a comprehensive internal exercise, operating in two stages. In stage one, focus on operational, organizational and financial restructuring of the units involved which aims at restoring their competitive efficiency.

In the second stage, after the banks have become self supporting and attract investor attention, privatization or mergers would assume.

Since the introduction of the banking reforms, there have been remarkable improvements in the various aspects of the financial health of the banks operating in Inida. Improvement in the asset quality has been a note worthy aspect of the financial performance of banks. During the past few years, the banking sector performance has been a remarkable one.

PART B

INSURANCE SECTOR REFORMS IN INDIA

Insurance regulation in India started with the passage of the Life Insurance Companies Act, 1912. A comprehensive legislation was introduced with the Insurance Act,1938 which provided strict state control over the insurance business in the country under the supervision of the Controller of Insurance. With the nationalization of the life insurance industry in 1956 and the General Insurance Industry in 1972, the role of the Controller of Insurance diminished over a period of time.

The move to initiate the process of liberalization of insurance in India commenced with the appointment of the Malhotra committee in 1993. The government's role as a facilitator of change is more evident with the opening up of the sector like insurance which was not only regulated but closely controlled for 45 years in case of Life Insurance and 27 years in case of non-life insurance.

After liberalization of the insurance sector in 1999, private players have entered both Life and non-life business in India. The government introduced the Insurance Regulatory Authority Bill, 1998 to provide for the establishment of an authority to protect the interests of the holders of insurance policies, to regulate, to promote and ensure orderly growth of the insurance industry and for the amendment of the Insurance Act, 1938, the LIC Act 1956 and the General Insurance Business Act, 1972.

The goals of the IRDA are to safeguard the interests of insurance policyholders, as well as to initiate different policy measures to help sustain growth in the Indian insurance sector.

Malhotra Committee (1993)

The formation of the Malhotra Committee in 1993 initiated reforms in the Indian insurance sector. The aim of the Malhotra Committee was to assess the functionality of the Indian insurance sector. This committee was also in charge of recommending the future path of insurance in India.

The Malhotra Committee attempted to improve various aspects of the insurance sector, making them more appropriate and effective for the Indian market.

The recommendations of the committee put stress on offering operational autonomy to the insurance service providers and also suggested forming an independent regulatory body.

The main terms of reference of the committees report were:

1. to examine the structure of the insurance industry and to assess its strengths and weaknesses;
2. to make recommendations for changes in the structure of the insurance industry;
3. to make specific suggestions regarding LIC and the GIC which would help to improve the functioning of these organizations in the changing economic environment;
4. to review the present structure of regulation and supervision of the insurance sector and make recommendations;
5. to review and make recommendations on the role and functioning of the surveyors, intermediaries and other ancillaries to the insurance sector;
6. to make recommendations on such other matters as the committee considers relevant for the health and long term development of the insurance sector.

India is a signatory to the WTO regime and to honour its commitments, it has to open the insurance, banking and accounting and legal services by January 1st 2005. Foreign insurance companies were allowed to hold up to 26 percent in joint ventures with Indian companies. It was in the recent budget increased to 49 percent by the Modi government in 2014.

The opening up of the insurance sector is crucial for liberalization. RBI has also taken a decision to allow entry of banks into insurance sector. This will result in higher domestic savings and investments, inflow of foreign capital and increased employment.

CONCLUSION

The reforms relating to financial sector began with the nationalization of banks in 1969. There were a number of reforms in the banking sector undertaken prior to 1991. The eighties were a period of gradual transition.

The 1991, Narasimham committee came up with a lot of recommendations which untied the controlling measures of the banking sector, followed by the recommendations made by the Narasimham Committee II.

Similar to this is visible in the Insurance arena with the recommendations of the Malhotra Committee and the subsequent liberalization of the insurance sector. To sum up, the financial sector reforms have improved the functioning of the financial system and also opened up the economy for foreign participants in both banking and insurance sectors.

To conclude it is examined that the reforms in the banking sector have helped the banks improve their performance and work efficiently, with this improved performance and the confidence the banks which opened branches abroad performed well and thus the trade in banking services improved. The reforms in the insurance sector also have an impact on the trade insurance services and India's contribution is good as compared to other countries and it has been increasing in the general insurance sector. Having covered the major reforms in this chapter, it would be of interest to examine their influence on trade which is covered in the next chapter.

The next chapter provides an analysis of the trends in the trade in banking services in India. The chapter not only discusses the business, profitability and performance aspects of Indian banks operating abroad and foreign banks in India but also in part two of the chapter does compare the efficiency of the domestic banks in comparison to the foreign banks. It studies the impact of the entry of the foreign banks on the efficiency of the domestic banks.

REFERENCES

1. Sri, Arya,"Banking and Financial Services", Tata McGraw Hill, 2002 pp. 40-45.

Trends in Trade in Banking Services

INTRODUCTION

As discussed earlier, the reforms in banking and insurance sector establishes that the trend of globalization, reinforced by liberalization policies and the removal of regulatory obstacles has fuelled steady growth of international investment and trade in services. The chapter studies the Indian banks operations abroad and foreign banks operations in India with reference to:

1. No of branches and No of employees
2. Business growth and profitability
3. foreign banks share in Indian Banking Business
4. Activity wise and Country wise trade in banking services; and the
5. Efficiency of foreign banks and domestic banks in India.

Eliminating discrimination between the treatment of foreign and domestic providers of financial services and removing barriers to the cross-border provision of financial services is of global interest. Empirical evidence supports the contention that financial sector opening contributes to improved financial sector performance and has important knock-on benefits for the rest of the economy.

International trade in services was brought under the common multilateral rule, General Agreement on Trade in Services (GATS), with the Uruguay Round of trade negotiations. GATS is the first set of multilaterally negotiated and legally enforceable rules covering international trade in commercial services. Following the entry into force of GATS, there has been an increasing demand for detailed and relevant and internationally comparable statistical information on trade in services. GATS cover twelve major groups of services including financial services.

Financial services broadly refer to the functions performed by financial institutions, viz. acceptance of deposits, lending, payment services, securities trading, asset management, financial advice/consultancy, settlement and clearing service, etc. and these functions carried out collectively with non-residents form international trade in financial services.

Financial services, particularly banking services, play an important role in promoting global, regional and bilateral economic integration. In order to facilitate international trade in banking services, considerable importance was given to this sector in the WTO negotiations under the aegis of GATS. Banking services includes, acceptance of deposits and lending (the core banking services), and the other financial services (para banking services) like payment services, securities trading, asset management, financial advice, settlement and clearing service, etc.

Essentially, banks have two options of expanding their operations in foreign markets. They can either service foreign clients through their domestic offices or they can establish a presence in the foreign markets. International trade in banking services occurs due to many reasons. Some possible reasons for international trade in banking services may be considered as:

1. currency substitution (currency substitution refers to the demand for domestic residents or selling domestic currency products to foreign residents); and
2. cost advantage in providing banking services either due to comparative advantage or regulatory advantage (Michael Francis, 2002).

Banking Services provided to residents through local presence of foreign banks and foreign affiliates is known as international trade in banking services (ITBS). Increasing globalization of the Indian economy is moving in line with the open financial market. The number of banks, branches/subsidiaries[1] across borders has increased to provide banking services in a cost effective manner. FDI in banking in the form of branches, agencies and subsidiaries or by means of cross-border mergers and acquisitions have increased the cross border presence of both domestic and foreign banks over the years. The cross-border branch network of both Indian and foreign banks has been expanded in the recent years.

It is pertinent to note that the existence of foreign banks in India today, such as Standard Chartered Bank and HSBC, found their roots in financing the growing trade between Asia and the rest of the world. Traditional trade items at the time were cotton from Mumbai, indigo and tea from Kolkata, rice from Burma, sugar from Java, tobacco from Sumatra, hemp from Manila and silk from Yokohama, all flowing to the west through Indian ports, making India an important destination for these banks.

Major American banking companies were at the time restricted by law from operating outside the US. The relaxation of these laws paved the way for the global expansion of American banks in the early 20th century. Citibank, or as it was known then, The National City Bank of New York, entered India in 1902, and JP Morgan, which had ambitions of entering India as early as 1902, did so in 1922 via an ownership stake in the Calcutta merchant banking firm Andrew Yule and Co. Ltd.

These issues have been examined with reference to 170 overseas branches and 180 overseas subsidiaries of Indian banks and 316 branches of foreign banks operating in India for a period of nine years i.e., from 2005-06 to 2013-14 (depending upon the availability of data). Trend analysis has been done for each aspect observing the domestic banks operating abroad and foreign banks operating in India.

The data of all the foreign banks operating in India and the domestic banks is taken from the RBI documents as available in the RBI website. The impact of the entry of foreign banks on the performance of domestic banks has been examined by using the Data Envelopment Analysis (a non-parametric method). The efficiency for all the banks for all the years was examined. The best and consistent performers of foreign banks and best and consistent performers of domestic banks have been identified. The study shows that despite the entry of the foreign banks the domestic banks are performing well.

COMPOSITION, TRENDS AND EFFICIENCY OF TRADE IN BANKING SERVICES

International trade in banking services refers to the banking services with non-residents that require a local presence of a foreign bank for functions such as retail deposit-taking, lending to firms, mortgage lending, consumer finance, and a host of non-asset based services such as securities underwriting, local currency bond trading, foreign exchange services for firms, brokering, custody services and funds collection and disbursal services. As all international transactions are directly or indirectly routed through banks, these services foster international trade in goods and services. For providing such banking services to residents of a country, ground presence of an overseas bank in that country would be required, which brings it face to face with the domestic banking policies of the host country.

The GATS framework envisages that the delivery of any commercial services can be through four different modes viz. Mode 1 –Cross Border Service, Mode 2 – Consumption abroad, Mode 3 – Commercial presence and Mode 4 – movement of natural persons. In Mode 3, the bank has a commercial presence in the territory of the service importing country and the service is delivered therein. The commercial presence can be through various investment vehicles like representative offices, branches, subsidiaries, associates and correspondents.

Banking services covered in this study include:

- **Deposit Account Management services** include fees and commissions charged to or received from the deposit account holders, for maintaining deposit accounts such as fee for cheque book, fee for internet banking, commission on draft and other instrument provided, penalty for not maintaining minimum balance, etc and any other fees charged to deposit account holders.
- **Credit related services** include fees received for credit-related or lending related services like credit processing fees, late payment or default charges and early redemption charges. Charges for facility and management fees, fees for renegotiating debt terms, mortgage fees, etc also to be reported here.
- **Financial Leasing services** include fees or commission received for arranging or entering into financial lease contracts. This also includes fees received directly or deducted from the proceedings.
- **Trade Finance related services** include commission or fees charged for arranging trade finance like buyers' and suppliers' credit, fees for establishing/originating, maintaining or arranging standby letters of credit, letter of indemnity, lines of credit, fees for factoring services, bankers acceptance, issuing financial guaranty, commitment fees, handling charges for trade bills.
- **Payment and Money Transmission services** include fees or charges for electronic fund transfer services like SWIFT, TT, wire transfer, etc. ATM network Services, annual credit/debit card fees, Interchange charges, fees for point of services, etc also have to be reported here. Further, Charges on the customer for making remittances abroad or receiving remittances from abroad have to be reported here.
- **Fund Management services** include fee or income received for managing or administering financial portfolios, all forms of collective investment management, pension fund management, custodial, depository and trust services. Commission or fees for safe custody of shares/equities, transaction fee for custodian account, communication cost or any other fees/charges related to custodian account should also be reported.
- **Financial Consultancy and Advisory services** include fees for advisory, intermediation and other auxiliary financial services including credit reference and analysis, portfolio research and advice, advice on mergers and acquisitions and on corporate restructuring and strategy. Arrangement/management fees for Pvt. Placement of share/ equities are also to be included.
- **Underwriting services** include underwriting fees, earning from buying and reselling an entire or substantial portion of newly issued securities.

- **Clearing and Settlement services** include settlement and clearance services for financial assets, including securities, derivative products, and other negotiable instruments.
- **Derivative, Stock, Securities, Foreign Exchange trading services** include commissions, margin fees, etc received for carrying out financial derivative transactions, placement services, and redemption fees. Earnings received on banks' own account as well as on behalf of customers for carrying out foreign exchange trading has to be reported under this item. Explicit brokerage fees and commissions for foreign exchange brokerage services are also to be reported. Earnings received on banks' own account for carrying out trading in derivative, stock, securities etc should not be reported.

Modes of Trade in Banking Services

International trade in banking services occurs due to many reasons. Some possible reasons for international trade in banking services may be considered as:

1. currency substitution (currency substitution refers to the demand for domestic currency by foreigners and foreign currency by domestic residents. From a bank's perspective, this means providing foreign currency products to domestic residents or selling domestic currency products to foreign residents); and
2. cost advantage in providing banking services either due to comparative advantage or regulatory advantage (Michael Francis, 2002).

The GATS framework envisages that the delivery of any commercial services can be through four different modes. Accordingly, banking services also can be delivered through four modes as given.

A technical Group on Statistics for International Trade in Banking Services (TG-SITBS) was set up by the Reserve Bank of India including members from Ministry of Finance, Ministry of Commerce and various departments (Department of Economic and Policy Research, Department of Banking Regulation and Department of Statistics and Information Management) of the Bank.

The TG-SITBS, after examining the different data sources available in the Reserve Bank, recommended collection of activity-wise international trade in services through annual surveys and suggested that initially the data may be collected on banking services from foreign banks operating in India and Indian banks having operations abroad. The TG-SITBS also recommended that a suitable questionnaire with explanatory notes should be prepared in consultation with the banks and suggested conducting annual survey for the financial year 2006-07 by June 2007. Accordingly, a survey schedule was prepared after detailed discussions with the major foreign banks operating in India and Indian banks functioning abroad.

Table 4.1: Modes of Trade in Banking Services

Mode of Delivery	Direction of Service	Example
Mode 1: Cross Border Service	Export	Banks in India provide custodial services to Foreign Institutional Investors.
	Import	Underwriting fees paid to foreign banks for ADR/GDR issues.
Mode 2: Consumption Abroad	Export	A foreign tourist opening an account with Indian Bank.
	Import	An Indian tourist availing banking services abroad.
Mode 3: Commercial Presence	Export	Indian banks lend abroad through its branches operating abroad.
	Import	Foreign banks lend in India through its branches operating in India.
Mode 4: Movement of Natural Persons	Export	Indian banks sending its employees abroad for working abroad in its branches.
	Import	Foreign bank branches in India appointing managers from its head office abroad.

Number of Branches and Employee Distribution

Table 4.1 gives the distribution of overseas branches of Indian banks and foreign banks operating in India. The number of employees in the overseas branches and subsidiaries of Indian banks increased consistently, contraction was witnessed in employee strength of foreign banks operating in India (after the global financial crisis in 2008).

The study covered 97.9 per cent and 98.7 per cent of overseas branches of Indian banks as at end-March 2010 and end-March 2011 respectively whereas in the case of foreign banks operating in India, the coverage stood at 97.4 per cent and 96.9 per cent, respectively. The survey covered 309 out of 319 branches of foreign banks operating in India and 153 of the 155 branches/offices of Indian banks operating abroad in 29 countries as at end-March 2011.

The number of branches of Indian banks operating abroad increased by nine branches from 112 to 121 in 2008, by 13 branches in 2009, 10 branches in 2010, 9 branches in 2011, 10 branches in 2012 and 7 branches in 2013. The above shows that probably because of the impact of the financial crisis the number of branches decreased with the decreased operations and decreased activity in the economy. The impact of the global financial turbulence is visible in the number of branches of both domestic banks abroad and foreign banks in India.

Table 4.2 (a): Details of Number of Branches and Employees for the period 2007 to 2013

Item	Indian Banks Operating Abroad								Foreign Banks Operating in India						
	2007	2008	2009	2010	2011	2012	2013	Item	2007	2008	2009	2010	2011	2012	2013
No. of Branches	112	121	134 (138)	144 (147)	153 (155)	163	170	No. of Branches	257	273	289 (295)	302 (310)	309 (319)	309	316
No. of Employees	4030	2629	2919	3084	3289	3489	3761	No. of Employees	25294	30159	29824	27945	28158	27342	25118
Local	2910	3461	2004	2070	2268	2313	2424	Local	25245	30062	28741	27848	28056	27235	25019
Indians	1054	1023	841	908	947	1074	1223	Indians	NA	NA	NA	NA	NA	NA	NA
Others	66	163	74	106	74	102	114	Others	49	97	83	97	102	107	99

Source: RBI Mothly Bulletin March 2014

Note: Figures in parenthesis indicate the total number of operating branches as reported in the RBI's annual publication Statistical Tables Relating to Banks in India for 2006- 07, 2007-08, 2008-09, 2009 -10, 2010-11, 2011-12 and 2012-13

NA – Not Applicable; Local – employees who are of origin of foreign country where the bank operates; Indians - employees who are Indians ; Others – other nation people other than home country and foreign country

The number of employees decreased from 4030 in 2007 to 2629 in 2008. This could be because of the financial crisis. The number of employees has been increasing from 2009 onwards and it picked up in 2013 where the increase is 272 employees from 20012 to 2013. On the other hand, the impact of global financial turbulence on foreign banks was visible on their Indian operations too as their employee strength in India contracted by 6.3 per cent in 2009-10 before recovering marginally by 0.8 per cent during 2010-11.

It is clearly visible that the Indian banks operating abroad, has more of locals as employees as compared to Indians. But the number of Foreign locals working has decreased and the number of Indians has increased this phenomenon is probably because of the payment to Indians is less than that paid to the foreign locals. When it comes to foreign banks operating in India, they employ mostly Indians and a very small percentage of people who are from other countries other than India and the respective foreign country.

The number of employees of Indian banks operating abroad increased successively by 5.7 per cent in 2009-10 and 6.6 per cent in 2010-11. On the other hand, the impact of global financial turbulence on foreign banks was visible on their Indian operations too as their employee strength in India contracted by 6.3 percent in 2009-10 before recovering marginally by 0.8 percent during 2010-11.

During 2012-13, Indian banks operating abroad employed 64.5 per cent of employees from local sources, 32.5 per cent from India and remaining 3 per cent from other countries. In case of foreign banks working in India, the share of local employees in total employees was much higher (99.6 per cent) in 2012-13. The number of employees of Indian banks operating abroad increased by 7.8 per cent and the number of employees of the foreign banks operating in India decreased by 8.1 per cent during 2012-13. Indian banks branches operating abroad employed 62.3 per cent of employees from local sources, 29.8 per cent from India and remaining 7.9 per cent from other countries in 2013-14. In contrast, foreign banks working in India had an overwhelming share of local employees (99.4 per cent) in their total employees. The number of employees in Indian banks' branches operating abroad increased by 5.5 per cent during 2013-14. In the case of foreign banks operating in India, number of employees declined by 1.6 per cent.

Of the 170 overseas branches of Indian banks in 2013, highest number of branches were located in the United Kingdom (30), followed by Hong Kong (19), Singapore (17), United Arab Emirates (13), Fiji (9), Sri Lanka (9) and Mauritius (9). State Bank of India (with 51 branches in 21 countries) and Bank of Baroda (51 branches in 13 countries) had the largest overseas presence, followed by Bank of India (25 branches in 13 countries). The number of branches of Indian banks operating abroad has increased in 2011 from 121 to 155 and the number of Foreign Banks Operating in India also has increased from 257 to 319. As per the balance sheets of Commercial banks operating abroad for March 2011, the highest number of branches of Indian banks were in the United Kingdom (28), followed by Hong Kong (18), Singapore (16), Fiji (9), United Arab Emirates (11), Mauritius (8), and Sri Lanka (8). Among Indian banks, Bank of Baroda had the largest overseas presence with 47 branches in 14 countries, followed by State Bank of India (45 branches in 19 countries) and Bank of India (24 branches in 12 countries).

Business Growth and Profitability Trend

Business Growth: Growth of Indian banks abroad is outpacing the growth of foreign banks in India. While the number of branches of foreign banks operating in India exceeds the number of Indian bank branches abroad, the growth in the latter has been more than the former in the recent years. As at end-March 2013, there were 43 foreign banks operating in India with 331 branches. As against this, there were 24 Indian banks with 171 branches abroad. Although Indian banks had a subsidiarised presence abroad, foreign banks operated only as branches with no subsidiaries as at end-March 2013. Taking into account the number of branches plus subsidiaries the presence of Indian banks in foreign markets has been growing at a much faster pace than the presence of foreign banks in India. Moreover, the expansion of overseas operations of Indian private sector banks has been relatively faster.

The subdued level of activity in the business of foreign banks operating in India was observed in 2012-13 following the economic slowdown in India.

The growth of assets/liabilities of Indian banks' branches operating abroad was 9.1 per cent during 2007-08 as against 55.8 per cent in the previous year. It slightly increased to 15.5% in the year 2009-10 and in the year 2010-11 it went up to 39.5% (Table 4.2). The credit extended and deposits mobilised by the Indian banks' branches abroad increased by 36.8 per cent and 9.9 per cent, respectively during 2007-08 compared to 48.8 per cent and 51.3 per cent, respectively in the previous year. The growth has picked up for credit extended and deposits mobilised in the year 2010 -11 to 39.5 and 30.5 as against 14.7 and 16.6 in the previous year. Thus, there was distinctive slow down in the banking activity of the overseas branches of the Indian banks in 2007-08 as compared to the previous year. The share of credit extended in total assets of Indian banks branches operating overseas increased by 57.6 per cent as at end March 2008 over the corresponding period of the previous year whereas the share of deposits mobilised in total liabilities of Indian banks increased marginally for the same period. The subdued level of activity in the global financial sector during 2009-10 was visible in the overseas operations of Indian banks. The consolidated balance sheet, of overseas branches of Indian banks, has increased by 15.5 per cent and 42.7 per cent in 2009-10 and 2010-11 respectively.

Table 4.2 (b): Growth in Credit extended and Deposits Mobilised of Indian Banks Operating Abroad for the period 2005-2013

(Percent)

Item	Growth (%) in 2006-07	Growth (%) in 2007-08	Growth (%) in 2008-09	Growth (%) in 2009-10	Growth (%) in 2010-11	Growth (%) in 2011-12	Growth (%) in 2012-13
Credit Extended	48.8	36.8	36.6	14.7	39.5	27.1	31.6
Deposits Mobilised	51.3	9.9	21.7	16.6	30.5	27.1	45.5
Total Assets	55.8	9.1	24.3	15.5	42.7	29.3	34.3

Source: RBI Mothly Bulletin March 2014

Table 4.3: Credit extended and Deposits Mobilised of Indian Banks Operating Abroad for the period 2006-2013

(Rs. Crores)

Item	2006	2007	2008	2009	2010	2011	2012	2013
Credit Extended	78657	117069	160185	218830	251000	350120	445110	585570
Deposits Mobilised	69078	104526	114826	139690	162900	212570	270090	393070
Total Assets	164310	256018	279300	347050	400900	572050	739920	993980

Source: RBI Monthly Bulletin March 2014

The credit extended grew by 48.8 per cent from 78657 crores in 2006 to 117069 crores in 2007. Further they grew by 32.6 per cent from 2012 to 2013. The growth in the credit extended is all through from 2006 to 2013. Despite the entry of the foreign banks the credit extended increased. Credit extended by Indian banks' branches operating overseas increased by 31.2 per cent to ' 7,684.4 billion (US$ 127.9 billion) in 2013-14. In contrast, credit by foreign banks in India declined by 3.1 per cent to ' 2,982.1 billion (US$ 49.6 billion). Deposits of Indian banks' branches operating abroad increased by 30.8 per cent to 5,143 billion during 2013-14 whereas deposit mobilisation by foreign banks operating in India recorded 23.5 per cent growth to 3,501 billion (US$ 58.2 billion) in March 2014.

The credit extended by Indian Banks operating abroad has grown by 48.8 % from 2005-06 to 2006-07. The rate of growth of credit extended started declining till 2009-10 where it was least but picked up in 2010-11 and finally it reached a growth rate of 31.6% in 2012-13. There has been a growth in the deposits mobilized but the growth rate has decreased from 51.3% in 2006-07 to 9.9% in 2007-08 finally the growth rate increased to 45.5%.

The balance sheet size of foreign banks operating in India saw an annual growth of 40.2% in 2006-07, 33.4% in 2007-08 and 22.8% in 2008-09. It contracted by 3.1 per cent during 2009-10, but increased subsequently by 13.3 per cent in the next year. Credit extended by them which recorded an annual growth of 30.5 in 2006-07 recorded a marginal decline during

2009-10 before recovering by 21.6 per cent in 2010-11. On the other hand, deposit growth which was 33.6% in 2006-07 came down to 11.1 per cent in 2009-10 moderated to 1.1 per cent in 2010-11.

The share of foreign banks in total assets/liabilities of SCB[2] in India increased from 7.0 in 2006 to 8.5 in 2009. It declined from 8.5 per cent in March 2009 to 6.8 per cent in March 2011 due to their lower business growth (deposit and credit) vis-à-vis other banks. Their share in credit declined from 6.3 per cent in March 2006 to 4.6 per cent in March 2011 whereas share in deposits declined from 5.1 per cent to 4.3 per cent over the same period.

The growth in income of foreign banks operating in India moderated from 18.5 per cent in 2011- 12 to 13.1 per cent in 2012-13. This is in synchrony with the contraction of their balance sheets and lower interest income.

Profitability: Profitability of foreign banks in India was more volatile but substantially higher than the overseas branches/subsidiaries of Indian banks, during the last five years. The profitability ratio as measured by return on assets (ROA: profit to total assets) increased for all the three categories during 2012-13 and their income to asset ratio in 2012 -13 was lower than respective 2008-09 level.

The share of foreign banks in total income of all commercial banks in India declined from 9.8 per cent in 2008-09 to 6.9 per cent in 2010-11, which was mainly attributable to the reduction in the share of interest income from 7.8 per cent to 5.8 per cent. During 2010-11, the share of interest income in total income was 72.5 per cent for foreign banks and 86.1 per cent for all SCBs. Total income of Indian banks' overseas branches and foreign banks operating in India declined during 2009-10 due to moderation in business and general decline in interest rates in the wake of global financial crisis but it recorded substantial rise in the next year .The expenses of Indian banks' operating abroad and foreign banks operating in India fell by 26.3 per cent and 38.7 per cent, respectively, in 2009-10. During 2010-11, however, their income and expenses increased substantially consistent with increase in their balance sheets.

The subdued level of activity in the business of foreign banks operating in India was observed in 2012-13 following economic slowdown in India. Growth of the consolidated balance sheet of foreign banks operating in India moderated to 5.2 per cent in 2012-13 from 17.5 per cent in the previous year. However, the business of the Indian banks' overseas branches continued to robust at 34.3 per cent in 2012-13 on top of 29.3 per cent growth in 2011-12.

The profitability ratios viz., net profit to total income and net profit to total assets of overseas branches of Indian banks increased sharply to 31.8 per cent and 1.1 per cent, respectively, in 2010-11 compared with 1.3 per cent and 0.1 per cent in 2008-09 (Table 4.5). The ratios of net profit to total income and net profit to total assets of branches of foreign banks operating in India increased to 44.9 percent and 3.8 percent, respectively, in 2009-10 before moderating to 28.6 per cent and 2.3 per cent in 2010-11. The income to total assets ratio for overseas branches of Indian banks and foreign banks' operating in India declined to 3.4 per cent and 8.0 per cent, respectively, in 2010-11 from 4.7percent and 8.7 percent in 2005-06.

Activity - wise and Country-wise Profitability of Indian Banks Branches Operating Abroad

Activity-wise Trade in Banking Services

Indian banks operating abroad generated major share of fee income by rendering service activity viz., credit related services, whereas in the case of foreign banks operating in India 'derivative, stock, securities, foreign exchange trading services', 'Financial consultancy and Advisory Services' and ' Trade Finance Related Services' occupied the major share of total trade in banking services.

The share of credit related services in total fee income, in case of Indian banks, increased significantly to 54.7 percent in 2007-08 from 43.8 per cent in 2006-07. In case of foreign banks operating in India, the share of trade finance related services increased from 10.2 per cent to 16.5 per cent during the same period. Indian banks operating abroad generated major share of fee income by rendering 'credit-related services' and 'trade-finance related services', which together accounted for 80.3 per cent and 78.6 percent to total fee income in 2009-10 and 2010-11, respectively. On the other hand, 'derivative, stock, securities, foreign exchange trading services' and 'financial consultancy and advisory services' were the major source of fee income for the foreign banks operating in India during the reference period. The share of fee income from 'credit-related services' in total fee income of Indian banks operating outside India, increased successively from 39.2 percent in 2008-09 to 54.4 per cent in 2010-11 whereas the share of 'trade-finance related services' declined from 40.3per cent to 24.2 per cent over the same period.

The share of 'trade-finance related services' in total fee income, of foreign banks operating in India declined from 17.7 per cent in 2008-09 to 11.1 per cent in 2010-11 (Table 4.3) but the share 'financial consultancy and advisory services' doubled during 2009-10 before declining marginally by 14.1 per cent in 2010-11. Indian banks operating abroad derived no fee income from 'underwriting services' during the reference period.

Table 4.4: Composition of Trade in Banking Services

(Percent)

Name of Banking Services	Indian Banks Operating Abroad								Foreign Banks Operating in India							
	2005-06	2006-07	2007-08	2008-09	2009-10	2010-11	2011-12	2012-13	2005-06	2006-07	2007-08	2008-09	2009-10	2010-11	2011-12	2012-13
Deposit Account Management Services	4.5	2.8	2	2.7	1.7	2.1	2.7	8.3	4.1	3	5	2.8	4.1	3.8	5.4	5.1
Credit Related Services	31.9	43.8	54.7	39.2	47.2	54.4	37.6	43.2	9.9	7.6	6.7	8.4	7.2	9	10.9	12.2
Finanacial Leasing Services	0	0	0	0	0.2	0	0	0	0	0	0	0.9	0	0	0	0
Trade Finance Related Services	31.7	21.7	14.1	40.3	33.1	24.2	26.8	36.7	13.6	10.2	16.5	17.7	14	11.1	19	22.1
Payment and Money Transmission Services	10.7	17.6	5.9	9.1	9.2	6	14.8	5.7	13	23.3	5	7	7	17.5	9.2	15
Fund Management Services	6.5	3.5	0	0.1	0.5	0	0	0	4.3	3.4	4.9	3.1	4.7	5.2	5.9	6.1
Financial Consultancy and Advisory Services	0	1.3	5	2.4	1.3	2.1	0.4	0.1	8.9	12.5	8.8	9.6	19.5	14.1	14.4	15
Underwriting Services Clearing and Settlement Services	0 -	0.3 -	0 0.6	0 0.6	0 0	0 0	0 2.8	0 0.3	0.5 4.5	1 5.4	0.6 1	0.8 3.4	0.4 2.2	0.4 2	0.4 3.7	0.2 1.2
Derivative, Stock, Securities, Foreign Exchange trading Services	13.3	8.4	7.9	4.4	5.9	10.2	14.1	3.5	35.8	28.5	34.1	35.2	18.7	27.1	21.5	17.6
Other Financial Services	1.3	0.7	9.8	1.2	0.9	1	0.9	2.3	5.4	5.2	17.4	11.1	22.1	9.8	9.6	5.6
All activities	100	100	100	100	100	100	100	100	100	100	100	100	100	100	100	100

Source: RBI Monthly Bulletin, Various Issues

Table 4.5: List of best and consistent performers of Domestic Banks for the period 2005 to 2013

	2005	2006	2007	2008	2009	2010	2011	2012	2013		
Decision Making Units [DMUs]s	Efficiency (Theta)	Efficiency (Theta)	Efficiency (Theta)	Efficiency (Theta)	Efficiency (Theta)	Efficiency (Theta)	Efficiency (Theta)	Efficiency (Theta)	Efficiency (Theta)	Standard Deviation	Coefficient of Variation
IDBI Bank Limited	1	1	1	**1**	1	1	0.664212	1	1	0.1119293	0.1162672
Yes Bank Ltd.	0.247212	1	1	**0.890674**	0.75572	0.755618	0.48022	1	1	0.2691266	0.3397375
Jammu & Kashmir Bank Ltd	0.820929	0.791668	0.635213	**0.723731**	0.735649	0.655204	0.395193	0.706752	0.813019	0.1307355	0.1874386
City Union Bank Limited	1	0.778414	0.6237	**0.675954**	0.691153	0.785735	0.50353	0.7925	0.828976	0.1404135	0.189181
Karur Vysya Bank Ltd.	0.669693	0.610307	0.587592	**0.624984**	0.662583	0.656018	0.422527	0.729896	0.7348	0.0931687	0.1471497
Oriental Bank of Commerce	0.779929	0.682761	0.6381	**0.754923**	0.734884	0.733495	0.515904	0.762979	0.832548	0.0930448	0.1301221
Federal Bank Ltd.	0	0.634678	0.447884	**0.645081**	0.677274	0.66701	0.395193	0.659468	0.677821	0.2260973	0.4235434
Indusind Bank Ltd.	1	0.599935	0.6801	**0.674416**	0.522465	0.550147	0.287477	0.695448	0.736379	0.1912135	0.29948
Vijaya Bank	0.681392	0.592719	0.536733	**0.662414**	0.657141	0.588043	0.329335	0.748018	0.836328	0.1427485	0.2281087
State Bank of Patiala	0.767465	0.64421	0.574061	**0.728328**	0.848651	0.802692	0.393476	0.694213	0.758224	0.1385084	0.2006942
Corporation Bank	0.583765	0.563946	0.517774	**0.605896**	0.67373	0.674162	0.44945	0.823044	0.965628	0.1589605	0.2442459
State Bank of Hyderabad	0.594206	0.539744	0.514766	**0.658849**	0.710501	0.781238	0.419196	0.693096	0.746691	0.1198503	0.1906324
Tamilnad Mercantile Bank Ltd.	0.815509	0.697085	0.578465	**0.557222**	0.569901	0.64809	0.40569	0.726358	0.876292	0.1442279	0.2209594
Uco Bank	0.55898	0.748455	0.844066	**0.594294**	0.643529	0.725084	0.442534	0.795623	0.962452	0.1590086	0.226615
Federal Bank Ltd.	0.613777	0.634678	0.557884	**0.606634**	0.647315	0.649034	0.419275	0.736496	0.828781	0.1128555	0.1783845

Source: Authors own work

The above are the domestic banks operating in India and are performing well consistently as indicated by their least Coefficient of Variation of the theta across a period of nine years.

Table 4.6: Efficiency of Foreign Banks for the period 2005 to 2013

	2005	2006	2007	2008	2009	2010	2011	2012	2013		
Decision Making Units [Dmus]	Efficiency (Theta)	Efficiency (Theta)	Efficiency (Theta)	Efficiency (Theta)	Efficiency (Theta)	Efficiency (Theta)	Efficiency (Theta)	Efficiency (Theta)	Efficiency (Theta)	Standard Deviation	Coefficient of Variation
Jpmorgan Chase Bank National Association	0.510944	1	1	**1**	1	1	1	1	1	0.163019	0.172386
Bank of Nova Scotia	0.829788	0.685874	0.99105	**1**	1	1	1	1	1	0.112189	0.118694
Mashreq Bank Psc	1	1	1	**0.84247**	0.862447	1	1	1	1	0.065251	0.067463
Krung Thai Bank Public Company Limited	0.197439	1	0.48832	**0.617772**	0.709526	0.640284	1	1	1	0.285903	0.386742
Bank of Ceylon	0.679368	0.482796	0.62549	**0.770246**	1	1	1	1	1	0.203801	0.242688
Antwerp Diamond Bank Nv	0.662626	1	1	**0.949575**	1	0.565541	0.42303	0.822482	0.597929	0.222516	0.285229
Credit Agricole Corporate and Investment Bank	0.517677	0.481939	0.66975	**0.751711**	0.973322	1	1	1	0.758489	0.209667	0.26381
Ab Bank Limited		0.951254	0.52952	**0.738588**	0.514368	1	0.900596	1	0.92593	0.201481	0.245698
State Bank of Mauritius Ltd.	1	1	0.7987	**0.693278**	0.824356	0.70696	0.742531	0.883786	1	0.126739	0.149112
Dbs Bank Ltd.	0.656733	0.960401	1	**1**	0.699706	0.926305	0.670216	0.636975	0.650479	0.165092	0.206342

Source: Authors own work

The above are the foreign banks operating in India and are performing well consistently as indicated by their least Coefficient of Variation of the theta across a period of nine years.

A dominant portion of the fee income of the Indian Bank's overseas branches came from non-residents. Overseas branches of Indian banks generated more fee income since 2009-10 by rendering banking services, mainly due to higher focus on 'Credit Related services' and 'Trade Finance Related Services'. Their fee income rose by nearly 2.8 times during the last three years. On the other hand, overseas subsidiaries of Indian banks recorded contraction in such fee income during 2009-10 and 2010-11 and its level in 2012-13 remains less than half of the fee income in 2008-09.

Indian banks' branches operating abroad generated major share of fee income by rendering 'credit related services' and 'trade finance related services', whereas foreign banks operating in India received major part of their fee income from 'Derivative, stock, securities, foreign exchange trading services', 'Financial Consultancy and Advisory Services' and 'Trade Finance Related services' (Table 4.3)

Total fee income generated by 170 branches of Indian banks operating outside India increased from 68.0 billion in 2011-12 to '93.5 billion in 2012-13 whereas, in case of foreign banks operating in India, total fee income generated by 316 branches declined from '94.3 billion in 2011-12 to '74.5 billion in 2012-13. A dominant portion of fee income of the Indian banks branches operating abroad came from rendering services to non-residents, whereas in case of Indian Banks overseas subsidiaries, it came from the residents. Profitability ratio of foreign banks in India was more volatile but higher than the overseas branches/subsidiaries of Indian banks, during the last five years.

Country wise Trade in Banking Services

Bahrain, Belgium, Hong Kong, Japan, Singapore, Sri Lanka, UAE, UK and USA were the major source countries which accounted together for nearly 92.2 per cent in total banking services provided by overseas branches of Indian Banks. Overseas subsidiaries of Indian banks were mainly present in Botswana, Canada, Russia and United Kingdom.

Country-wise return on assets, i.e., net profit to total assets of Indian banks operating abroad is presented in Chart 4.1. It has been observed that country-wise return on assets in majority of countries, where the Indian banks were operating, improved during 2006-07 over the previous year. Return on assets of Indian banks operating in Oman was the highest at 2.4 per cent in 2006- 07, followed by in Singapore (1.9 per cent) and UAE (1.7 per cent). However, the return on assets of Indian banks operating in the countries like Fiji, Hong Kong, Thailand and USA declined during 2006-07 as compared with the previous year. The return on assets of Indian banks operating in Sri Lanka was the highest at 2.4 per cent in 2007-08, followed by Singapore (1.8 per cent) and Oman (1.7 per cent). It was observed that return on assets of Indian banks' overseas branches improved in 2007-08 over the preceding year in case of Sri Lanka, Bahrain, Belgium, France and Hong Kong and declined in case of Japan, Mauritius, Thailand, the UK and the US. Indian banks operating in Maldives recorded highest return on assets of 4.6 per cent and 5.1 per cent, respectively, in 2009-10 and 2010-11. The return on assets of Indian banks' overseas branches in Australia, Hong Kong, Japan, Oman, Singapore, Thailand, UK and USA improved in 2009-10 and 2010-11 but it declined in Sri Lanka, Fiji, Mauritius, Belgium, Bahrain and France.

Cross-border presence of both Indian and foreign banks have increased in the recent years. The consolidated balance sheet of overseas branches of Indian banks, which moderated after the global financial crisis, recovered in subsequent years whereas that of foreign banks operating in India is continuing to grow at a relatively moderate pace. The share of non-interest income in total income of foreign banks in India was more than that for overseas branches of Indian banks, as the former had more non-fund-based activities whereas the latter generated major share of their fee income by rendering 'credit related services' and 'trade finance related services'.

EFFICIENCY OF FOREIGN BANK ENTRY AND DOMESTIC BANKS

Several studies have found that the entry of foreign bank can bring potential benefits in terms of better resource allocation and higher efficiency (Levine, 1996; Walter and Gray, 1983; Goldberg and Saunders, 1981; Gelb and Sagari, 1990). Moreover, the study of Levine (1996) had mentioned that allow the entry of foreign banks may (i) enhance domestic financial development by promote improvement of domestic financial infrastructure and financial policy, (ii) improve a country's access to international capital markets, (iii) improve the financial services quality in domestic bank by stimulate bank competition and subsequently encourage the domestic banks implement more advance banking skills and technology.

However, the foreign banks entry has certain disadvantages too. According to Stiglitz (1993), the entry of foreign bank can bring impact to domestic banks in term of potential costs. The researcher found that domestic banks have to incur more costs in order to compete with foreign banks by applying more advance banking skills and technology. In addition, the results of Claessens et al (2001) shown that the foreign banks entry has brought certain risks to domestic banks by making the competition more intense and thereby reduce the earnings of domestic banks.

The present study identifies the gap that there is no study so far identifying the efficiency of foreign banks operating in India and the efficiency of the domestic banks exploring the impact of foreign bank entry on the domestic bank performance.

Method and Analysis - Data Envelopment Analysis

In general there are two basic approaches that estimate efficiency, the parametric and the non- parametric ones. The parametric methods require explicit assumptions about the function that convert inputs into outputs and about the distribution of the error terms. On the other hand the non parametric methods (including Data Envelopment Analysis) do not require functional form. DEA requires only the necessary data, input variables and output variables. Due to the advantages of non parametric methods, in recent years DEA has gained researchers' and managers' interest. The method is used to estimate the relative efficiency of homogenous decision making units such as hospitals, public institutions, banks, financial institutions, schools, farms etc. DEA is a mathematical programming approach calculating the technical efficiency expressed by the ratio of the weighted sum of outputs to the weighted sum of inputs.

Measurement efûciency of decision-making units (DMUs) such as hospitals, banks, universities etc. that use multiple inputs and produce multiple outputs is complex. Charnes et al.(1978) introduced a non-parametric approach in such situations to measure the technical efûciency of a set of comparable DMUs – data envelopment analysis (DEA).DEA uses input= output variables to construct an efûcient frontier from a set of observed DMUs. Then the efûciency of each DMU is calculated by measuring the distance of the DMU to the efûcient frontier. Over the last decade DEA has gained considerable attention as a powerful managerial tool for performance measurement and it has been widely used for assessing the efûciency of the public and private sectors (Emrouznejad *et al.*, 2008).

Data Envelopment Analysis is a decision making tool based on linear programming for measuring the relative efficiencies of a set of comparable units. DEA is initially developed by Charnes, Cooper, Rhodes (1978). The basic DEA model is called the CCR model. It is important to mention that the CCR model is used only in problems with constant returns to scale (CRS). Literature shows that the competition of foreign banks compel domestic banks to be more efficient but, although foreign banks may have higher productivity in the primary stage, domestic banks learn from foreign banks and imitate their operating skills following a time variance. Thus, the productivity of domestic banks will improve, and the advantages of foreign banks may gradually disappear. In particular, this result occurs easily in both rapidly developed and close developed countries.

About DEA

DEA is a method for measuring efficiency of DMUs using linear programming techniques to envelop observed input–output vectors as tightly as possible (Boussofiane, Dyson, and Thanassoulis 1991). DEA allows multiple inputs–outputs to be considered at the same time without any assumption on data distribution. In each case, efficiency is measured in terms of a proportional change in inputs or outputs. A DEA model can be subdivided into an input-oriented model, which minimizes inputs while satisfying at least the given output levels, and an output- oriented model, which maximizes outputs without requiring more of any observed input values. DEA models can also be subdivided in terms of returns to scale by adding weight constraints. Charnes, Cooper, and Rhodes (1978) originally proposed the efficiency measurement of the DMUs for constant returns to scale (CRS), where all DMUs are operating at their optimal scale. Later Banker, Charnes, and Cooper (1984) introduced the variable returns to scale (VRS) efficiency measurement model, allowing the breakdown of efficiency into technical and scale efficiencies in DEA.

DEA is a nonparametric linear programming method for assessing the efficiency and productivity of DMUs. DEA application areas have grown since it was first introduced as a managerial and performance measurement tool in the late 1970s. Since then, new applications with more variables and complicated models have been and are being introduced. Stata equipped with the dea command will provide the user with a new nonparametric tool to analyze productivity data. From within Stata, users will be able to produce DEA scores and analyze them. The dea command introduced in this article is a new application in Stata and is a powerful managerial tool for measuring the efficiency and productivity of DMUs.

The DMU is called efficient when the DEA score equals 1 and all slacks are 0 (Cooper, Seiford, and Tone 2006).

In the present study attempts to measure the change in the efficiency of foreign banks operating in India during 2005-2013. By using frontier based non-parametric technique, i.e., Data Envelopment Analysis (DEA).

This study uses the DEA method according to the production approach in order to evaluate the 44 foreign banks and 57 domestic banks that participate in the Indian banking system estimating the relative efficiency of each one. The period of the study is nine years from 2005 to 2013. The input variables considered for the study are number of offices, number of employees and operating expenses and output variables taken for analysis are profit per employee, interest income and return on assets.

On performing DEA, the efficiency as indicated by theta (θ) is obtained and the ranks for banks based on their efficiencies are obtained. The most efficient bank is one that obtains the highest efficiency score.

Then all the domestic banks and foreign banks performing consistently across a period of time based on the theta are identified. After identifying the theta values and the ranks are generated for the foreign banks and domestic banks standard deviation and coefficient of variation are calculated for each bank across a period of nine years.

Standard deviation (α) signifies the variability and shows the deviation in the efficiency of the bank. The coefficient of variation (CV) is a normalized measure of dispersion of a probability distribution or frequency distribution. It is defined as the ratio of the standard deviation to the mean. The lower the CV the more consistent the banks are in their performance. Through this method of all the foreign banks operating in India the best and consistent performers are identified. Similarly the domestic banks which are best performers and consistent in their performance are identified.

Also a comparison among the foreign and domestic banks shows that despite the entry of the foreign banks the performance of the domestic banks is not much affected merely by the entry.

The following table shows the list of best performing domestic banks. IDBI Bank, SBI Commercial International, Karur Vysya Bank, City Union Bank, Yes Bank, Jammu and Kashmir Bank Ltd and Oriental Bank of Commerce have been consistent performers despite of the entry of foreign banks and their increase in the operations. Among the foreign banks Bank of Nova Scotia, JPMORGAN Chase Bank National Association, MASHREQ BANK PSC,Bank Internasional Indonesia, DBS Bank Ltd and State Bank of Mauritius Ltd. are good and consistent performers.

The following are the charts showing the top five efficient and best and consistent performers of foreign banks. The time period is taken on the X-axis and the efficiency as indicated by theta which ranges from 0 to 1 is taken on the Y-axis.

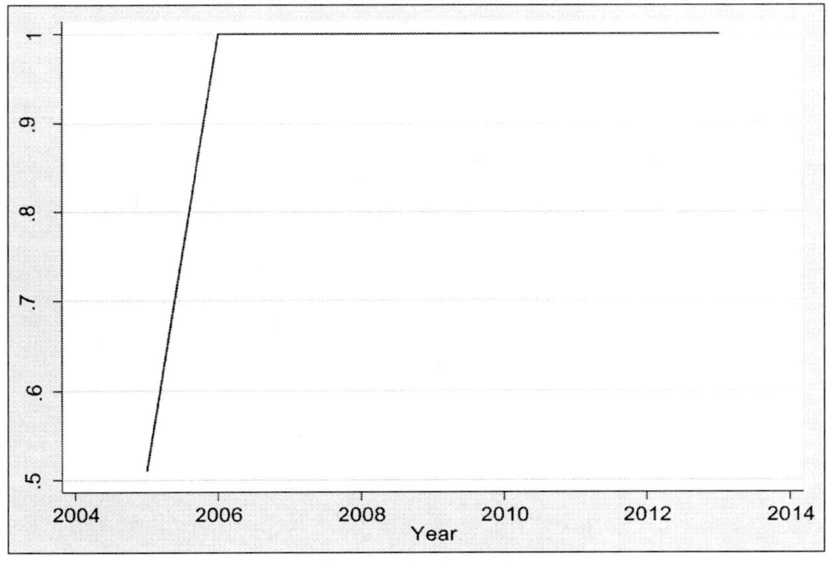

Chart 4.1: Efficiency of JP Morgan Chase International

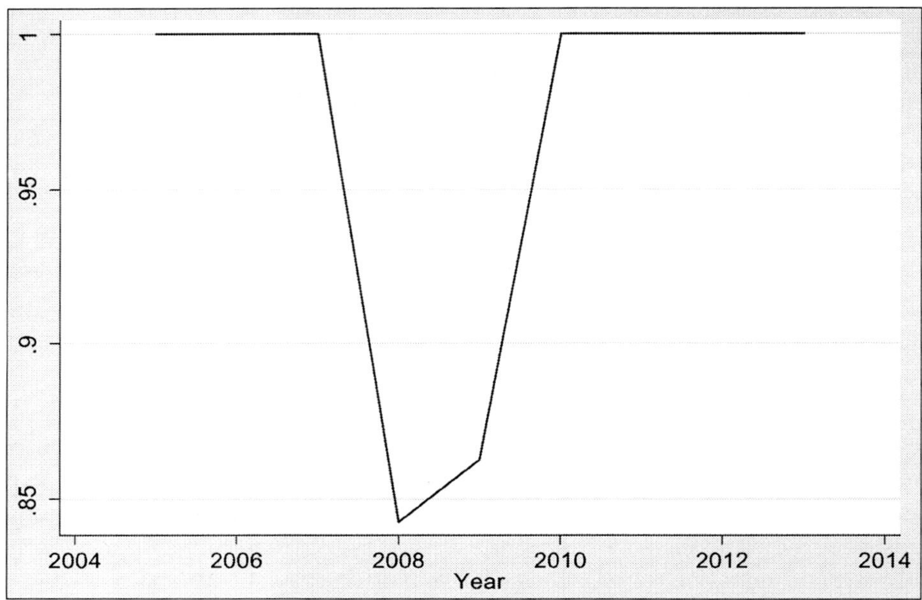

Chart 4.2: Efficiency of Mashreq Bank PSC

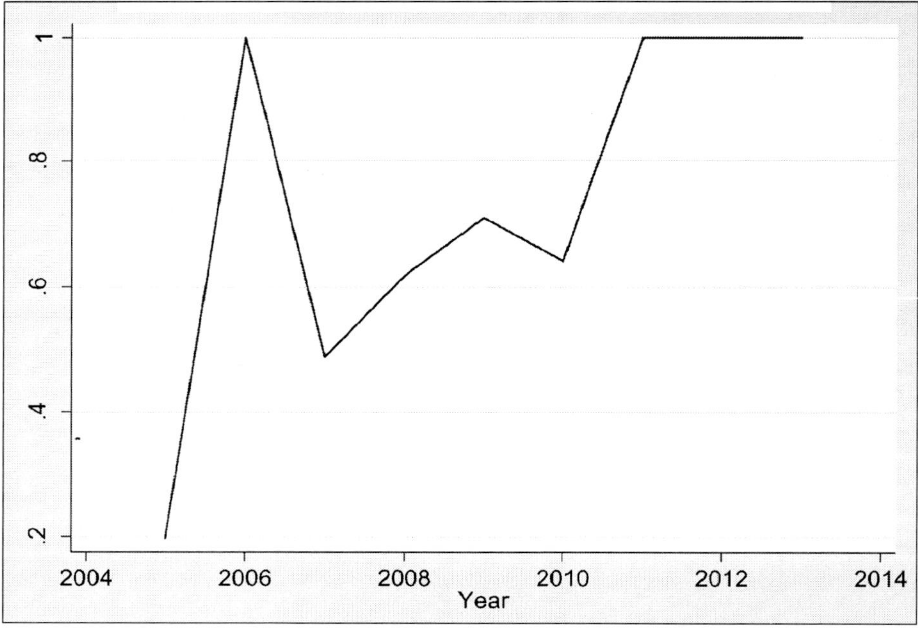

Chart 4.3: Efficiency of Krung Thai Bank Public

The above chart shows the efficiency of Krung Thai Bank, a bank of Thailand. As it is seen from the chart it has improved its efficiency since 2004 and has been performing efficiently with score of 1 in the year 2.3

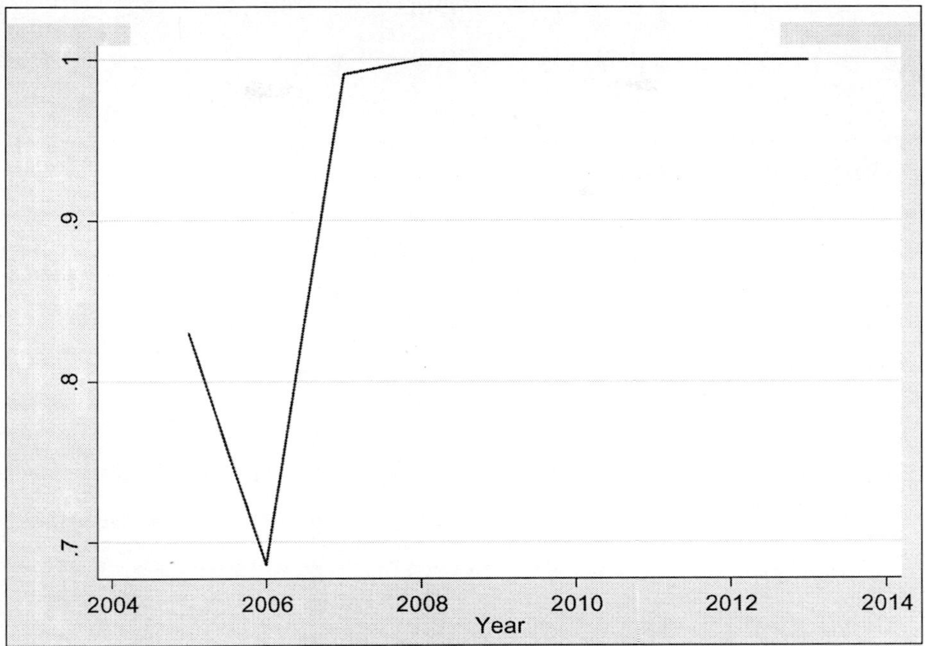

Chart 4.4: Efficiency of Bank of Nova Scotia

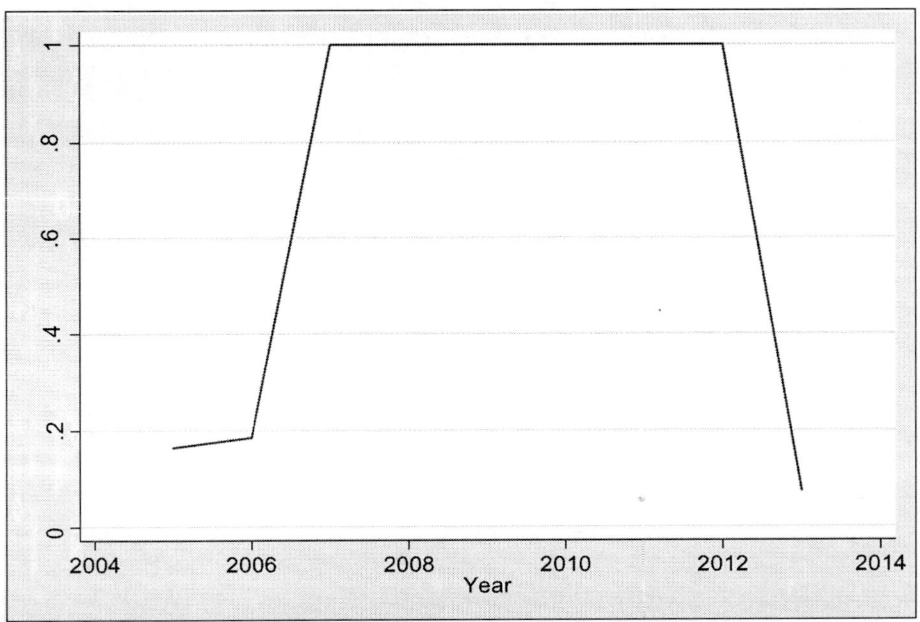

Chart 4.5: Efficiency of Bank of International Indonesia

Best and consistent performers of Domestic Banks

The following are the charts which show the best and consistent performing domestic banks in terms of efficiency as indicated by theta (θ) the efficiency score derived by performing DEA.

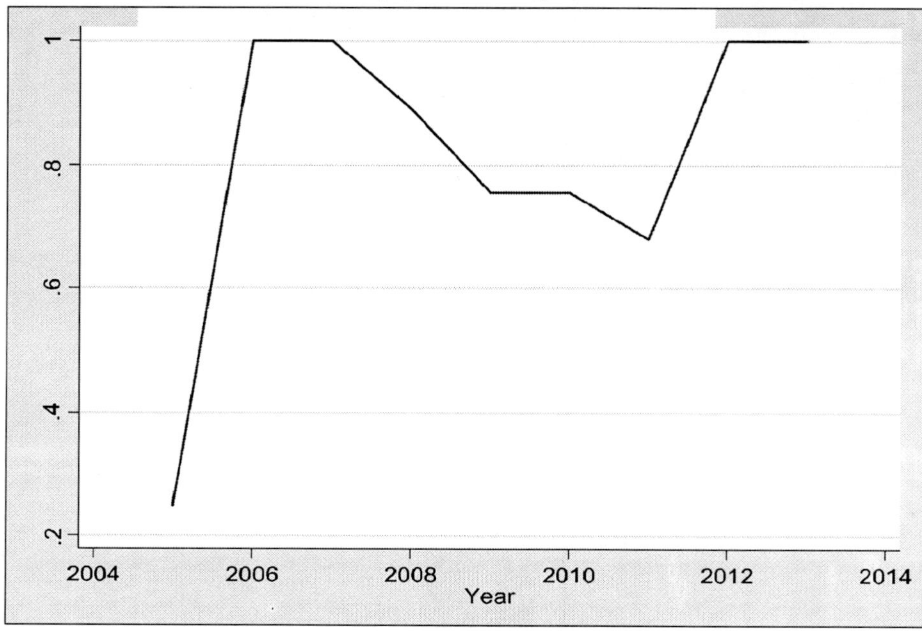

Chart 4.6: Efficiency of Yes Bank Ltd.

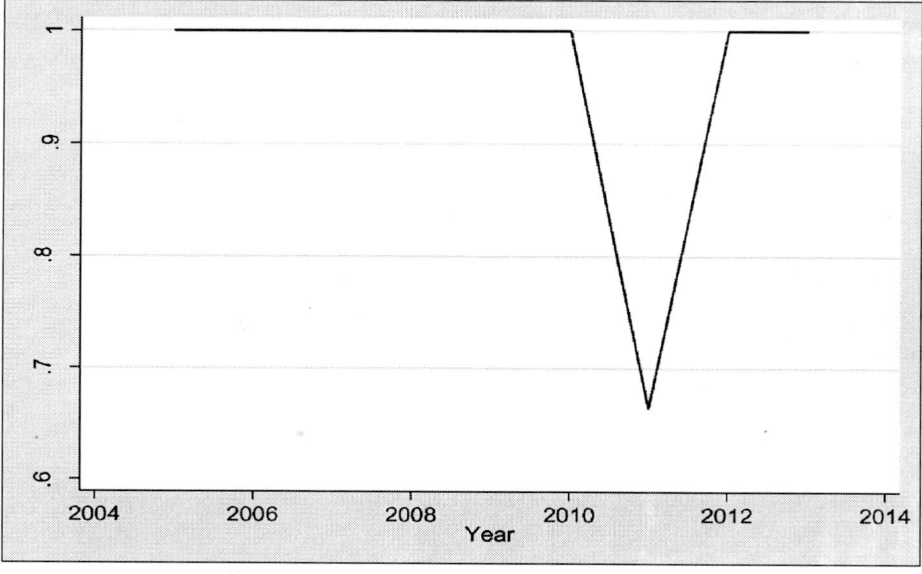

Chart 4.7: Efficiency of IDBI Bank

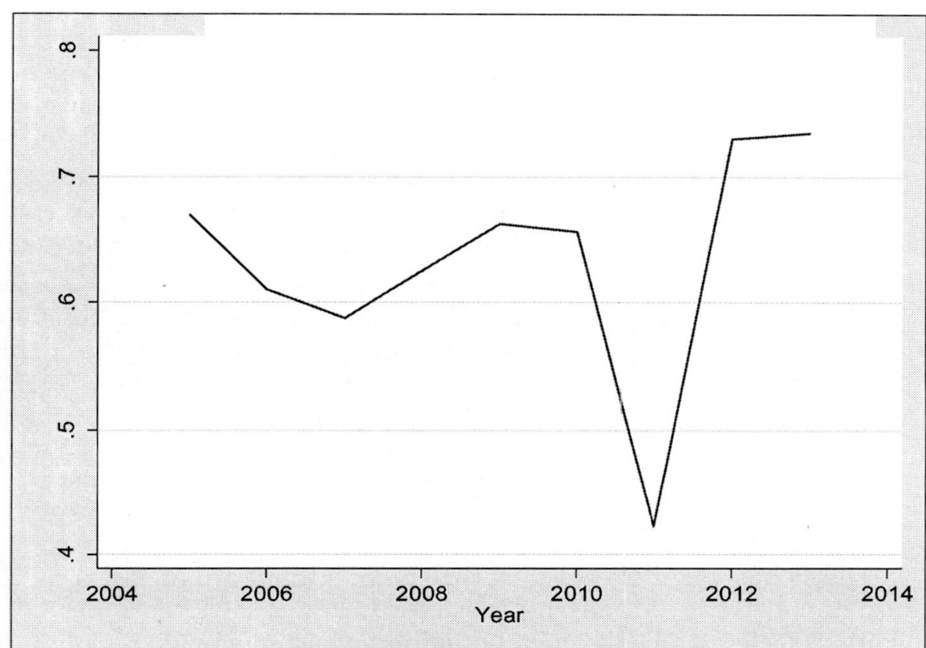

Chart 4.8: Efficiency of Karur Vysya Bank

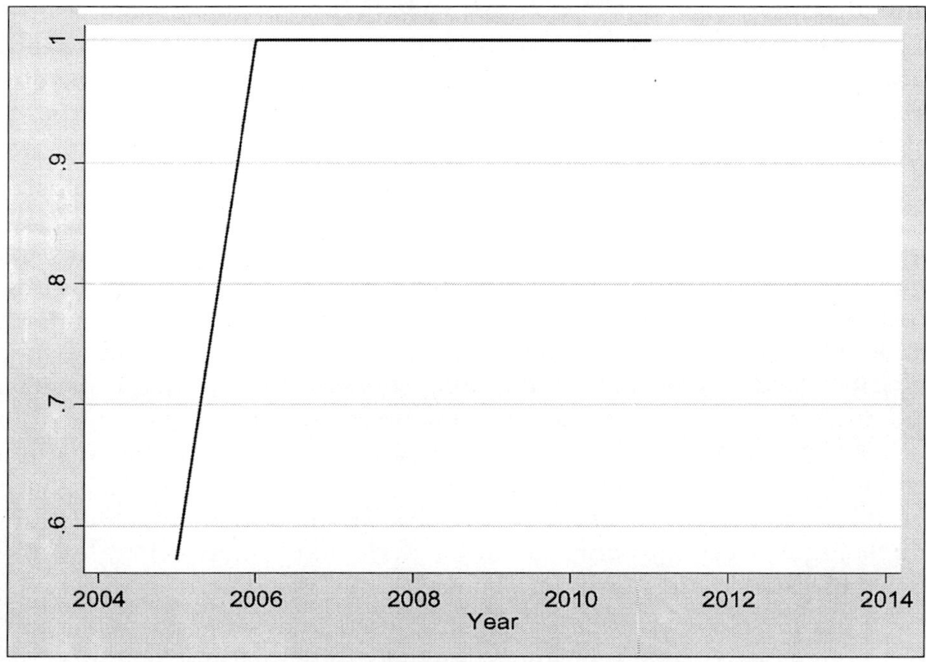

Chart 4.9: Efficiency of SBI Commercial & International

The chart 4.7 shows the efficiency of IDBI bankwhich has been most efficient in almost all years with a theta score of 1 except for the year 2011. The chart 4.8 shows the efficiency of Karur Vysya Bank which has been performing well in almost all years except 2011. Though it has never got an efficiency score of 1 it is always above 0.6 and has been a consistent performer.

The chart 4.8 is of Karur Vysya Bank with time period on X-axis and the efficiency as indicated by theta on the Y-axis it shows that excepting for one year it has always been getting an efficiency score above 0.60 or above.

The chart 4.9 shows the efficiency of SBI Commercial & International Bank Ltd. it has been consistently performing with an efficiency of from the year 2006 to 2013.

The above banks are the best and consistent performing domestic banks, showing that there is not much impact on the entry of foreign banks on the performance of the domestic banks.

FINDINGS AND CONCLUSION

There has been an adverse effect of global financial crisis on international trade in banking services during 2008-11 as reflected in operations of foreign banks operating in India and some moderation in the operations of overseas branches/subsidiaries of Indian banks operating abroad. These were reflected in changes in size of their balance sheets, activity-wise and country wise composition of fee income, profitability ratios. Foreign banks' operations in India were subdued in the wake of the crisis and their balance sheet which contracted during 2009-10 expanded later in 2010-11.

Overseas branches of Indian banks continued to expand their business as credit-related services constituted a major portion of their overseas operations. The fee income of overseas branches of Indian banks from rendering services to residents, non-residents in India and non-residents from other countries was evenly distributed whereas a dominant portion of fee income of foreign banks came from residents. 'Derivative, stock, securities, and foreign exchange trading services and financial consultancy and advisory services' were the major sources of foreign banks' fee income in India and the size of operations of foreign banks in India was much larger than the operations of overseas operations of India banks during the reference period. As such, income from trade in banking services was much higher foreign banks in India than that generated by overseas branches/ subsidiaries of Indian banks.

Data Envelopment Analysis method used to examine the efficiency of the foreign banks and the domestic banks and to study if the entry of foreign banks has affected the performance of domestic banks. The theta values show the efficiency. The standard deviation is done for both the banks to identify the deviation in the performance if any over a period of 9 years. The Coefficient of Variation is calculated to identify the consistent performers among the best both in domestic banks and also in foreign banks in India.

Data for 44 foreign banks operating in India and 57 domestic banks used to conduct the analysis of relative efficiency. Our findings indicate that:

1. the efficiency of Foreign banks and Domestic banks in India and identify the best performers;
2. the efficiency scores, standard deviation and Coefficient of variation show the best performers and those consistent among them;
3. shows that the entry of the foreign banks and the growth of foreign banks in India is not exactly affecting the performance of the domestic banks in India.

The following table shows the list of best performing domestic banks. IDBI Bank, SBI Commercial International, Karur Vysya Bank, City Union Bank, Yes Bank, Jammu and Kashmir Bank Ltd and Oriental Bank of Commerce have been consistent performers despite of the entry of foreign banks and their increase in the operations. Among the foreign banks Bank of Nova Scotia, JPMORGAN Chase Bank National Association, MASHREQ BANK PSC, Bank Internasional Indonesia, Krung Thai Bank Public Company Limited, DBS Bank Ltd and State Bank of Mauritius Ltd. are good and consistent performers.

The latest opportunity foreign banks see is in the retail sector. The government recently allowed overseas companies in multi-brand retail and removed the cap on foreign direct investment (FDI) in single-brand retail. India is a profitable market as well for foreign lenders. The country is the fifth most profitable market for Deutsche Bank globally and its most profitable emerging market. Foreign banks are also preparing for the internationalization of Indian business. As Indian companies go global they need banking support and it is not possible for Indian banks to be present all over the world. Foreign banks have the network.

The performance of the domestic banks and the entry of the foreign banks is affected by macro-economic variables. The impact of these variables and the fluctuations in the performance of the banks can considered as scope a further study.

The international trade in insurance services a study of the insurance penetration and insurance density is examined in the next chapter.

REFERENCES

1. As per IMF's Balance of Payments Manual and International Investment Position Manual Sixth Edition (BMP6), a subsidiary is a direct investment enterprise (DIE) over which direct investor is able to exercise control, which is assumed to exist if the investor has more than 50% equity in the enterprise investment. An associate is a DIE over which the direct investor own's from 10 to 50% of the equity shares in the investment enterprise.
2. Scheduled Banks in India are those banks which have been included in the Second Schedule of Reserve Bank of India (RBI) Act, 1934 . RBI in turn includes only those banks in this schedule which satisfy the criteria laid down vide section 42 (6) (a) of the Act. As on 30 June 1999, there were 300 scheduled banks in India having a total network of 64,918 branches. Scheduled commercial banks in India include State Bank of India and its associates (5), nationalised banks (20), foreign banks (45), private sector banks (32), co-operative banks and regional rural banks.

Trends in Trade in Insurance Services

INTRODUCTION

The present chapter discusses the trends in the trade in insurance services. The various aspects like insurance services and regulatory standards, insurance services and GATS commitments, trends in insurance penetration and density in India, global picture of insurance penetration and density in India are discussed in this chapter.

The insurance industry is an important component of the financial infrastructure of an economy. The viability and strengths of this industry have far reaching consequences for not only its money, capital market and also real sector. Risk has increased enormously in our lives and hence insurance occupies an important place in the complex modern world. This has led to growth in the insurance business and evolution of various types of insurance covers. It plays a significant role in the economic development of a country, while economic development itself also facilitates the growth of the insurance sector.

Insurance development realized the entry of international insurers with the proliferation of innovative products and distribution channels, as well as the raising of supervisory standards. The insurance industry in India has come a long way since the time when businesses were tightly regulated and concentrated in the hands of a few public sector insurers till 1999. The year of 1999 was a significant year in the history of insurance industry in India as it allowed the market access to private and foreign players. Recently, government has increased the FDI cap to 49% in 2013 from the existing 26%.

The insurance sector acts as a mobilizer of savings, a financial intermediary, a promoter of investment activities, a stabilizer of financial markets and a risk manager in the economy. Presently, the insurance sector has a share of 17.1 per cent in the total Gross Domestic Product (GDP) and is growing at a healthy rate of 16.82% in 2012-13. According to IBEF, India is ranked 10th among 156 countries in the life insurance business, with a share of 2.3 per cent during the financial year 2012 and 19th among 156 countries in the non-life premium income, with a share of 0.62 per cent in the financial year 2012 (India Brand Equity Foundation (IBEF - 2013)).

Following the Financial Stability Forum,[1] one can classify insurance into three major categories: life insurance, non-life insurance and reinsurance. The WTO W/120 Sectoral Classification List breaks down financial services into (a) all insurance and insurance related services and (b) banking and other financial services. The former is further broken down into life, accident and health insurance services; non-life insurance services; reinsurance and retrocession; insurance intermediation; and services auxiliary to insurance. The Annex on Financial Services ("the Annex") defines financial services as any services of a financial nature offered by a financial services supplier. It specifies the inclusion of insurance and insurance-related products. The Annex goes on to list insurance and insurance-related products as:

- Direct insurance, both life and non-life;
- Reinsurance and retrocession;
- Insurance intermediation, such as brokerage and agency services;
- Services auxiliary to insurance, such as consultancy, actuarial, risk assessment and claim settlement services.

This broad listing of insurance products, coupled with technological developments and the creation of newer hybrid products, has in the current round of negotiations raised issues of classification.[2] Essentially there are three types of stakeholders in the insurance process: the insured (the consumer), the insurer (the provider of a service) and the regulator (generally the Government or an independent authority). Other stakeholders in the sector include actuaries and auditors.

In India, the life insurance, public sector is monopolized by the Life Insurance Corporation of India (LIC) which has captured the 71% market in the total premium and 72% market in the first year premium. As against, only 29% and 28% market served by the private players in the total premium and first year premium respectively. In the non-life insurance also the public sector dominates half of the market (58%), while private sector caters 43% of the market.

Insurance plays a crucial role in economic development: a well-functioning insurance sector is a vital piece of national infrastructure. Insurance liberalization when successfully managed will help to attract foreign direct investment and drive the development in financial services, in turn spurring overall economic development, financial security and levels of prosperity.

The insurance sector is an infrastructural pillar of the financial services sector and the economy as a whole. It plays a key role in economic development. Several empirical studies suggest a strong correlation between the development of financial intermediaries and economic growth. According to Patrick (1966)[3] there are two, possibly coexisting, relationships between the financial sector and economic growth. The first is the case where the financial sector has a supply-leading relationship with growth, and where economic growth can be induced through the supply of financial services. The second is a demand-following relationship where the demand for financial services can induce growth of financial institutions and their assets. Developing countries have supply-leading patterns of causality of development and have considered locally incorporated insurance institutions or State-owned monopolies an essential element of economic development.[4]

Given the importance of the insurance sector, its potential for growth, rapidly emerging trends within the sector including the trend towards liberalization of insurance services, it is essential to clearly understand the challenges and opportunities that arise from both the development of the insurance sector as well as its liberalization for developing countries. It was with this objective in mind that UNCTAD, at the behest of its member States and in accordance to its mandate pursuant to the ninth session of the Commission on Trade in Goods and Services, and Commodities, held in Geneva from 14 to 18 March 2005, held an ad hoc expert meeting on insurance services on 24 November 2005. The discussions indicated that while insurance service liberalization and globalization can be beneficial, they have different impacts on developed and developing countries. Country experiences seemed to indicate that liberalization of insurance services needs to be accompanied by a strategic and clearly defined national policy on the financial services sector in general and the insurance sector in particular.

The insurance sector is closely linked with macroeconomic factors (e.g. inflation, currency controls and the national income of a country), regulation and supervision, and the achievement of national development objectives, as well as the international trade regime. Given its dual infrastructural and commercial role, the sector has attracted great interest in the context of privatization and liberalization. There are several ways in which insurance services contribute to economic development[5]. The Government plays an important role in ensuring that insurance services can generate benefits. In developed countries, the Government's key role is to act as a regulator to ensure security and stability in the sector. In developing countries, it also has the role of providing insurance services as a public good.

Consistent growth in the insurance sector depends on a few factors. Some of these are:

1. Effective distribution channels – The efficiency and cost of the various distribution strategies used by companies are significant to their success in the insurance business. This particularly holds true for the retail business.
2. Focus on overall financial inclusion – As time evolves, so must the approach of the insurance sector in India. The objective of the insurance sector should ideally be to offer a broader range of activities to a wider populace.
3. Consumer needs and preferences – The growth of India's insurance industry can be attributed to product innovation, dynamic distribution channels, and vibrant publicity and promotional campaigns run by insurance companies. Benefits attached to the products and the manner in which they are delivered (through various marketing tie-ups) have helped bring customers and insurance companies closer to each other and made the latter more relevant.

The process of opening up the insurance sector was initiated against the background of Economic Reform process which commenced from 1991. For this purpose Malhotra Committee was formed during this year who submitted their report in 1994 and Insurance Regulatory Development Act (IRDA) was passed in 1999. Resultantly Indian Insurance was opened for private companies and Private Insurance Company effectively started operations from 2001. Insurance sector in India has become one of the most favored investment destinations both for Indians and NRIs. India is the fifth largest insurance market among the globally emerging insurance economies. Growing interest towards insurance among people, innovative products and distribution channels are sustaining the growth of the insurance sector.

The rising importance of insurance in the globalized world is evident from increased number of players in both domestic and international market (IRDA). India, being one of the fastest- growing economies in the world after china and an upcoming attractive foreign direct investment (FDI)[6] destination from major developed economies has the potential to significantly increase the market of its insurance industry. India's constantly increasing disposable income, coupled with the high potential demand for insurance offerings, has opened many doors for both domestic and foreign insurers.

There is a growing empirical literature seeking to assess the relationship between macroeconomic performance of the insurance sector and economic growth which contributes to increase the international trade among countries. Insurance sector is a central element of the trade and development matrix and is considered as one of the key pillars of the financial services.

A sound national insurance sector represents an essential feature of a proper economic system, contributing to economic growth and fostering high employment (UNCTAD, 1964). As both, an infrastructural and commercial service, a well-functioning insurance sector plays a crucial role in economic development not just at a macro-economic level but also in terms of the activities of individuals and businesses (UNCTAD, 2007). From an infrastructural perspective it promotes financial and social stability which mobilizes and channel savings, supports trade, commerce and entrepreneurial activity and improves the quality of the lives of individuals (Puri 2007).

Liberalization and privatization helps bring substantial financial strength, technological and industry know how. At the same time, good risk management and asset liability management skills are required especially in the context of developing countries (Puri 2007). He mentioned the following areas of concerns in the insurance sector which is needs to be consider on priority basis: security and stability of the insurance sector; the importance of building supply side capacity; the role of regulation frameworks; current negotiations on insurance services within the GATS; the role of the Government as a provider of insurance services and the extent of its role as a provider of insurance services.

"The development of the life insurance market has a positive effect on economic growth." Chen, Lee, Chang, Feng has taken the conditional variables of middle-income countries which are savings, the real interest rate, social security, the stock market turnover ratio, and the young dependency ratio to show the positive impacts of the development of the life insurance market on growth. According to their study, a country with a well-developed financial system does not necessarily enhance (and maybe lessens) the positive effects of the development of the life insurance market on economic growth.

"Improved access to insurance services, given their importance to global growth and development would be tangible way to underpin the recovery of the global economy."

Recently many developing countries such as India have taken initiatives to promote their state and private sector insurance providers to bolster regional trade. This will also help enhance the growth of their economies. Arkell (2011) explained that these initiatives involve restrictions to the opportunities for abroad based insurers which would affect their potential benefit. Further, the new limitations affect both national insurers and affiliates in which investment has been made from abroad, which might even reduce the market access accorded to foreign insurers under GATS commitment of the WTO on trade in services. Moreover, insurance can increase saving rate, create deeper financial markets which lead to greater working capital; where capital markets are not well developed they might benefit from the long term investment (Arkell 2011).

This chapter provides an overview of the insurance sector in India, its origin and growth. It begins by defining insurance as a concept, followed by a discussion on the importance of insurance for individuals, households, and the economy. The penetration of the insurance business and insurance density in India are compared with those in other countries.

TRADE IN INSURANCE SERVICES

In the Uruguay Round, WTO members made more commitments in financial services than any other sector, except tourism. About 60 members made commitments in life and non-life insurance, and only three of these had no commitments in life insurance, and only one in non-life. Nearly 70 members made commitments in "reinsurance and retrocession", but only just over 40 for "insurance intermediation" and "services auxiliary to insurance".

For market access in Mode 1, about two thirds of the developing countries and almost all least developed countries made no commitments. Just over half the developed countries made only partial commitments, and a third none. The averages for national treatment were slightly less liberal.

The figures for the modes of supply were broadly not much different. For Modes 3 & 4 about nine out of ten developed countries made partial commitments for market access and three quarters for national treatment whereas the figures for developing countries were about four in ten in each case, and for the LDCs, three in ten.

The commitments related to the more internationalized services such as reinsurance and services to corporate businesses, rather than to retail services or new products.

Banks report to the Reserve Bank under Foreign Exchange Transaction - Electronic Reporting System (FET-ERS) which is the primary source of trade data in services Receipts covers:

- receipts on account of freight insurance (i.e., relating to import and export of goods)
- premium on life and non-life policies
- reinsurance premium from foreign insurance companies
- receipts on account of settlement of claims and auxiliary services (commission on insurance).

The reverse holds good for Payments under Insurance services. As per BPM6, "insurance services" has been re-classified as "insurance and pension services". A separate code is being introduced to capture the "pension services" to comply with the IMF's BPM6 categorization of "insurance and pension services".

A number of economies have started to compile their balance of payments statistics according to the sixth edition (2009) of the IMF Balance of Payments Manual (BPM6). In August 2012, the IMF has started to publish annual and quarterly figures according to the new methodology, with the new series beginning in 2005.Starting with 2009 data, UNCTAD and WTO have been converting trade in commercial services figures from BPM6 to BPM5 for the economies which only report BPM6-based data. The objective of this conversion is three-fold: (i) ensuring to the fullest extent cross-country comparability; (ii) providing users with the longest possible time series (which are currently only available on a BPM5 basis); (iii) comparability with the more detailed EBOPS and partner statistics.

Insurance Services and International Regulatory Standards

Insurance markets in developing countries have a number of particular features. These include small size, undercapitalization and institutions that are underdeveloped or do not exist, as well as insufficient experience and know-how. In many developing countries, insurance services are not yet considered a key component of the financial services sector. Recently the size of developing countries insurance markets has been growing substantially.

Regulators in both developed and developing countries are facing newer regulatory challenges arising from the increasingly heterogeneous and complex nature of the insurance sector, challenges from technological developments and those from the new and hybrid insurance products.

GATS Commitments on Insurance Services

The globalization of trade in services is an important objective of India as a signatory to the agreement establishing the World Trade Organization. The WTO W/120 sectoral classification list7 breaks down financial services into (a) all insurance and insurance related services and (b) banking and other financial services. The former is further broken down into life, accident and health insurance services; non-life insurance services; reinsurance and retrocession; insurance intermediation; and services auxiliary to insurance.

In the Uruguay round, WTO undertakes GATS to regulate the functioning of services sector in 1995. Under GATS, there are four modes of supply i.e.

1. Cross border supply;
2. Consumption abroad;
3. Commercial presence; and
4. Presence of Natural persons which facilitate trade in services.

The GATS commitments on the four modes of supply of insurance services are as follows:

Table 5.1: All insurance and insurance-related Services GATS Commitments

Limitations on Market Access	Limitations on National Treatment
Non-life, limited to insurance of freight Ex.5(a) (i)(B)	
1. Unbound except in the case of insurance of freight,where there is no requirement that goods in transit to and from India should be insured with Indian insurance companies only. Insurance is taken by the buyer or seller in accordance with the terms of the contract. This position will be maintained. Once under a contract the Indian importer or exporter agrees to assume the responsibility for insurance such as in the case of f.o.b contracts for imports into India or c.i.f contracts for exports from India, insurance has to be taken only with anIndian insurance company.	1. Unbound
2. Unbound	2. Unbound
3. Unbound	3. Unbound
4. Unbound except as indicated in the horizontalsection	4. Unbound except as indicated in the horizontalsection
Reinsurance and retrocession 5(a)(ii)	
1. Reinsurance can be taken with foreign to the extent of the residual uncovered risk after obligatory or statutory placements domestically with Indian insurance companies.	1. Unbound
2. Reinsurance can be taken with foreign to the extent of the uncovered risk after obligatory or statutory placements domestically with Indian insurance companies.	2. Unbound
3. Unbound	3. Unbound
4. Unbound except as indicated in the horizontal section.	4. Unbound except as indicated in the horizontalsection.

(Table Contd...)

Insurance intermediation, limited to reinsurance Ex.5(a)(iii)	
1. Reinsurance of domestic risks can be placed with foreign reinsurers through overseas brokers, to the extent mentioned underreinsurance and retrocession.	1. Unbound
2. Reinsurance of domestic risks can be placed with foreign reinsurers through overseas brokers, to the extent mentioned underreinsurance and retrocession.	2. Unbound
3. (i) Overseas brokers are allowed to have resident representatives and representative offices who can procure reinsurance business from Indian insurance companies to the extent mentioned above. They can also place reinsurance business from abroad with Indian insurance companies. (ii) Except for the business indicated above, the resident representatives and representative offices cannot undertake any other activity in India. (iii) All expenses of the resident representatives and representative offices have to be met by remittances from abroad and no income can be received in India from Indian residents.	3. Unbound
4. Unbound except as indicated in the horizontal section.	4. Unbound except as indicated in the horizontal section.

The economic environment and financial markets in 2012 were challenging for insurers. Economic growth slowed in most advanced markets and Western Europe even fell back into recession. Emerging markets held up better, but growth slowed due to their reliance on exports to advanced markets. Expansionary monetary policies kept interest rates low, but boosted equity markets. Weak economic growth weighed on exposure growth of non-life insurance, elevated unemployment figures in many advanced markets and reduced the demand for life insurance, while low interest rates continued to be a drag on profitability.

TRENDS IN INSURANCE PENETRATION AND INSURANCE DENSITY IN INDIA

The potential and performance of the insurance sector is universally assessed with reference to two parameters, viz., insurance penetration and insurance density. These two are often used to determine the level of development of the insurance sector in a country.

1. level of insurance penetration which is measured as the percentage of insurance premium in gross domestic product (GDP); and
2. insurance density ratio (wherein insurance density is defined as the per capita expenditure on insurance premium and is directly correlated with per capita GDP).

The potential and performance of the insurance sector is universally assessed with reference to two parameters, viz., insurance penetration and insurance density. These two are often used to determine the level of development of the insurance sector in a country. Insurance penetration is defined as the ratio of premium underwritten in a given year to the Gross Domestic Product (GDP).

Insurance Penetration

Insurance penetration explains the growth of premium with the growth of the gross domestic product in the economy. It is measured as ratio of premium to GDP.[7] Insurance penetration (both life and non-life) in the post liberalization period are shown in Chart 5.1. Total insurance penetration has increased from 2.71% in 2001 to 3.90% in 2013. Life insurance dominates the insurance penetration in India; however, the share is declining after 2010; increase from 2.15% in 2001 to 4.60% in 2009 and stood at 3.10% in 2013. While the share of non-life insurance penetration in the total insurance penetration increased from 0.56% in 2001 to 0.80% in 2013.

The opening up of the insurance sector marked an improvement since 2000 with consistent increase in the total penetration levels. India's growing consumer class, rising insurance awareness, increasing domestic savings and investments are among the most critical factors that have positively driven the market penetration of the insurance products among its consumer segments.

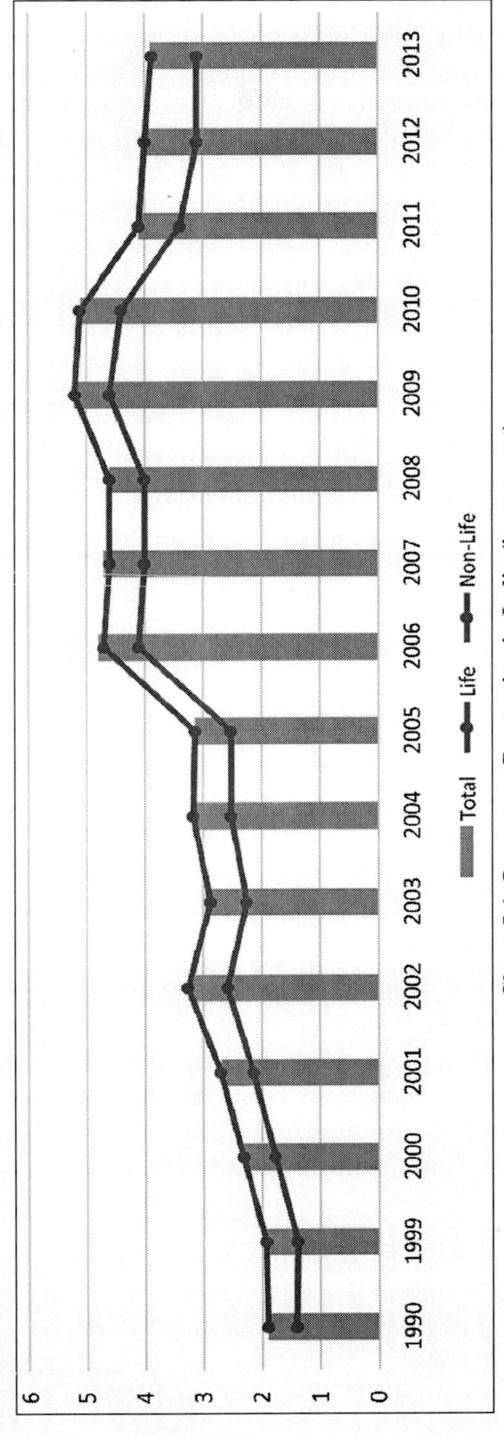

Chart 5.1: Insurance Pentration in India (in per cent)

Source: Swiss Re, Various Issues

However, there are many impediments such as lack of awareness and financial illiteracy which is hampering the growth of the insurance industry. As the industry penetration level is on the downward path since 2010; 5.10% in 2010 to 4.10% in 2011. Global re-insurer Swiss Re's sigma study on world insurance in 2013 said India stood at 15th position in the world in terms of premium volume. In 2012, it was at 14th position. The study showed insurance penetration in India fell to 3.9 per cent in 2013 compared to four per cent in 2012.

Table 5.2: Insurance Penetration and Density in India

Year	Life		Non-Life		Industry	
	Density (USD)	Penetration (%)	Density (USD)	Penetration (%)	Density (USD)	Penetration (%)
2001	9.1	2.15	2.4	0.56	11.5	2.71
2002	11.7	2.59	3.0	0.67	14.7	3.26
2003	12.9	2.26	3.5	0.62	16.4	2.88
2004	15.7	2.53	4.0	0.64	19.7	3.17
2005	18.3	2.53	4.4	0.61	22.7	3.14
2006	33.2	4.10	5.2	0.60	38.4	4.80
2007	40.4	4.00	6.2	0.60	46.6	4.70
2008	41.2	4.00	6.2	0.60	47.4	4.60
2009	47.7	4.60	6.7	0.60	54.3	5.20
2010	55.7	4.40	8.7	0.71	64.4	5.10
2011	49.0	3.40	10.0	0.70	59.0	4.10
2012	42.7	3.17	10.5	0.89	53.2	3.96
2013	41.0	3.10	11.0	0.80	52.0	3.90

1. Insurance density is measured as ratio of premium (in USD) to total population.
2. Insurance penetration is measured as ratio of premium (in USD) to GDP (in USD)
3. The data of Insurance penetration is available with rounding off to one digit after decimal from 2006.

Source: Swiss Re, SIGMA,Various issues

There are a number of studies that show that a relationship between the per capita GDP and total insurance penetration. The data also supports that there is positive relationship; penetration increases from 1.90% in 1990 to 5.10% in 2010, similarly per capita GDP rises from Rs. 6987.03 billion in 1990 to Rs. 65727.77 billion in 2010. In 2011, the growth in the insurance penetration is on the lowed side while the total GDP follows the same upward trend. However, there are various demand (socio-demographic characteristics of policy holders, risk appetite, etc.) and supply (quality of distribution channel, product innovation, etc.) driven factors to boost the insurance penetration level in India (IRDA).

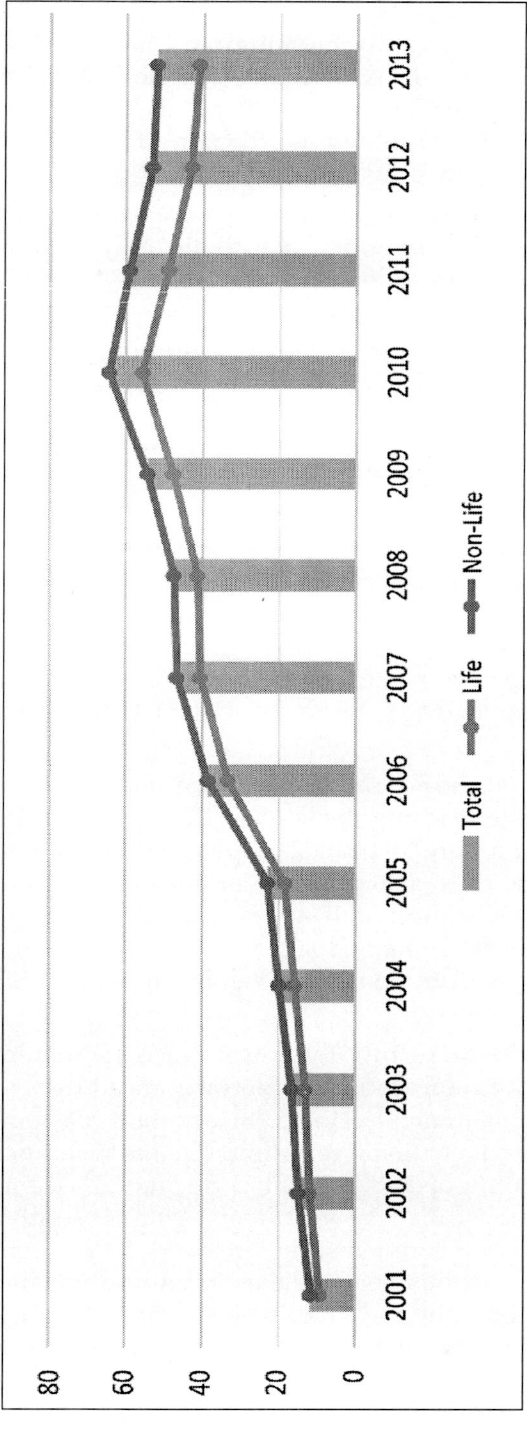

Chart 5.2: Insurance Density in India (in USD

Source: Swiss Re, Various Issues

Insurance Density

Insurance density is known as per capita premium and measured as ratio of premium (in US Dollars) to total Population. After liberalization, total insurance density has experienced an upward trend. However, the life insurance sector serves the population more than the non-life insurance as it capture the greater share in the total insurance density.

Non-life insurance density line shows an upward trend after the privatization of the insurance sector. The entry of private players may support the non-life insurance density in India as it rises from 2.40 USD in 2001 to 10 USD in 2011.

Table 5.6 explains the international comparison of insurance density in 2011. The international comparison of insurance density suggests that the density in India which stands at $59 is well below the World average of $661 in 2011. It is interesting to note that the insurance density in china is three times as high as in India. Pakistan, Sri Lanka and Bangladesh are laggards in terms of their insurance density.

India has reported consistent increase in insurance density every year since the sector was opened up for private competition in the year 2000. However, for the first time in 2011, there was a fall in insurance density. The life insurance density in India has gone up from USD 9.1 in 2001 to USD 52.0 in 2013 though it reached the peak of USD 55.7 in 2010. The insurance density of non-life sector reached the peak of USD 11.0 in 2013 from its level of USD 2.4 in 2001.

The insurance density of life insurance sector had gone up from USD 9.1 in 2001 to USD 49.0 in 2011 while reaching the peak at USD 55.7 in 2010. Similarly, life insurance penetration surged from 2.15 per cent in 2001 to 4.60 per cent in 2009, before slipping to 4.40 per cent in 2010 and further slipping to 3.40 per cent in 2011. Over the last 10 years, the penetration of nonlife insurance sector in the country remained steady within the narrow range of 0.56-0.71 per cent. However, its density has gone up from USD 2.4 in 2001 to USD 10.0 in 2011.

As at end-September 2012, there are fifty-three insurance companies operating in India; of which twenty four are in the life insurance business and twenty-eight are in non-life insurance business. In addition, General Insurance Corporation (GIC) is the sole national reinsurer. The life insurance industry recorded a premium income of 2, 87,072 crore during 2011-12 as against 2, 91,639 crore in the previous financial year, registering a negative growth of 1.57 per cent. While private sector insurers posted 4.52 per cent decline (11.08 per cent growth in previous year) in their premium income, Life Insurance Corporation (LIC), the fully state owned insurance company, recorded 0.29 per cent decline (9.35 per cent growth in previous year), in its total premium underwritten.

The operational expense ratio of the Indian non-life industry deteriorated further in fiscal 2010-11 despite already being the highest globally. This deterioration was evident among both public and private insurers. Operational expenses increased as insurance players continued to invest in the expansion of their business and to compete with incoming international players. Government of India in its new budget declared the increase in the limit on foreign direct investment in insurers to 49% from 26%. If global players acquire larger stakes in domestic operations, it could lead to more widespread adoption of best practices, and resultant operational efficiencies in the long run. The acquisition ratio of India's non-life insurers declined in fiscal 2010-11 as new and low-cost distribution channels emerged, especially among private-sector providers, where acquisition costs are lower than among public insurers. As a result, total commission expenses rose by only 9.7% despite GWP growth of 19.8%. Investment income for India's non-life industry remained stable in fiscal 2010-11.

Premium Underwritten Outside India

All public sector insurers (except United India) are underwriting non-life insurance business outside India. United India ceased operations outside India in 2003-04. The total premium underwritten outside the country by the three public sector insurers stood at 1,703 crore in 2011- 12 as against 1,265 crore in 2010-11 registering a growth of 34.60 per cent against 5.86 per cent in the previous year. The premium underwritten outside India accounted for 3.12 per cent of total premium underwritten by the non-life insurance companies.

New India continued to be the largest public sector non-life insurer underwriting premium outside India, with the premium underwritten outside India constituting 15.20 per cent of the total premium underwritten by the insurer in 2011-12. In case of Oriental, the contribution of outside India premium to the total premium works out to be 2.37 per cent in 2011-12, marginally higher than 2.02 per cent in 2010-11. National Insurance continued to have a small component of overseas business at 0.32 per cent in 2011-12, slightly lower than 0.39 per cent reported in 2010-11. Of the total premium of 1,703 crore written outside India in 2011-12, New India underwrote a higher premium of 1,531 crore (1,128 crore in 2010-11), its market share in the total outside India premium of public sector non-life insurers increased to 89.92 per cent in 2011-12 from 89.17 per cent in 2010-11. National underwrote a premium of 25 crore in 2011-12 (24.47 crore in 2010-11). The outside India premium underwritten by Oriental Insurance stood at 147 crore higher than previous year's 113 crore, recording an increase of 30.08 per cent.

Table 5.3: Ratio of India's Premium to Total Premium

Insurer	2001-02	2002-03	2003-04	2004-05	2005-06	2006-07	2007-08	2008-09	2009-10	2010-11	2011-12	2012-13
National	3.3	0.22	0.26	0.28	0.36	0.33	0.37	0.37	0.45	0.39	0.32	0.31
New India	16.33	18.52	17.80	17.49	16.36	15.49	14.22	14.67	14.88	13.72	15.19	15.46
Oriental	2.09	2.26	2.33	2.35	2.29	2.29	2.36	2.79	2.43	2.02	2.37	2.75
United*	4.55	0.05	–	–	–	–	–	–	–	–	–	–

* Ceased operations in 2003-04

New India continued to be the largest public sector non-life insurer underwriting premium outside India, with the premium underwritten outside India constituting 15.46 per cent of the total premium underwritten by the insurer in 2012-13 marginally higher than the 15.19 in the previous year. It reached a peak in 2004-05 at 17.49 per cent but in 2010-11 it was at its least with 13.72 per cent. In case of Oriental the contribution of outside India premium to the total premium works out to be 2.75 per cent in 2012-13, as compared to 2.09 per cent in 2001-02. National Insurance continued to have a small component of overseas business at 0.31 percent in 2012-13, slightly higher than 0.23 reported in 2001-02. (Table 5.3).

Table 5.4: Gross Direct Premium from Business Outside India: Non-Life Insurers

Insurer	2001-02	2002-03	2003-04	2004-05	2005-06	2006-07	2007-08	2008-09	2009-10	2010-11	2011-12	2012-13
National	73.95 (-33.00)	6.29 (-91.00)	8.86 (41.00)	10.74 (21.09)	12.670 (17.99)	12.70 (0.24)	14.74 (16.05)	15.95 (8.21)	20.81 (30.49)	24.47 (17.56)	25.00 (2.18)	28.89 (15.56)
New India	685.73 (52.00)	891.55 (30.00)	875.79 (-2.00)	892.35 (1.89)	937.38 (5.05)	919.58 (4.02)	874.55 (-4.90)	946.95 (8.28)	1056.63 (11.58)	1128.37 (6.79)	1531.01 (35.68)	1835.53 (19.89)
Oriental	52.15 (10.00)	64.74 (24.00)	67.63 (4.00)	72.77 (7.60)	82.66 (13.59)	92.26 (11.61)	92.07 (-0.20)	113.64 (23.43)	117.97 (3.81)	112.54 (-4.60)	146.71 (30.45)	185.26 (26.28)
United*	12.65 (53.00)	1.57 (-99.00)	–	–	–	–	–	–	–	–	–	–
Total	824.48	964.04 (16.93)	952.28 (-1.21)	975.86 (2.47)	1032.71 (-5.80)	1024.54 (0.79)	981.36 (-4.22)	1076.54 (9.70)	1195.41 (11.04)	1265.38 (5.85)	102.72 (34.56)	2049.68 (20.38)

Figures in bracket indicate the growth (in percent) over previous year.

Source: IRDA

The public sector non-life insurers who have operations outside India underwrote premium of Rs. 2049.68 crore in 2012-13 as against Rs. 824.48 crore in 2001-02. New India has its operations in countries outside India through a network of branches, agencies, associate companies and subsidiaries. 16.33 per cent in 2001-02 as against 15.46 per cent in 2012-13 of its premium is being underwritten abroad. National Insurance Company underwrote a premium of Rs. 6.89 crore in 2001-02 (Rs. 28.89 crore in 2012-13,). New India too increased the premium underwritten abroad with Rs. 685.83 crore (as against Rs. 1835.53 crore in the financial year 2012-13). Oriental Insurance underwrote a premium of Rs. 52.15 crore (as against Rs. 185.26 crore in 2012-13. United India has ceased foreign operations since 2003-04 (Table 5.4)

GLOBAL PICTURE OF INSURANCE PENETRATION AND DENSITY

Globally, the share of life insurance business in total premium was 56.2 per cent. However, the share of life insurance business for India was very high at 79.6 per cent while the share of non- life insurance business was small at 20.4 per cent.

In life insurance business, India is ranked 11th among the 88 countries, for which data is published by Swiss Re. India's share in global life insurance market was 2.00 per cent during 2013. However, during 2013, the life insurance premium in India declined by 0.5 per cent (inflation adjusted) when global life insurance premium increased by 0.7 per cent.

The Indian non-life insurance sector witnessed a growth of 4.1 per cent (inflation adjusted) during 2013. During the same period, the growth in global non-life premium was 2.3 per cent. However, the share of Indian non-life insurance premium in global non-life insurance premium was small at 0.66 per cent and India ranks 21st in global non-life insurance markets.

At global level, life premiums grew by just 0.7 per cent in 2013 to $2,608 billion — down from 2.3 per cent growth in 2012. Premiums in the US contracted sharply by 7.7 per cent due to the non-recurrence of large corporate deals which had boosted group annuity business in 2012.

The study said life premium growth was expected to resume in the advanced and improve in the emerging markets. The firming economy and labour markets in the advanced markets will support the life and non-life sector, and growth in the emerging markets should hold up also. The Sigma Re study said "In the life sector, China and India in particular should see a return to higher growth rates. Overall profitability has improved in the life and non-life sectors". However, the study said investment returns, an important component of insurers' earnings, remain low given the very low level of interest rates since the 2008 financial crisis.

Table 5.5: International Comparison of Insurance Penetration

Countries	2007			2008			2009			2010			2011			2012		
	Life	Non-Life	Total	Life	Non-Life	Total	Life	Non-Life	Total	Life	Non-Life	Total	Life	Non-Life	Total	Life	Non-Life	Total
Australia	9.15	5.70	3.44	8.48	5.02	3.46	5.90	3.10	2.80	6.00	3.00	3.00	6.0	3.0	3.0	5.6	2.8	2.8
Brazil	3.00	1.40	1.60	3.00	1.40	1.60	3.10	1.60	1.50	3.20	1.70	1.50	3.2	1.7	1.5	3.7	2.0	1.7
France	10.30	7.30	3.00	9.20	6.20	3.00	10.50	7.40	3.10	9.50	6.20	3.30	9.5	6.2	3.3	8.9	5.6	3.3
Germany	6.60	3.10	3.60	6.60	3.10	3.60	7.20	3.50	3.70	6.80	3.20	3.60	6.8	3.2	3.6	6.7	3.1	3.6
Russia	2.40	0.10	2.40	2.40	0.10	2.40	2.30	0.00	2.30	2.40	0.10	2.30	2.4	0.1	2.3	1.3	0.1	1.2
South Africa	17.97	15.19	2.78	18.78	15.92	2.86	14.80	12.00	2.80	12.90	10.20	2.70	12.9	10.2	2.7	9.6	5.3	4.3
Switzerland	10.30	5.70	4.60	9.90	5.50	4.40	9.90	5.50	4.40	10.00	5.50	4.50	10.0	5.5	4.5	—	—	—
UK	15.70	12.60	3.00	15.70	12.80	2.90	12.40	9.50	2.90	11.80	8.70	3.10	11.8	8.7	3.1	11.3	8.4	2.8
USA	8.90	4.20	4.70	8.70	4.10	4.60	8.00	3.50	4.50	8.10	3.60	4.50	8.1	3.6	4.5	8.2	3.7	4.5
Asian Countries																		
Bangladesh	0.70	0.50	0.20	0.90	0.70	0.20	0.90	0.70	0.20	0.90	0.70	0.20	0.9	0.7	0.2	–	–	–
Hong Kong	11.80	10.60	1.20	11.20	9.90	1.30	11.40	10.10	1.40	11.40	10.10	1.40	11.4	10.1	1.4	12.4	11.0	14.0
India	**4.70**	**4.00**	**0.60**	**4.60**	**4.00**	**0.60**	**5.10**	**4.40**	**0.70**	**4.10**	**3.40**	**0.70**	**4.1**	**3.4**	**0.7**	**4.0**	**3.2**	**0.8**
Japan	9.60	7.50	2.10	9.80	7.60	2.20	10.10	8.00	2.10	11.00	8.80	2.20	11.0	8.8	2.2	11.4	9.2	2.3
Malaysia	4.30	2.80	1.50	4.60	3.10	1.50	4.80	3.20	1.60	5.10	3.30	1.80	5.1	3.3	1.8	4.8	3.1	1.7
Pakistan	0.70	0.30	0.4	0.80	0.30	0.40	0.70	0.30	0.30	0.70	0.40	0.30	0.7	0.4	0.3	0.7	0.4	0.3
PR China	2.90	1.80	1.10	3.30	2.20	1.00	3.80	2.50	1.30	3.00	1.80	1.20	3.0	1.8	1.2	3.0	1.7	1.3
Singapore	7.60	6.20	1.50	7.80	6.30	1.60	6.10	4.60	1.60	5.90	4.30	1.50	5.9	4.3	1.5	6.0	4.4	1.6
Srilanka	1.50	0.60	0.90	1.40	0.60	0.90	1.40	0.60	0.90	1.20	0.60	0.60	1.2	0.6	0.6	1.2	0.5	0.7
Taiwan	15.70	12.90	2.80	16.20	13.30	2.90	18.40	15.40	3.00	17.00	13.9	3.10	17.0	13.9	3.1	18.2	15.0	3.2
Thailand	3.40	1.80	1.50	3.30	1.80	1.50	4.30	2.60	1.70	4.40	2.70	1.70	4.4	2.7	1.7	5.0	3.0	2.1
World	7.50	4.40	3.10	7.10	4.10	2.90	6.90	4.00	2.90	6.60	3.80	2.80	6.6	3.8	2.8	6.2	3.7	2.8

Source: Swiss Re, SIGMA reports

Table 5.6: International Comparision of Insurance Density (in USD)

Countries	2010			2011		
	Total	Life	Non-Life	Total	Life	Non-Life
Australia	3369.2	1766.3	1603.0	4094.0	2077.0	2017.0
Brazil	327.6	169.9	157.7	398.0	208.0	189.0
France	4186.6	2937.6	1249.0	4041.0	2638.0	1403.0
Germany	2903.8	1402.2	1501.6	2967.0	1389.0	1578.0
Russia	296.8	6.4	290.4	303.0	8.0	295.0
South Africa	1054.7	854.6	200.1	1037.0	823.0	215.0
Switzerland	6633.7	3666.8	2966.9	8012.0	4421.0	3591.0
United Kingdom	4496.6	3436.3	1060.2	4535.0	3347.0	1188.0
United States	3758.9	1631.8	2127.2	3846.0	1716.0	2130.0
Asian Countries						
Bangladesh	5.8	4.4	1.4	7.0	5.0	2.0
Hong Kong	3635.5	3197.3	438.2	3904.0	3442.0	462.0
India	64.4	55.7	8.7	59.0	49.0	10.0
Japan	4390.2	3472.8	917.4	5169.0	4138.0	1031.0
Malaysia	421.1	282.8	138.3	502.0	328.0	175.0
Pakistan	6.1	3.2	2.9	8.0	4.0	4.0
PR China	158.4	105.5	52.9	163.0	99.0	64.0
Singapore	2823.4	2101.4	722.1	3106.0	2296.0	810.0
South Korea	2339.4	1454.3	885.1	2661.0	1615.0	1045.0
Sri Lanka	34.2	13.7	20.6	33.0	15.0	18.0
Taiwan	3296.2	2756.8	539.3	3371.0	2757.0	614.0
Thailand	199.4	121.9	77.5	222.0	134.0	88.0
World	627.3	364.3	263.0	661.0	378.0	283.0

Source: Swiss Re reports

The international comparison of insurance penetration shows that across the countries in the world the insurance penetration has been decreasing from 2007 to 2012 and India is no exception to this trend. The world insurance penetration in Life insurance which was 7.5 per cent in 2007 came down to 6.2 per cent in 2012. The world insurance premium in Non-Life section which was 4.40 per cent in 2007 came down to 3.7 per cent and the total insurance penetration of the world came down from 3.10 per cent to 2.8 per cent from 2007 to 2012. This shows that the overall trend is declining. While Brazil showed an increase in all the three sections life, non-life and total from 2007 to 2012, many of the developed nations including USA, UK, France, Germany, Australia and others showed a decline in all the three sections Life, Non-Life and the total insurance penetrations.

India's overall insurance penetration was 0.6 per cent in 2007 increased to 0.8 per cent in 2012. India's life insurance penetration came down from 4.7 per cent to 4.0 per cent and non-life insurance penetration came down from 4.00 per cent to 3.2 percent.

GLOBAL PICTURE OF INSURANCE DENSITY

As per the World Insurance Report, published by the reinsurance major "Swiss Re", the global direct premium during 2011 dropped by 0.8 per cent against a surge at 2.7 per cent growth witnessed in the previous year. Globally, life insurance premium accounted for 57 per cent of total insurance premium. This share is higher in advanced economies than in the emerging markets. During 2011, global life insurance premium dropped by 2.7 per cent to USD 2627 billion. The premium volume fell in Western Europe, China and India, whereas, it rose in Middle East and Latin America.

On the other hand, the premium in non-life insurance business grew by 1.9 per cent. Latin America reported remarkably high growth. The Report mentions that the year 2011 witnessed exceptionally high catastrophe losses in Japan, Australia, and the United States, while European countries generally enjoyed low catastrophe claims. In 2011, total economic losses to Society due to disasters (both insured and uninsured) reached an estimated USD 370 billion, compared to USD 226 billion in 2010. The earthquake in Japan, the country's worst on record in terms of magnitude, alone accounted for 57 per cent of global economic losses. The insured losses from natural catastrophes appeared to be to the tune of USD 110 billion. As at end-September 2012, there are fifty-two insurance companies operating in India; of which twenty four are in the life insurance business and twenty-seven are in non-life insurance business. In addition, General Insurance Corporation (GIC) is the sole national reinsurer.

The life insurance industry recorded a premium income of Rs. 2, 87,072 crore during 2011-12 as against Rs. 2, 91,639 crore in the previous financial year, registering a negative growth of 1.57 per cent. While private sector insurers posted 4.52 per cent decline (11.08 per cent growth in previous year) in their premium income, Life Insurance Corporation (LIC), the fully state owned insurance company, recorded 0.29 per cent decline (9.35 per cent growth in previous year), in its total premium underwritten. While the renewal premium accounted for 60.31 per cent (56.66 per cent in 2010-11) of the total premium received by the life insurers, first year premium contributed the remaining 39.69 per cent (43.34 per cent in 2010-11).

During 2011-12, the growth in renewal premium was 4.77 per cent (6.23 per cent in 2010-11). First year premium registered a decline of 9.85 per cent in comparison to growth of 15.02 per cent during 2010-11. In the non-life segment, the insurers underwrote gross direct premium of Rs. 52,876 crore in India for the year 2011-12 as against Rs. 42,576 crore in 2010-11, registering a growth of 24.19 per cent as against an increase of 22.98 per cent recorded in the previous year. The public sector insurers exhibited growth in 2011-12 at 21.50 per cent; as against the previous year's growth rate of 21.84 per cent. The private sector general insurers registered a growth of 28.06 per cent, which is higher than 24.67 per cent achieved during the previous year.

INDIAN INSURANCE COMPANIES ABROAD

The Insurance Regulatory and Development Authority (IRDA) has allowed insurance companies in India to conduct business overseas. The companies can do business in the life insurance, non- life insurance and in re-insurance space. The regulator has allowed insurance companies to open a company as well as branches abroad. But this will also be dictated by the local regulations. There are some countries, such as India, that don't allow foreign insurers to open branches but the UK, for instance, allows branches. According to IRDA foreign company would mean a company registered outside India whose paid-up capital is subscribed to by an Indian insurance company and shall include a foreign subsidiary company wherein the Indian insurance company has a holding of more than 50% of its paid-up capital or is in a position to control the composition of its board of directors. It shall also include a branch office of the Indian insurance company. In order to open offices abroad, IRDA needs insurers to be at least three years old with a net worth of at least Rs.500 crore in case of a life insurance company and Rs. 250 crore in case of a non-life company. In the case of reinsurance companies, the net worth should be Rs. 750 crore. In order to ensure that these companies have sound financial health, IRDA has also stipulated that these companies should have made profits for at least three years out of the last five years. In addition to this, the insurer should have a clear track record of regulatory compliances for three years out of the last five years.

Except LIC (Life Insurance Corp. of India) there aren't many companies with a profit record of more than three years. Also private insurers already have foreign partners who are operating in most markets of the world, it makes little sense for these companies to go abroad just yet. Seeking to safeguard the interest of domestic policyholders, IRDA further said the insurer setting up overseas business will not be allowed to utilise the fund of domestic policyholder. "The Indian insurance company shall have in place appropriate arrangements to ensure that the policyholder's liabilities that arise for foreign operations are adequately ring-fenced in order to protect the Indian policyholder," the guidelines said.

There are 52 companies in life, general insurance and reinsurance business in India. Most of them have foreign partners.

An insurance company desirous of setting up foreign insurance company (including branch office) "should not suffer from any adverse report of the Authority on its track record of regulatory compliances, for 3 years out of the last 5 years from the date of application," the IRDA said. The guidelines also said the Indian insurers should formulate an 'Investment Policy' to suit the scale, nature and area of operations of the foreign branch offices.

As per the IRDA, a 'foreign insurance company means a company registered outside India whose paid-up capital is subscribed to by an Indian insurance company. It shall include a foreign subsidiary company wherein the Indian insurance company has a holding of more than 50 of its paid-up capital or is in a position to control the composition of its Board of Directors. It shall also include a branch office of the Indian insurance company.

Even as the insurance regulator has allowed insurers to set up offices abroad, the products that they are able to offer will depend upon the local jurisdiction of the country they are operating in. The products they can offer will depend on the local jurisdiction of the country they are operating in. So as a non-resident Indian (NRI), if one is looking to buy rupee-denominated insurance products, he will have to buy it from India. For NRIs who live in countries such as the US, the UK and Singapore, insurance products are cheaper. For instance, term product rates in the US are about 25% cheaper than India. Also insurance products in most countries come with tax incentives. The tax rules of the country in which the insurer operates will apply. Most countries are offering generous tax breaks on insurance products. Insurers who operate abroad so far only state-owned insurers have offices abroad. For instance, in the life insurance space, only LIC has offices in the Gulf countries and sell dollar-denominated products such as term insurance plans, traditional insurance-cum-investment plans and unit-linked insurance plans (Ulips). In addition to offering products, these offices also provide service to NRIs that have LIC policies from India. LIC has a separate website for its international business (www.licinternational.com). State-owned general insurer New India Assurance Co. Ltd has 23 offices abroad. Most of these offices were set up before IRDA came into being in 2000.

CONCLUSION

Insurance companies around the globe have worked diligently since the global financial crisis to reduce operational costs, and improve effectiveness. Undoubtedly those initiatives are now paying dividends, but market conditions remain tough, with few insurers able to raise rates as much as they would like, if at all, and investment income is still lagging.

Insurance sector has immense potential in terms of contribution to the growth momentum. The underinsured and unsaturated markets need to be taped in order to realize its full impact on the Indian economy. The study identifies the low level of insurance penetration and density levels vis-à-vis various advanced and emerging economies. It has also shown the correlation between the insurance penetration and economic development. The increased penetration with the opening up of the sector in 2000 gives a clear indication that the private and the foreign players have ability to enhance the size, structure and participation in the insurance market worldwide.

The growing need for financial education for the families to take better financial decision and to increase their economic security has been widely recognized. It is felt that well informed and well educated customers can create economic ripples as is generally known. They make better financial decisions for themselves and their families, increasing their economic security and wellbeing. Secured families are more involved in their communities as home owners and voters. They are more involved as parents with their children's schools and teachers, enabling better educational and economic outcomes for their children. They contribute to vital, thriving communities, further fostering community economic development. Thus, being financially literate is not only important to the individual household and family, it is also important to communities and societies. (Hogarth, Jeanne M., 2006).

Insurance sector demands huge investment, working capital and in-depth knowledge of the market. The gestation period in the insurance industry both life and non-life is reasonably long (ranges from 10 to 15 years) which underestimates the efficiency of private and foreign players.

India continues to be an under-insured state compared to middle income countries such as China, Brazil and the developed countries such as United States of America and the United Kingdom. Hence, both private and public sector insurance companies are making enormous efforts to create insurance awareness. Since the insurance sector is still in a nascent stage of development, the insurance industry in India has witnessed negligible growth during the past few years [Chart 5.1 & 5.2].

A low and uneven development of insurance, especially in the non-life lines of business, increases the level of risk in the economic decisions taken by individuals and firms which hampers the economic activities. The declining level of penetration is a matter of concern. There is a need to make the insurance sector competitive at global level. The regulatory environment for insurance should encourage risk-based pricing. Government should act as a promoter and facilitator of insurance services with privatization and liberalization of insurance services so that the level of insurance in the country could improve vis-à-vis the standards in the international market.

A recent study by McKinsey & Company indicates that consumers have an unmet need for long- term savings products and a preference for insurance vis-à-vis other investment products. Consumers rank insurance higher than other investment options because of the ease and convenience in investing, and in obtaining tax benefits and protection cover. Indian consumers perceive life insurance as a low-risk and high-return investment, this being a perception driven by the awareness of LIC's performance and its record of delivering stable returns over the years. India's insurance market has grown over the past six years. Liberalisation of the sector has enabled the entry of a number of new players who have contributed to the growth (over 40 per cent per annum), by enhancing product awareness and promoting consumer education and information. However, the market is still in a nascent stage.

The study identifies low level of insurance penetration and density levels vis-à-vis advanced and emerging economies. It also shows the correlation between the insurance penetration and economic development. The increased penetration with the opening up gives a clear indication that the private and foreign players have an ability to enhance the size, structure and participation in the insurance market worldwide.

Having discussed trends of trade in insurance services is discussed in detail with respect to insurance penetration and insurance density and the banking and insurance performance and its relationship with economic growth is studied in the next chapter.

REFERENCES

1. The Financial Stability Forum (FSF) brings together Senior Representatives of National Financial Authorities, International Financial Institutions Groupings (including sector specific ones), Committees of Central Bank Experts and the European Central Bank. It was Convened in April 1999 to prom Information Exchange and International Cooperation in Financial Supervision and Surveillance. The FSF seeks to Coordinate the efforts of these vario Financial Stability, Improve the Functioning of Markets, and Reduce Systemic Risk. See http://www.fsforum.org.
2. Examples of Hybrid Products Encompassing different Financial Services include bancassurance and insurance-linked derivates.
3. Patrick (1966), Financial Development and Economic Growth in Underdeveloped Countries, Economic Development and Cultural Change, Vol. 14 (2), pp. 174-189.

4. The Stream of Literature on the Interrelationship between Economic Growth and the Financial Services Sector also includes Levine Ross, Financial Development and Economic Growth: Views and Agenda, October 1996.
5. Das, Davies and Podpiera (2003), Insurance and issues in Financial Soundness, IMF Working Paper WP/03/138.
6. FDI refers to the long Term Capital Inflows from Abroad that Invest in the Production Capacity of any Economy and is a Preferred over other forms of External Finance because they are non-debt Creating as Oppose to the Foreign Institutional investment which is Highly Volatile in Nature.
7. IRDA Annual Report 2011-12.

Economic Growth and Banking and Insurance Performance

INTRODUCTION

The present study examines the dynamic relation between growth, domestic credit and money and quasi money to banking and insurance as a percentage of total trade in services for the select Asian countries which fall in the Low and Middle income groups using time-series data from 2005 to 2012. There is however no study which considers the financial deepening, GDP percapita and the domestic credit as a percentage of GDP and their impact on the increase or decrease in the Banking and Insurance performance in the total trade in services.

Domestic Credit to GDP: measures the degree of bank intermediation towards private sector. This is one of the widely used measures of financial intermediation.

Domestic credit provided by the financial sector includes all credit to various sectors on a gross basis, with the exception of credit to the central government, which is net. The financial sector includes monetary authorities and deposit money banks, as well as other financial corporations where data are available (including corporations that do not accept transferable deposits but do incur such liabilities as time and savings deposits). Examples of other financial corporations are finance and leasing companies, money lenders, insurance corporations, pension funds, and foreign exchange companies[1].

The Domestic credit provided by banking sector (% of GDP) varies by country. The country with the highest value in the world is Japan, with a value of 341.69. The country with the lowest value in the world is Libya, with a value of -65.93.

The following table shows the value of domestic trade and the rank of the countries. While Japan, Cyprus, United States, Ireland, United Kingdom, Netherlands, Hong Kong, Denmark and Portugal stand in the first ten ranks in the amount of Domestic credit provided by the financial sector (% to GDP), the select eight countries only Malaysia and Thailand are in ranks below 30, India with 60 rank all the others range from 60 to 110th rank in the world ranking.

Table 6.1: World Ranking of the Domestic Credit Provided by Financial Sector (% GDP) ratio

Rank	Country	Value	Year
1	Japan	341.69	2011
2	Cyprus	330.e	2011
3	United States	232.51	2011
4	Spain	230.91	2011
5	Ireland	225.67	2011
6	United Kingdom	212.62	2011
7	Netherlands	211.37	2011
8	Hong KongSAR, China	207.06	2011
9	Denmark	205.45	2011
10	Portugal	204.10	2011
60	India	74.12	2011
110	Indonesia	38.51	2011
28	Malaysia	128.74	2011
106	Maldives	39.53	2011
86	Philippines	51.83	2011
102	Pakistan	43.28	2011
95	Sri Lanka	46.18	2011
16	Thailand	159.21	2011

GDPP (Per Capita GDP) is a measure of the total output of a country that takes the gross domestic product (GDP) and divides it by the number of people in the country. The per capita GDP is especially useful when comparing one country to another because it shows the relative performance of the countries.

M2 to GDP (Money and Quasi Money Growth (%))

The financial intermediation is also measured by M2 to GDP, which is an indicator of the financial deepening and indicates the deposit mobilization role of the financial system. It measures the average annual growth rate in money and quasi money. Money and quasi money comprise the sum of currency outside banks, demand deposits other than those of the central government, and the time, savings, and foreign currency deposits of resident sectors other than the central government. This definition is frequently called M2. The change in the money supply is measured as the difference in end-of-year totals relative to the level of M2 in the preceding year. This measures the financial deepening of the economy.

The present study identified the gap that most of the studies examine the relationship and impact of the banking and insurance performance on the economic growth of economies. Having identified the gap the present study examines the relationship of the economic growth on the banking and insurance trade performance. Most of the studies are on developed countries, as India is a developing country located in Asia, the present study considers select Asian countries of the low and middle income group.

In the present study economic growth is considered as depended and it is represented by three variables. They are DOMCREDIT, GDPP and M2GDP and the banking and insurance performance as represented by BIPER is considered as the independent variable. The study examines the relationship between the dependent and independent variables for select eight Asian Countries i.e., India, Indonesia, Malaysia, Maldives, Philippines, Pakistan,Thailand and Sri Lanka.

The data was tested grouped into panel data thus combining time series and Cross section data. The data was tested with Panel Unit Root test. Panel Unit roots are performed to check whether the series is stationary or not. [Series means - each variable data]. Panel Unit roots are done and not time series unit roots. Time Series Unit roots don't give BLUE estimates, they give inconsistent and biased estimate. Hence Panel Unit Root tests are conducted. Stationarity means Mean and Variance is consistent over a period of time.

METHODOLOGY USED

The data was tested grouped into panel data thus combining time series and Cross section data. The data was tested with Panel Unit Root test. Panel Unit roots are performed to check whether the series is stationary or not. [Series means - each variable data]. Panel Unit roots are done and not time series unit roots. Time Series Unit roots don't give BLUE estimates, they give inconsistent and biased estimate. Hence Panel Unit Roots are done. Stationarity means Mean and Variance is consistent over a period of time.

Panel Unit Root Tests Performed are:

1. Levin, Lin, Chu t-statistic test
2. Im, Pesaran and Shin w-statistic test
3. ADF – Fisher Chi square
4. PP – Fisher Chi square

The above tests were performed at 95% confidence level or " level. If P < 0.05 the null hypothesis is rejected. If P>0.05 the alternate hypothesis is accepted. The Null Hypothesis for Panel Unit Root - Series is having unit root. Unit roots should also be checked for (variables) series which are also having linear trend. Two tests are performed for each variable. They are i) Panel Unit Roots: - individual effects and ii) Panel unit roots – with individual effects and linear trend.

Mostly in econometric series data appear to be in trend, to safeguard against this trended data is taken. If individual effects and linear trend give the same results then estimate in good and efficient.

In the present study eight countries of Asian region – covering both Low and Middle group (also based on the availability of data) are chosen. They are Indonesia, India, Sri Lanka, Maldives, Malaysia, Pakistan, Phillipines and Thailand. Therefore time series of eight countries for the time period from 2005-06 to 2012-13 is considered for four variables. The time period for the study is from 2005 to 2012. The following variables are considered for the study:

1. BIPER – Banking and Insurance percentage of Service Exports
2. Dom Credit to GDP – Domestic Credit provided by financial sector as a percentage of GDP
3. GDPP – GDP percapita
4. M2 to GDP – Money and Quasi Money as a percentage of GDP - financial deepening

If there are unit roots then the First Difference is taken to eliminate i.e., if null hypothesis is accepted. After 1st difference again unit roots are calculated to check if the unit roots still exist or not. Unit roots exist it means the variables are not stationery. For Individual effects four test panel unit root tests and for Normal Data Linear trend four tests panel unit root tests are conducted. Again for First Difference, individual effects for each variable panel unit root tests are conducted and for linear trend also for all four variables panel unit root tests are conducted.

Therefore as there are four variables and four tests in total 16 tests are conducted.

For normal data:

Ifp > α, then H_0 should be accepted

For First difference data:

Ifp < α, then H_1 should be accepted Thus showing that the series is stationery.

Basic requirement for Panel Co-integration is that all the series should be stationery at their first difference. Since it is confirmed that all the series are stationery at their first difference, panel cointegration can be conducted.

Co-integration: means series are moving together. $H_{0:}$ There is No cointegration. $H_{1:}$ Cointegration exists. The null hypothesis if $P < \alpha$ is rejected and alternate Hypothesis is accepted. SEven cointegration tests are done, out of which majority count is taken. Pedroni Co-integration are conducted which have the following tests:

1. Panel v –statistic
2. Panel rho – statistic
3. Panel PP – statistic (Phillip Perron)
4. Panel ADF – statistic (Augmented Dickey Fuller)
5. Group rho – statistic
6. Group PP statistic
7. Group ADF statistic

Equations

BIPER= f (GDPP M2GDP DOMCREDIT) (1)

Definitions:

BIPER = Banking and insurance share as percentage of total services

GDPP = Gross domestic Product Per capita

M2GDP = Ratio of M2 to Gross Domestic Product

DOMCREDIT = Domestic Credit as percentage of Gross Domestic Product

In the equation form our the researcch model can be written as

$BIPER = GDPP + GDPP + DOMCREDIT + u_t$

BIPER = Banking and insurance share as percentage of total services

GDPP = Gross domestic Product Per capita

M2GDP = Ratio of M2 to Gross Domestic Product

DOMCREDIT = Domestic Credit as percentage of Gross Domestic Product

u_t = independently distributed random error term, with zero mean and constant variance at time t

And defined that

, , , , = parameters to be estimated

$BIPER_{it} = + (GDPP_{it} +_{(D1} *(GDPP_{it))} + (1_2*(GDPP_{it}))\ _3*(GDPP_{it} + (D_4*(GDPP_{it))}$
$1_5*(GDPP_{it})) + (D_6*(GDPP_{it})) + (D_7*(GDPP_{it} + u_{it}$

$BIPER_{it\,=} + (M2GDP_{it}) + (D_1* (M2GDP_{it}))\ _+ (D_2*(M2GDP_{it}))\ (D_3*M2GDP_{it}))$
$_+ (D_4* (M2GDP_{it\,+}\ (D_5*(M2GDP_{it})) + (D_6*(M2GDP_{it}))\ _+ (D_7*M2GDP_{it})) + u_{it}$

$BIPER_{it} = + (DOMCREDIT_{it})) + (D_1* DOMCREDIT_{it})) +$
$((D_2*(DOMCREDIT_{it} + (D_3*(DOMCREDIT_{it})) + (D_4*(DOMCREDIT_{it})) +$
$(D_5*(DOMCREDIT_{it})) + (D_6*(DOMCREDIT_{it})) + (D_7*(DOMCREDIT_{it})) + + u_{it}$

Where

i = cross-section-data (the choosen country) t = time series data

$BIPER_{it}$ = Banking and insurance share as percentage of total services of country i at time t;

$GDPP_{it}$ = Gross domestic Product Per capita of country i at time t; $M2GDP_{it}$ = Ratio of M2 to Gross Domestic Product of country i at time t;

$DOMCREDIT_{it}$ = Domestic Credit as percentage of Gross Domestic Product of country i at time t;

u_{it} = independently distributed random error term, with zero mean and constant variance number i at time t;

D_1 = 1 is India, D_1 = 0 is otherwise;

D_2 = 1 is Indonesia, D_2 = 0 is otherwise;

D_3 = 1 is Malaysia, D_3 = 0 is otherwise;

D_4 = 1 is Maldives, D_4 = 0 is otherwise;

D_5 = 1 is Pakistan, D_5 = 0 is otherwise;

D_6 = 1 is Philippines, D_6 = 0 is otherwise;

D_7 = 1 is Srilanka, D_7 = 0 is otherwise;

ECONOMIC GROWTH AND BANKING AND INSURANCE PERFORMANCE

There is a lot of literature on the impact of banking and insurance trade performance on the economic growth of an economy. The present study examines the gap and studies the impact of economic growth on the banking and insurance trade performance. Also the low and middle income countries on Asia are considered for the study. The reason for conducting the study on the Low and Middle Income group is that most of the studies in this area are done on developed economies and hence the study considers low and middle income countries, also identifying that no study is done with South Asian countries in this aspect.

The study examines the relationship between the independent variable BIPER and the dependent variables DOMCREDIT, GDPP and M2GDP by conducting one to one using Pedroni Residual Cointegration Test.

(i) Relationship between BIPER and DOMCREDIT

The table below shows the results of the Pedroni Residual Cointegration conducted for the variables BIPER and DOMCREDIT.

Table 6.2: Panel Cointegration results between BIPER and DOMCREDIT

			Weighted	
	Statistic	Probability	Statistic	Probability
Panel v-Statistic	1.747726	0.0403	-0.49014	0.688
Panel rho-Statistic	-1.85058	0.0321	-0.76459	0.2223
Panel PP-Statistic	-5.38524	0	-3.8641	0.0001
Panel ADF-Statistic	-5.28529	0	-3.70654	0.0001
	Statistic	Probability		
Group rho-Statistic	0.306304	0.6203		
Group PP-Statistic	-3.85954	0.0001		
Group ADF-Statistic	-4.035	0		

The above table shows that the null hypothesis is rejected and the alternate hypothesis is accepted showing that there is a relationship among the variables BIPER and DOMCREDIT.

The table 6.3 shows the cross section specific results giving the co-integration in the relationship between BIPER and DOMCREDIT.

Table 6.3: Cross Section specific results – BIPER and DOMCREDIT

Phillips-Peron results (non-parametric)				
Cross ID	Variance	HAC	Bandwidth	Obs
India	0.273171	0.172637	6	7
Indonesia	0.250836	0.209568	2	7
Malaysia	0.031005	0.024575	2	7
Maldives	0.021406	0.007401	6	7
Pakistan	0.398884	0.460992	1	7
Philippines	0.045951	0.035193	3	7
Sri Lanka	0.077753	0.094074	1	7
Thailand	0.022552	0.022552	0	7
Augmented Dickey-Fuller results (parametric)				
Cross ID	Variance	Lag	Max lag	Obs
India	0.273171	0	0	7
Indonesia	0.250836	0	0	7
Malaysia	0.031005	0	0	7
Maldives	0.021406	0	0	7
Pakistan	0.398884	0	0	7
Philippines	0.045951	0	0	7
Sri Lanka	0.077753	0	0	7
Thailand	0.022552	0	0	7

Since in majority of tests p value is less than alpha (0.05) null hypothesis (series is not cointegrated) is rejected. As null hypothesis is rejected alternative hypothesis is accepted and it can be concluded that series BIPER and the series DOMCREDIT are cointegrated.

(ii) Relationship between BIPER & GDPP

The relationship between independent variable BIPER and the dependent variable GDPP is checked for using the Pedroni Cointegration (a panel cointegration method).

Table 6.4: Panel Cointegration results for variables BIPER and GDPP

	Statistic	Probability	Statistic	Probability
Panel v-Statistic	1.873808	0.0305	0.54905	0.2915
Panel rho-Statistic	-2.19173	0.0142	-1.19623	0.1158
Panel PP-Statistic	-5.52701	0	-3.91482	0
Panel ADF-Statistic	-5.47001	0	-3.87328	0.0001

	Statistic	Probability
	0.173041	0.5687
Group rho-Statistic	-5.01776	0
Group PP-Statistic	-3.75355	0.0001
Group ADF-Statistic		

The above table shows that the null hypothesis is rejected and the alternate hypothesis is accepted showing that there is a relationship among the variables BIPER and GDPP.

Table 6.5: Cross Section specific results – BIPER and GDPP

Cross ID	Variance	HAC	Bandwidth	Observations
India	0.200547	0.224873	1	7
Indonesia	0.130221	0.027666	6	7
Malaysia	0.032602	0.029852	1	7
Maldives	0.022998	0.013084	4	7
Pakistan	0.460615	0.460615	0	7
Philippines	0.040231	0.027968	3	7
Sri Lanka	0.121755	0.164479	1	7
Thailand	0.030334	0.034632	1	7

Cross ID	Lag	Max lag	Obs
India	0	0	7
Indonesia	0	0	7
Malaysia	0	0	7
Maldives	0	0	7
Pakistan	0	0	7
Philippines	0	0	7
Sri Lanka	0	0	7
Thailand	0	0	7

Since in majority of tests p value is less than alpha (0.05) null hypothesis (series is not co-integrated) is rejected. As null hypothesis is rejected alternative hypothesis is accepted and it can be concluded that series BIPER and GDPP are co-integrated

(iii) Relationship between BIPER and M2GDP

The table below shows the Pedroni Panel Cointegration results for verifying the relationship using variables BIPER and M2GDP.

Table 6.6: Panel Cointegration Results for BIPER and M2GDP

	Statistic	Probability	Statistic
Panel v-Statistic	1.677109	0.0468	-0.25232
Panel rho-Statistic	-1.77301	0.0381	-0.63403
Panel PP-Statistic	-4.39433	0	-4.58718
Panel ADF-Statistic	-4.35997	0	-4.04933
	Statistic	**Probability**	
Group rho-Statistic	0.417868	0.662	
Group PP-Statistic	-5.32673	0	

Table 6.7: Cross Section Specific Results of BIPER and M2GDP

Cross ID	AR1	Variance	Observations
India	-0.189	0.217638	7
Indonesia	-0.57	0.208958	7
Malaysia	-0.173	0.026149	7
Maldives	-0.134	0.015077	7
Pakistan	-0.51	0.505835	7
Philippines	-0.167	0.046812	7
Sri Lanka	0.142	0.199607	7
Thailand	-0.536	0.019042	7
Augmented Dickey Fuller Test			
Cross	**AR 1**	**Variance**	**Observations**
India	-0.189	0.217638	7
Indonesia	-0.57	0.208958	7
Malaysia	-0.173	0.026149	7
Maldives	-0.134	0.015077	7
Pakistan	-0.51	0.505835	7
Philippines	-0.167	0.046812	7
Sri Lanka	0.142	0.199607	7
Thailand	-0.536	0.019042	7

Since in majority of tests p value is less than alpha (0.05) null hypothesis (series is not co-integrated) is rejected. As null hypothesis is rejected alternative hypothesis is accepted and it can be concluded that series BIPER and M2GDP is co-integrated

The present study examined the relationship between economic growth and banking and insurance performance. The study is done for select Asian countries for a period of nine years from 2005 to 2013.

Most of the literature shows that banking and insurance performance has an impact on the economic growth of the economy. But we believe and wanted to check the relationship other way round. When an economy grows it does have an impact on the level of activities, international trade and thus has an impact on banking and insurance trade performance also.

To check this relationship banking and insurance performance [BIPER] has been taken as the independent variable and three variables [GDPP, M2GDP, DOMCREDIT] representing economic growth have been taken as dependent variables.

In this study the variables like Domestic credit provided by financial sector as a percentage of GDP, Money and Quasi money as a percentage of GDP and GDP per capita is measured for eight Asian countries including low developed and middle developed countries by using fixed-effect panel data regression. The analysis is done for the period between the years 2005-2013.

Panel unit root tests are conducted to check the data for stationarity and then Panel cointegration was performed. The Pedroni co-integration test (Panel Co-integration) test when performed shows that there is significant relationship between Banking and Insurance performance and the variables like Domestic Credit provided by financial sector, Money and Quasi money and GDP. Thus, it shows the relationship between economic growth and banking and insurance performance of an economy. Which shows that as the economy grows the banking and insurance trade performance also grows.

The second part of the analysis is to check for which countries there is a strong relationship between the dependent and independent variables. Taking India as the reference country the relationship of the variables in India is checked and also checked if the relationship shows a similar pattern in other countries.

In this study Banking and Insurance Performance and its relationship with variables like Domestic credit provided by financial sector as a percentage of GDP, Money and Quasi money as a percentage of GDP and GDP percapita is measured for 8 Asian countries including low developed and middle developed countries by using fixed-effect panel data co-integration. The analysis is done for the period between the years 2005-2012. Panel unit root tests have been performed on all the four variables BIPER, GDPP, M2 to GDP, DOMCREDIT. The following Panel unit root tests have been performed on all the variables (Levin, Lin & Chu, Im, Pesaran and Shin, ADF - Fisher Chi-square, PP - Fisher Chi-square, PP - Fisher Chi-square). From the panel unit root values it can be concluded that there are unit roots in all the series. Since all the series had unit roots they undergo 1st difference to eliminate the unit roots. Panel unit root tests for first difference values were done. When first difference was taken for all the series unit roots have been eliminated. Hence it can be concluded that all the series have become stationary at Level1 or they can be called as Level (1) series. After understanding that the series has become stationary at level1, co-integration tests were carried out.

Pedroni Panel co-integration tests (as shown in tables 6.2 to 6.7) are carried out on independent and dependent variables. It has been found and concluded that the independent variable Banking and Insurance trade performance [BIPER] and the dependent variables [DOMCREDIT], BIPER and M2GDP, BIPER and GDPP series are co-integrated. They all move in the same direction. They show that the growth and development of the country has impact on the banking and insurance performance.

The relationship between the independent variable BIPER and the dependent variable representing economic growth DOMCREDIT is examined with panel co-intergration and it is found that there is a strong relationship between the two. Similarly the relationship between BIPER and the M2toGDP has been examined and found that there is also a strong relationship between the variables. The relationship between BIPER and GDPP (another variable representing the Economic Growth) is also being checked for and it is found that there is a strong relationship between all the three variables of Economic Growth and the Banking and Insurance Performance.

RELATIONSHIP BETWEEN DEPENDENT AND INDEPENDENT VARIABLES FOR SOUTH ASIAN COUNTRIES

In the present chapter it is examined if there is significant relationship between dependent variable (economic growth) and independent variable (banking and insurance performance) of sample countries using Panel Regression.

The present chapter checks if there is any significant relationship between the dependent variable Banking and Insurance performance (BIPER) and the independent variables, GDPP (Gross Domestic Product Percapita), M2 to GDP percentage and Domestic Credit provided by financial sector as a percentage of GDP for all the select Asian countries

Indonesia, India, Maldives, Malaysia, Srilanka, Phillippines, Pakistan and Thailand. And also checks if the relationship is the same as in the case of the reference country. In the present study India is taken as the reference country.

As a first step WALD test is conducted to understand whether fixed effects model or OLS test should be conducted.

Table 6.8: Wald Test coefficients

Test Statistic	Value	DF	Probability
F-statistic	61.52575	(7, 53)	0
Chi-square	430.6802	7	0
Null Hypothesis Summary:			
Normalized Restriction (= 0)		Value	Std. Err.
C(5)		3.797988	0.343074
C(6)		3.197606	0.468279
C(7)		1.919094	0.417819
C(8)		-0.35315	0.49819
C(9)		1.729015	0.420529
C(10)		-1.24549	1.041886
C(11)		-2.38287	0.796307

Table 6.9: Cross Section Data Analysis – Fixed Effects

Country code	Coefficient	Std. Error	t-Statistic	Prob.
C(1)	2.814913	1.053349	2.672345	0.01
C(2)	-0.00015	9.45E-05	-1.60186	0.1151
C(3)	0.008299	0.012936	0.641531	0.5239
C(4)	0.031122	0.020763	1.498918	0.1398
C(5)	-0.60038	0.610493	-0.98344	0.3299
C(6)	-1.8789	0.524386	-3.58304	0.0007
C(7)	-4.15114	0.617941	-6.7177	0
C(8)	-2.06897	0.584555	-3.5394	0.0008
C(9)	-5.04348	0.951621	-5.29988	0
C(10)	-6.18086	0.609165	-10.1464	0
C(11)	-3.79799	0.343074	-11.0705	0
R-squared	0.925049	Mean dependent var		2.122964
Adjusted R-squared	0.910908	S.D. dependent var		1.683897
S.E. of regression	0.502616	Akaike info criterion		1.617177
Sum squared resid	13.38899	Schwarz criterion		1.988235
Log likelihood	-40.7497	Hannan-Quinn criter.		1.763355
F-statistic	65.41307	Durbin-Watson stat		2.10744
Prob(F-statistic)	0			

From the above table since the value of p is less than alpha. It indicates that Fixed effect model is better than Pooled OLS model.

Fixed Effects Model

BIPER = C(1) + C(2)*GDPP + C(3)*DOMCREDIT + C(4)*M2GDP + C(5)*D1 + C(6)*D2 + C(7)*D3 + C(8)*D4 + C(9)*D5 + C(10)*D6 + C(11)*D7

India has been taken as the base country. All other countries have been compared taking Indian values as the reference. Based on the p-values for the dummy coefficients, it can be said that only Sri Lanka with a p value(0.3299) which is greater than 0.05does not have intercepts that differ significantly from Indian intercept of 2.8149. Which shows that in SriLanka the relationship of the independent variable BIPER and the dependent variables is not significant and it is also not as it is in the reference country, India.

Using fixed effect dummy variable regression, India was taken as the reference country and the relationship between banking and insurance performance and economic growth as indicated by the variables BIPER, DOMCREDIT, GDPP and M2GDP is checked. The test reveals if the relationship is same as in the reference country. The Fixed effects test reveals that there is significant country effects meaning the relationship in all the countries are in the similar direction as in India except for SriLanka. The results reveal that variables BIPER, DOMCREDIT, GDPP and M2GDP have strong effect in the countries Pakistan, Maldives, Indonesia, Malaysia, Thailand and Philippines.

The coefficients for the countries Pakistan, Maldives, Indonesia, Malaysia, Thailand and Philippines were found to be significant. Only SriLanka doesn't not show significant relationship among the dependent and independent variables. It also does not show a similar trend in the relationship between the variables BIPER, GDPP, DOMCREDIT and M2GDP.

In this study Banking and Insurance Performance and its relationship with variables like Domestic credit provided by financial sector as a percentage of GDP, Money and Quasi money as a percentage of GDP and GDP per capita is measured for 8 Asian countries including low developed and middle developed countries by using fixed-effect panel data regression. The analysis is done for the period between the years 2005-2012. Using fixed effect dummy variable regression, the coefficients for the following countries Pakistan, Maldives, Indonesia, Malaysia, Thailand and Philippines were found to be significant. It is concluded that there is significant country effects. The results reveal that variables BIPER, DOMCREDIT, GDPP and M2GDP have strong effect in the above countries.

Having understood the relationsip between Banking and Insurance performance and the development in the Asian Countries in this chapter, the concluding remarks are given in the final chapter.

REFERENCE

1. The World bank, World Development Indicators.

Trade in Financial Services

The purpose of this chapter is to synthesize the various aspects of trade in banking and insurance and its relationship with the economic growth of economy as examined in the foregoing chapters, and to provide an integrated view of the findings and conclusions.

Reforms in the Banking and Insurance Sectors

Financial sector reforms all over the world have been driven by two apparently contradictory forces. The first is a thrust towards liberalisation, which seeks to reduce if not eliminate a number of direct controls over banks and other financial market participants. The second is a thrust in favour of stronger regulation of the financial sector.

The reforms cover the following aspects:

1. the need for specific financial, disclosure or corporate governance requirements for foreign banks;
2. the optimal degree of separation and segmentation of international activities from domestic bank activities;
3. requirements on subsidiarization and ring-fencing;
4. the best modalities for international liquidity and lender of last resort facilities;
5. mitigating cross-border financial turmoil; and
6. the optimal institutional framework and burden sharing arrangements.

All branches of economic activity today are fundamentally dependent on access to financial services. A healthy and stable financial system, accompanied by sound macroeconomic management and prudential regulation, is an essential ingredient for sustained growth.

Conversely, macroeconomic instability arising from weaknesses in the financial sector can undermine the process of development.

First, reform measures were initiated and sequenced to create an enabling environment for banks to overcome the external constraints – these were related to administered structure of interest rates, high levels of pre-emption in the form of reserve requirements, and credit allocation to certain sectors. Sequencing of interest rate deregulation has been an important component of the reform process which has imparted greater efficiency to resource allocation. The process has been gradual and predicated upon the institution of prudential regulation for the banking system, market behavior, financial opening and, above all, the underlying macroeconomic conditions.

Second, as regards the policy environment of public ownership, it must be recognized that the lion's share of financial intermediation was accounted for by the public sector during the pre- reform period. As part of the reforms programme, initially, there was infusion of capital by the Government in public sector banks, which was followed by expanding the capital base with equity participation by the private investors. Diversification of ownership has led to greater market accountability and improved efficiency. Since the initiation of reforms, infusion of funds by the Government into the public sector banks for the purpose of recapitalisation amounted, on a cumulative basis, to less than one per cent of India's GDP, a figure much lower than that for many other countries.

Third, one of the major objectives of banking sector reforms has been to enhance efficiency and productivity through competition. Guidelines have been laid down for establishment of new banks in the private sector and the foreign banks have been allowed more liberal entry. As a major step towards enhancing competition in the banking sector, foreign direct investment in the private sector banks is now allowed up to 74 per cent, subject to conformity with the guidelines issued from time to time.

Fourth, consolidation in the banking sector has been another feature of the reform process. This also encompassed the Development Financial Institutions (DFIs), which have been providers of long-term finance while the distinction between short-term and long-term finance provider has increasingly become blurred over time. While guidelines for mergers between non-banking financial companies and banks were issued some time ago, guidelines for mergers between private sector banks have been issued recently.

Fifth, impressive institutional and legal reforms have been undertaken in relation to the banking sector. In 1994, a Board for Financial Supervision (BFS) was constituted comprising select members of the RBI Board with a variety of professional expertise to exercise 'undivided attention to supervision'. The BFS also ensures an integrated approach to supervision of commercial banks, development finance institutions, non-banking finance companies, urban cooperatives banks and primary dealers.

Sixth, there have been a number of measures for enhancing the transparency and disclosures standards. Illustratively, with a view to enhancing further transparency, all cases of penalty imposed by the RBI on the banks as also directions issued on specific matters, including those arising out of inspection, are to be placed in the public domain.

Seventh, while the regulatory framework and supervisory practices have almost converged with the best practices elsewhere in the world, two points are noteworthy. This was prescribed at a time when interest rates were falling and banks were realizing large gains out of their treasury activities.

Eighth, of late, the regulatory framework in India, in addition to prescribing prudential guidelines and encouraging market discipline, is increasingly focusing on ensuring good governance through "fit and proper" owners, directors and senior managers of the banks. Banks have also been asked to ensure that the nominated and elected directors are screened by a nomination committee to satisfy `fit and proper' criteria. The listed banks are also required to comply with governance principles laid down by the SEBI – the securities markets regulator.

Globalization, financial deregulation and improvement in technology have had a profound effect on the financial landscape in recent years. These developments have intensified competition and resulted in financial engineering through product innovation and business strategies. While market participants have now greater scope to diversify risk and manage it efficiently, this has also posed new risks and challenges to the financial system. Growth of financial firms across different business lines and across national boundaries has made the task of designing appropriate policies more challenging. Regulatory and supervisory policies are, therefore, constantly assessed regarding their capabilities to meet the challenges of containing systemic risk in the financial system. The main challenge for the supervisory authorities has been to maintain financial stability without curtailing the incentive to innovate.

In view of the inherent potential for sustained growth in the domestic economy and also growing integration into the global economy there needs to be commensurate expansion in the presence of foreign banks in India. However, post crisis, the support for domestic incorporation of foreign banks through the subsidiarisation route has acquired importance. Comprehensive policy in this regard is being proposed.

The present study covers the potential benefits of foreign bank presence in India over a period of nine years from 2005-2006 to 2013-2014. Yet little is known about the channels by which foreign banks can improve the efficiency of domestic financial systems, increase financial sector development and access to financial services, and enhance countries' overall economic growth. Further, the recent financial crisis has highlighted again that there can be risks associated with cross-border banking and foreign banks presence. These developments have led to an increased demand among policy makers and interest among academics for more analyses of the benefits and risks of foreign bank presence to help guide regulatory reforms.

One of the major objectives of reforms was to bring in greater efficiency by permitting entry of private sector banks, liberalised policy on entry of new foreign banks and increased operational flexibility to banks. Keeping these in view, several measures were initiated to infuse competition in the banking sector. Through the lowering of entry barriers, competition has significantly increased since the beginning of the 1990s, with the Reserve Bank allowing entry of new banks in the private sector.

State Bank of India (SBI), at the 38th position, and ICICI Bank at 99th position, are the only banks from India appearing in the top 100 banks (Brand Directory League Tables 2013).

With regard to globalisation, there is an opposing view that instead of looking outwards, Indian banks should look inwards through financial deepening. In this context, it needs to be noted that looking outwards for global presence and looking inwards for deeper financial penetration are not mutually exclusive. It should be possible to aim for both. This opportunity for larger Indian banks which are looking for growth and looking outwards for global presence is initiated and made possible by the reforms in the banking and insurance sector in India.

To conclude it is examined that the reforms in the banking sector have helped the banks improve their performance and work efficiently, with this improved performance and the confidence the banks which opened branches abroad performed well and thus the trade in banking services improved. The reforms in the insurance sector also have an impact on the trade insurance services and India's contribution is good as compared to other countries and it has been increasing in the general insurance sector.

Trends in Trade in Banking Services

The annual survey on International Trade in Banking Services (ITBS) provides information on the branches/subsidiaries of Indian banks operating abroad and foreign banks operating in India. Cross-border presence of both Indian and foreign banks have increased in the recent years. The consolidated balance sheet of overseas branches of Indian banks, which moderated after the global financial crisis, recovered in subsequent years whereas that of foreign banks operating in India is continuing to grow at a relatively moderate pace.

The growth of cross-border trade not only depends on the willingness of consumers to use alternative delivery systems, but also on their willingness to transact with foreign financial services providers. The necessary change in behaviour may occur as providers find new ways to foster a climate of trust between themselves and their customers.

The number of branches of Indian banks operating abroad increased by nine branches from 112 to 121 in 2008, by 13 branches in 2009, 10 branches in 2010, 9 branches in 2011, 10 branches in 2012 and 7 branches in 2013. The above shows that probably because of the impact of the financial crisis the number of branches decreased with the decreased operations and decreased activity in the economy. The impact of the global financial turbulence is visible in the number of branches of both domestic banks abroad and foreign banks in India.

The number of employees decreased from 4030 in 2007 to 2629 in 2008. This could be because of the financial crisis. The number of employees has been increasing from 2009 onwards and it picked up in 2013 where the increase is 272 employees from 2012 to 2013. On the other hand, the impact of global financial turbulence on foreign banks was visible on their Indian operations too as their employee strength in India contracted by 6.3 per cent in 2009-10 before recovering marginally by 0.8 per cent during 2010-11.

It is clearly visible that the Indian banks operating abroad, has more of locals as employees as compared to Indians. But the number of Foreign locals working has decreased and the number of Indians has increased this phenomenon is probably because of the payment to Indians is less than that paid to the foreign locals. When it comes to foreign banks operating in India, they employ mostly Indians and a very small percentage of people who are from other countries other than India and the respective foreign country.

The amount accrued from ITBS operations of banks from UK, Hong Kong, USA was higher than the amount accrued to India from such overseas operations by Indian banks in these countries. However, the amount accrued to India from ITBS was more than the amount accrued to countries like Bahrain, Belgium, Singapore and UAE from their operations in India.

The share of non-interest income in total income of foreign banks in India was more than that for overseas branches of Indian banks, as the former had more non-fund-based activities whereas the latter generated major share of their fee income by rendering 'credit related services' and 'trade finance related services'.

Total fee income generated by 170 branches of Indian banks operating outside India increased from '68.0 billion in 2011-12 to '93.5 billion in 2012-13 whereas, in case of foreign banks operating in India, total fee income generated by 316 branches declined from '94.3 billion in 2011-12 to '74.5

billion in 2012-13. A dominant portion of fee income of the Indian banks branches operating abroad came from rendering services to non-residents, whereas in case of Indian Banks overseas subsidiaries, it came from the residents. Profitability ratio of foreign banks in India was more volatile but higher than the overseas branches/subsidiaries of Indian banks, during the last five years.

Foreign Banks in India always brought in the culture of prompt services to customers. After the set up foreign banks in India, the banking sector in India also become more competitive and accurate. India is expected to find a place in the strategy of these banks given the country's growth prospects. India's GDP is seen growing at a robust pace of around 7 per cent over the next few years, throwing up opportunities for the banking sector. RBI provided a launch pad to foreign banks for greater business expansion after 2009.

The present study measured the efficiency change of foreign banks operating in India during 2005-2013. By using the non-parametric technique, i.e., Data Envelopment Analysis (DEA). IDBI Bank, YES bank, SBI Commercial and International Bank, City Union Bank, Jammu & Kashmir Bank, Oriental Bank of Commerce have been identified as the best and consistent performers among the domestic banks. Among the foreign banks JP Morgan Chase Bank (USA), Bank of Nova Scotia (Canada), Krung Thai Bank PSU Ltd., (Thailand), Mashreq Bank (UAE), Bank of Ceylon (Sri Lanka) are identified as the best and the consistent performers. The best and consistent performers are identified based on the efficiency as given by theta value. They are also check for standard deviation and co-efficient of variation to identify the consistency in the performance.

Overall, it is concluded that the competition of foreign banks compel domestic banks to be more efficient but, although foreign banks may have higher productivity in the primary stage, domestic banks learn from foreign banks and imitate their operating skills following a time variance. Thus, the productivity of domestic banks will improve, and the advantages of foreign banks may gradually disappear. In particular, this result occurs easily in both rapidly developed and close developed countries.

The chapter on international trade in banking provides empirical evidence that a larger foreign ownership share of banks indeed reduces the profitability of domestically owned banks. The foreign bank entry has improved the functioning of national banking markets, with positive welfare implications for banking customers. The relaxation of restrictions on foreign bank entry may reduce domestic banking profits, but with positive overall welfare implications for the domestic economy. Literature also shows and highlights an interesting point that the number of entrants matters rather than their market share.

The economic growth of the country is an apt indicator for the growth of the banking sector. The Indian economy is projected to grow at a rate of 5-6%[1] and the country's banking industry is expected to reflect this growth.

Data Envelopment Analysis method has been used to examine the efficiency of the foreign banks and the domestic banks and to study if the entry of foreign banks has affected the performance of domestic banks. The theta values show the efficiency. The standard deviation is done for both the banks to identify the deviation in the performance if any over a period of 9 years. The Coefficient of Variation is calculated to identify the consistent performers among the best both in domestic banks and also in foreign banks in India.

Data for 44 foreign banks operating in India and 57 domestic banks used to conduct the analysis of relative efficiency. Our findings indicate that:

1. the efficiency of Foreign banks and Domestic banks in India and identify the best performers;
2. the efficiency scores, standard deviation and Coefficient of variation show the best performers and those consistent among them;
3. shows that the entry of the foreign banks and the growth of foreign banks in India is not exactly affecting the performance of the domestic banks in India.

The study reveals that the best performing domestic banks are IDBI Bank, YES bank, SBI Commercial and International Bank, City Union Bank, Jammu & Kashmir Bank, Oriental Bank of Commerce. They have been identified as the best and consistent performers among the domestic banks. Among the foreign banks JP Morgan Chase Bank (USA), Bank of Nova Scotia (Canada), Krung Thai Bank PSU Ltd., (Thailand), Mashreq Bank (UAE), Bank of Ceylon (Sri Lanka) are identified as the best and the consistent performers. The best and consistent performers are identified based on the efficiency as given by theta value. They are also check for standard deviation and co-efficient of variation to identify the consistency in the performance.

The performance of the domestic banks and the entry of the foreign banks is affected by macro-economic variables. The impact of these variables and the fluctuations in the performance of the banks can be taken up for further research.

International Trade in Insurance Services

Insurance sector has immense potential in terms of contribution to the growth momentum. The underinsured and unsaturated markets need to be tapped in order to realize its full impact on the Indian economy. The study identifies the low level of insurance penetration and density levels vis-à-vis various advanced and emerging economies. It has also shown the correlation between the insurance penetration and economic development. The increased penetration with the opening up of the sector in 2000 gives a clear indication that the private and the foreign players have ability to enhance the size, structure and participation in the insurance market worldwide.

Insurance penetration increased from 1.9% in 1990 to 3.9% in 2013. Life Insurance dominates the Insurance Penetration in India from 1.41% in 1990 o 3.1% in 2013. The non-life penetration increased from 0.49% in 1990 to 0.78% in 2013.

The insurance density increased from 11.5 USD in 2000 to 52 USD in 2013. The life Density increased from 9.1 USD in 2000 to 41 USD in 2013. The non-life density increased from 2.4 USD in 2000 to 11 USD in 2013. All public sector insurers (except United India) are underwriting non-life insurance business outside India. United India ceased operations outside India in 2003-04. Total Premium underwritten outside the country by 3 public sector insurers is 1703 crores in 2012 as against 1265 crores in 2011.

Globally, the share of life insurance business in total premium was 56.2 per cent. However, the share of life insurance business for India was very high at 79.6 per cent while the share of non-life insurance business was small at 20.4 per cent.

In life insurance business, India is ranked 11th among the 88 countries, for which data is published by Swiss Re. India's share in global life insurance market was 2.00 per cent during 2013. However, during 2013, the life insurance premium in India declined by 0.5 per cent (inflation adjusted) when global life insurance premium increased by 0.7 per cent.

The Indian non-life insurance sector witnessed a growth of 4.1 per cent (inflation adjusted) during 2013. During the same period, the growth in global non-life premium was 2.3 per cent. However, the share of Indian non-life insurance premium in global non-life insurance premium was small at 0.66 per cent and India ranks 21st in global non-life insurance markets.

New India continued to be the largest public sector non-life insurer underwriting premium outside India, with the premium underwritten outside India constituting 15.46 per cent of the total premium underwritten by the insurer in 2012-13 marginally higher than the 15.19 in the previous year. It reached a peak in 2004-05 at 17.49 per cent but in 2010-11 it was at its least with 13.72 per cent. In case of Oriental the contribution of outside India premium to the total premium works out to be 2.75 per cent in 2012-13, as compared to 2.09 per cent in 2001-02. National Insurance continued to have a small component of overseas business at 0.31 percent in 2012-13, slightly higher than 0.23 reported in 2001-02.

The public sector non-life insurers who have operations outside India underwrote premium of Rs.2049.68 crore in 2012-13 as against Rs.824.48 crore in 2001-02. New India has its operations in countries outside India through a network of branches, agencies, associate companies and subsidiaries. 16.33 per cent in 2001-02 as against 15.46 per cent in 2012-13 of its premium is being underwritten abroad. National Insurance Company underwrote a premium of Rs. 6.89 crore in 2001-02 (Rs. 28.89 crore in 2012-13,). New India too increased the premium underwritten abroad with Rs. 685.83 crore (as against Rs. 1835.53 crore in the financial year 2012-13). Oriental Insurance underwrote a premium of Rs. 52.15 crore (as against Rs. 185.26 crore in 2012-13 United India has ceased foreign operations since 2003-04.

The international comparison of insurance penetration shows that across the countries in the world the insurance penetration has been decreasing from 2007 to 2012 and India is no exception to this trend. The world insurance penetration in Life insurance which was 7.5 per cent in 2007 came down to 6.2 per cent in 2012. The world insurance premium in Non-Life section which was 4.40 per cent in 2007 came down to 3.7 per cent and the total insurance penetration of the world came down from 3.10 per cent to 2.8 per cent from 2007 to 2012. This shows that the overall trend is declining. While Brazil showed an increase in all the three sections life, non-life and total from 2007 to 2012, many of the developed nations including USA, UK, France, Germany, Australia and others showed a decline in all the three sections Life, Non-Life and the total insurance penetrations.

India's overall insurance penetration was 0.6 per cent in 2007 increased to 0.8 per cent in 2012. India's life insurance penetration came down from 4.7 per cent to 4.0 per cent and non-life insurance penetration came down from 4.00 per cent to 3.2 percent.

The survival of the banking system in India through the financial crisis has demonstrated its strengths and most foreign banks present in India believe that India is a market with undeniable potential. However, like their predecessors, they continue to look for the best possible role they can play amidst the challenging political economy, heightened competition and changing financial services regulations

Insurance sector demands huge investment, working capital and in-depth knowledge of the market. The gestation period in the insurance industry both life and non-life is reasonably long (ranges from 10 to 15 years) which underestimates the efficiency of private and foreign players.

A low and uneven development of insurance, especially in the non-life lines of business, increases the level of risk in the economic decisions taken by individuals and firms which hampers the economic activities. The declining level of penetration of new business in the broad state categories however is a matter of concern. There is a need to fasten up the insurance sector to make it competitive at global level. The regulatory environment for insurance should encourage risk-based pricing. Government should act as a promoter and facilitator of insurance services with privatization and liberalization of insurance services so that the level of insurance in the country could improve vis-à-vis the standards in the international market.

IRDA needs to address issues related to the policy framework that needs to be put in place for risks associated with dealing in derivatives by insurance companies. It also needs to make a beginning by introducing a risk-based capital requirement for the insurance sector in order to progress towards adopting a risk-based supervisory cycle for the insurance companies.

The Indian insurance industry faces an inadequate supply of specialised skilled professionals, particularly in the areas of treasury management and actuarial and underwriting skills in non- traditional areas. Adequate initiatives need to be taken in this regard. IRDA too needs to continue taking steps to enhance the skill sets as well as retain its skilled staff. The recent global financial turmoil has brought into sharp focus the liquidity and contagion risks facing the financial institutions. In this context, there is a requirement for an integrated risk management approach which takes into account all facets of risk and their contiguous properties and increased regulatory co-operation and information sharing.

New India continued to be the largest public sector non-life insurer underwriting premium outside India, with the premium underwritten outside India constituting 15.46 per cent of the total premium underwritten by the insurer in 2012-13 marginally higher than the 15.19 in the previous year. It reached a peak in 2004-05 at 17.49 per cent but in 2010-11 it was at its least with 13.72 per cent. In case of Oriental the contribution of outside India premium to the total premium works out to be 2.75 per cent in 2012-13, as compared to 2.09 per cent in 2001-02. National Insurance continued to have a small component of overseas business at 0.31 percent in 2012-13, slightly higher than 0.23 reported in 2001-02.

The public sector non-life insurers who have operations outside India underwrote premium of Rs. 2049.68 crore in 2012-13 as against Rs. 824.48 crore in 2001-02. New India has its operations in countries outside India through a network of branches, agencies, associate companies and subsidiaries. 16.33 per cent in 2001-02 as against 15.46 per cent in 2012-13 of its premium is being underwritten abroad. National Insurance Company underwrote a premium of Rs. 6.89 crore in 2001-02 (Rs. 28.89 crore in 2012-13,). New India too increased the premium underwritten abroad with Rs. 685.83 crore (as against Rs. 1835.53 crore in the financial year 2012-13). Oriental Insurance underwrote a premium of Rs. 52.15 crore (as against Rs. 185.26 crore in 2012-13. United India has ceased foreign operations since 2003-04.

The survival of the banking system in India through the financial crisis has demonstrated its strengths and most foreign banks present in India believe that India is a market with undeniable potential. However, like their predecessors, they continue to look for the best possible role they can play amidst the challenging political economy, heightened competition and changing financial services regulations.

The BJP government in the present budget increased the foreign direct investment (FDI) limit to 49 per cent from the current level of 26 per cent. There is, however, a rider that management and control of the company will remain with the Indian partner.

Currently, Indian promoters are finding it difficult to continue investing additional capital required for growth. Experts say, 49 per cent increase should be positive and will help the industry to gain additional Rs. 7,800 crores. According to data on the website of Life Insurance Council, an umbrella body of life insurers, as on March 2013, insurers have deployed around Rs. 34,200 crore as capital in the life insurance industry.

However, unlike the existing automatic route, the additional investment has to follow the Foreign Investment Promotion Board (PFIPB) route. This move will help the industry, particularly existing players-old and middle-level companies. Insurers have welcomed the move considering it would lead to product innovation, better customer service mechanism and higher insurance penetration in the country.

From an insurance industry standpoint, the increase in the FDI cap in insurance will bring in the requisite growth capital from foreign promoters and will help deepen penetration of insurance solutions in the Indian rural markets.

Economic Growth and Banking and Insurance Performance

The present study examined the relationship between economic growth and banking and insurance performance. The study is done for select asian countries for a period of nine years from 2005 to 2013.

Most of the literature shows that banking and insurance performance has an impact on the economic growth of the economy. But we believe and wanted to check the relationship other way round. When an economy grows it does have an impact on the level of activities, international trade and thus has an impact on banking and insurance trade performance also.

To check this relationship banking and insurance performance [BIPER] has been taken as the independent variable and three variables [GDPP, M2GDP, DOMCREDIT] representing economic growth have been taken as dependent variables.

In this study the variables like Domestic credit provided by financial sector as a percentage of GDP, Money and Quasi money as a percentage of

GDP and GDP per capita is measured for eight Asian countries including low developed and middle developed countries by using fixed-effect panel data regression. The analysis is done for the period between the years 2005-2013.

Panel unit root tests are conducted to check the data for stationarity and then Panel cointegration was performed. The Pedroni co-integration test (Panel Co-integration) test when performed shows that there is significant relationship between Banking and Insurance performance and the variables like Domestic Credit provided by financial sector, Money and Quasi money and GDP. Thus, it shows the relationship between economic growth and banking and insurance performance of an economy. Which shows that as the economy grows the banking and insurance trade performance also grows.

The second part of the analysis is to check for which countries there is a strong relationship between the dependent and independent variables. Taking India as the reference country the relationship of the variables in India is checked and also checked if the relationship shows a similar pattern in other countries.

First Wald test was performed to check if fixed effects test has to be performed or random effects test has to be performed. The results show that fixed effects have to be done.

India has been taken as the base country. All other countries have been compared taking Indian values as the reference. Based on the p-values for the dummy coefficients, it can be said that only Sri Lanka with a p value(0.3299) which is greater than 0.05does not have intercepts that differ significantly from Indian intercept of 2.8149. The analysis done by using Fixed effects model for the eight Asian countries shows that in Sri Lanka the relationship of the independent variable BIPER and the dependent variables is not significant and it is also not as it is in the reference country, India.

Using fixed effect dummy variable regression, India was taken as the reference country and the relationship between banking and insurance performance and economic growth as indicated by the variables BIPER, DOMCREDIT, GDPP and M2GDP is checked. The test reveals if the relationship is same as in the reference country. The Fixed effects test reveals that there is significant country effects meaning the relationship in all the countries are in the similar direction as in India except for Sri Lanka. The results reveal that variables BIPER, DOMCREDIT, GDPP and M2GDP have strong effect in the countries Pakistan, Maldives, Indonesia, Malaysia, Thailand and Philippines.

The coefficients for the countries Pakistan, Maldives, Indonesia, Malaysia, Thailand and Philippines were found to be significant. Of the Asian countries selected for the study Sri Lanka doesn't not show significant relationship among the variables.

CONCLUSION

Given the general robustness of the regulatory and supervisory environment complemented by a gradual approach towards financial sector reforms, India has remained relatively less affected by financial crises which have impacted the international financial system at different points in time, from the 1990s till date. As many parts of the developing world remain poorly integrated both domestically and internationally trade facilitation seems just as relevant today as it did during the colonial period in India.

The important aspect at this point of time is that regulation must become tighter and the supervision must become more controlled. The study identifies low level of insurance penetration and density levels vis-à-vis advanced and emerging economies. It has also shown the correlation between the insurance penetration and economic development. The increased penetration with the opening up of the section in 2000 gives a clear indication that the private and foreign players have an ability to enhance the size, structure and participation in the insurance market worldwide.

Structural reforms are crucial in three areas for building an efficient and stable financial sector. Trade liberalization in the financial services sector can play a supportive role in relation to these structural reforms, through pre-commitment to market opening.

The reforms in the Indian Banking sector and the recommendations made by the respective committees helped the industry to remain abreast of the international practices. The recommendation of encouraging competition by way of allowing more private players and allowing mergers of the small banks with the big and the capable and finally allowing more foreign players into the banking system through branch, subsidiary, representative office or other forms helps in bringing in better technology and encourages competition.

With regard to globalisation, there is an opposing view that along with of looking outwards, Indian banks should look inwards through financial deepening. In this context, it needs to be noted that looking outwards for global presence and looking inwards for deeper financial penetration are not mutually exclusive. It should be possible to aim for both. This opportunity for larger Indian banks which are looking for growth and looking outwards for global presence is initiated and made possible by the reforms in the banking and insurance sector in India.

It is examined that the reforms in the banking sector have helped the banks improve their performance and work efficiently, with this improved performance and the confidence the banks which opened branches abroad performed well and thus the trade in banking services improved.

The reforms in the insurance sector also have an impact on the trade insurance services and India's contribution is good as compared to other countries and it has been increasing in the general insurance sector.

Indian banking sector is constantly growing. The study reveals that the foreign banks increased the efficiency of the local banking system by bringing more sophisticated financial services. Their entry also enhanced financial stability by permitting greater diversification and improving risk management. The foreign banks are also not very sensitive to the host country cycles. They are also more resilient to currency crisis.

The RBI is relooking at the priority sector lending norms for the foreign banks and a possible solution that RBI is thinking of is to involve domestic banks into more of agricultural lending and foreign banks into more of SME lending.

When the efficiency of the domestic and foreign banks was examined using Data Envelopment Analysis for a period of nine years from 2005 to 2013 it was observed that domestic banks performance has not been affected by the entry of the foreign banks. The analysis also identified the best and consistent performers of the domestic and foreign banks operating in India.

IDBI Bank, YES bank, SBI Commercial and International Bank, City Union Bank, Jammu & Kashmir Bank, Oriental Bank of Commerce have been identified as the best and consistent performers among the domestic banks. Among the foreign banks JP Morgan Chase Bank (USA), Bank of Nova Scotia (Canada), Krung Thai Bank PSU Ltd., (Thailand), Mashreq Bank (UAE), Bank of Ceylon (Sri Lanka) are identified as the best and the consistent performers. The best and consistent performers are identified based on the efficiency as given by theta value. They are also check for standard deviation and co-efficient of variation to identify the consistency in the performance.

Keeping in view the changing landscape in the financial sector, the Reserve Bank has been suitably focusing its regulatory and supervisory framework to promote a stable and efficient financial sector. The main focus of the Reserve Bank is recent regulatory and supervisory initiatives has been on prudential regulation and financial infrastructure broadly in line with international best practices. However, while focusing on a globally competitive and the robust banking sector, the Reserve Bank has also emphasized financial inclusion, whereby banking services are accessed easily by the underprivileged sections of the society. Various reform measures initiated from time to time have imparted resilience to the financial system.

Foreign banks are seeing growth opportunities in Asia's third largest economy. Some of the Janpanese and Indonesian banks are planning to enter India through the WOS route ahead of others.[2] The latest opportunity that foreign banks see in India is the retail sector. The government recently allowed overseas companies in multi-brand retail and removed the cap on FDI in single brand retail. Foreign banks are also preparing for the internationalization of Indian business. As Indian go global they need banking support and it is not possible for Indian banks to be present all over the world.

The RBI's Discussion policy talks about creating an environment favorable to foreign banks being encouraged to set up WOS almost at par with domestic banks. With this liberal branch expansion policy, WOS would have access to the areas, which until now remained unexplored by foreign banks in India. Thus, there is ample growth opportunities for foreign banks under the WOS set up.

India has traditionally been a savings-oriented country and insurance plays a crucial role in the development of the Indian economy. But whether it is in terms of life insurance premiums or general insurance premium as a percentage of GDP or premium per capita – the market is under penetrated and people are under insured.

India as compared to many developed nations is not a very globalised economy in terms of market share of global trade. Economies should understand the impact of services revolution which is presently our growth engine and also understand that integration of financial markets is essential for globalization. A sound national insurance and reinsurance market is a necessity for economic growth.

While insurance service liberalization and globalization can be beneficial, they have different impacts on developed and developing countries. This is definitely a challenge for developing countries like India, as the international trade in banking and insurance services has potential impact on the economy as a whole. The introduction of competition from foreign insurers has woke up the large state owned company (LIC). Foreign participation has created benefits not only for the new entrants but also for the players already in the market.

Insurance sector is a central element of the trade and development matrix and is considered as one of the key pillars of the financial services. A sound national insurance sector represents an essential feature of a proper economic system, contributing to economic growth and fostering high employment. As both, an infrastructural and commercial service, a well-functioning insurance sector plays a crucial role in economic development not just at a macro-economic level but also in terms of the activities of individuals and businesses. From an infrastructural perspective it promotes financial and social stability which mobilizes and channel savings, supports trade, commerce and entrepreneurial activity and improves the quality of the lives of individuals.

Liberalization and privatization helps bring substantial financial strength, technological and industry knowhow. At the same time, good risk management and asset liability management skills are required especially in the context of developing countries.

Coming to the relationship between economic growth and the banking and Insurance performance, the analysis helps us to conclude that there is a significant relationship as shown by the Pedroni Panel Co-integration Test.

India has been taken as the base country. All other countries have been compared taking Indian values as the reference. Based on the p-values for the dummy coefficients, it can be said that only Sri Lanka with a p value(0.3299) which is greater than 0.05 does not have intercepts that differ significantly from Indian intercept of 2.8149.

The analysis done by using Fixed effects model for the eight Asian countries shows that in Sri Lanka the relationship of the independent variable BIPER and the dependent variables is not significant and it is also not as it is in the reference country, India.

All the other countries except Sri Lanka show significant relationship among the dependent and independent variables and also show a similar trend between the variables as is visible from the results of fixed effects – a panel regression test.

With the lessons learnt from the crisis, many countries have been reviewing their banking structures post crisis. It is important to review the banking structure in the Indian context also with a view to enabling the banking sector to cater to the needs of a growing and globalizing economy as well as furthering financial inclusion.

SUGGESTIONS

1. It is suggested to spread financial literacy across all citizens of the country equipping them with knowledge, skills and confidence required to make an informed choice while choosing any financial product. This would help increase the insurance density and penetration in India.
2. FDI restrictions in reinsurance sector could also be removed and foreign reinsurance companies should be allowed to set up their representative offices and function in India through a network of branches and divisions.
3. A review of the regulations for establishing re-insurance companies is necessary for increasing the foreign direct investment to 74-100 percent. This would facilitate higher retention of premium within the county. In addition, it would also result in attracting reinsurance business from the neighboring countries; thereby there is probably a possibility of moving India to the position of a regional reinsurance hub in Asia in due course.

4. As recommended by Narasimham committee if India can consider more mergers and acquisitions of banks especially small banks merging with relatively big ones The merger of smaller banks with big ones may also be attributed to an extent for the declining profitability, in case of some major banks. But in the long run this would help the banking system and the economy as a whole.
5. As the analysis showed that the entry of foreign banks has not impacted the profitability or the efficiency of the banks rather the domestic banks are performing better and consistently to survive the competition. So it is suggested that more and more liberal policies be brought in enabling foreign banks to open branches in India such that the economy and the banking system are benefited and flow of money increases with extended credit and other advisory and important services being used for our benefit.
6. India is doing well in the insurance sector with respect to penetration and density. India is doing better in the non-life sector. As suggested by the Malhotra committee more beneficial and liberal policies towards health, motor and reinsurance will help in further improvement in the penetration in these areas and all help in more savings for the economy.
7. With this liberal branch expansion policy, WOS would have access to those areas, which so far remained unexplored by foreign banks in India. Thus, there are ample growth opportunities for foreign banks under the WOS set up. RBI and the Government of India should come up with more of such policies.

REFERENCES

1. Business Standard – Finance Minister to Lower GDP Projection in mid-year Economic Review.
2. Tanmay Bandopadhyay "Global Banks' Local Woes in India", Live Mint, 24th December 2014.

Annexure - 1

WORLD TRADE ORGANIZATION

RESTRICTED
MTN.GNS/W/1201
0 July 1991
(98-0000)

Special Distribution

SERVICES SECTORAL CLASSIFICATION LIST

Note by the Secretariat

The secretariat indicated in its informal note containing the draft classification list (24 May 1991) that it would prepare a revised version based on comments from participants. The attached list incorporates, to the extent possible, such comments. It could, of course, be subject to further modification in the light of developments in the services negotiations and ongoing work elsewhere.

SERVICES SECTORAL CLASSIFICATION LIST

SECTORS AND SUB-SECTORS	CORRESPONDING CPC
1. BUSINESS SERVICES	Section B
A. Professional Services	
a. Legal Services	
b. Accounting, auditing and bookeeping services	862
c. Taxation Services	863
d. Architectural services	8671
e. Engineering services	8672
f. Integrated engineering services	8673
g. Urban planning and landscape architectural services	8674
h. Medical and dental services	9312
i. Veterinary services	932
j. Services provided by midwives, nurses, physiotherapists and para-medical personnel	93191
k. Other	
B. Computer and Related Services	
a. Consultancy services related to the installation of computer hardware	841
b. Software implementation services	842
c. Data processing services	843
d. Data base services	844
e. Other	845+849
C. Research and Development Services	
a. R&D services on natural sciences	851
b. R&D services on social sciences and humanities	852
c. Interdisciplinary R&D services	853
D. Real Estate Services	
a. Involving own or leased property	821
b. On a fee or contract basis	822
E. Rental/Leasing Services without Operators	
a. Relating to ships	83103
b. Relating to aircraft	83104
c. Relating to other transport equipment	83101+83102+
d. Relating to other machinery and equipment	83106-83109
e. Other	832
F. Other Business Services	
a. Advertising services	871
b. Market research and public opinion polling services	864
c. Management consulting service	865
d. Services related to man. consulting	866

e. Technical testing and analysis serv.	8676
f. Services incidental to agriculture, hunting and forestry	881
g. Services incidental to fishing	882
h. Services incidental to mining	883+5115
i. Services incidental to manufacturing	884+885 (except for 88442)
j. Services incidental to energy distribution	887
k. Placement and supply services of Personnel	872
l. Investigation and security	873
m. Related scientific and technical consulting services	8675
n. Maintenance and repair of equipment (not including maritime vessels, aircraft or other transport equipment)	633+ 8861-8866
o. Building-cleaning services	874
p. Photographic services	875
q. Packaging services	876
r. Printing, publishing	88442
s. Convention services	87909*
t. Other	8790
2. <u>COMMUNICATION SERVICES</u>	
A. <u>Postal services</u>	7511
B. <u>Courier services</u>	7512
C. <u>Telecommunication services</u>	
a. Voice telephone services	7521
b. Packet-switched data transmission services	7523**
c. Circuit-switched data transmission services	7523**
d. Telex services	7523**
e. Telegraph services	7522
f. Facsimile services	7521**+7529**
g. Private leased circuit services	7522**+7523**
h. Electronic mail	7523**
i. Voice mail	7523**
j. On-line information and data base retrieval	7523**
k. electronic data interchange (EDI)	7523**
l. enhanced/value-added facsimile services, incl.	7523**

* The (*) indicates that the service specified is a component of a more aggregated CPC item specified elsewhere in this classification list.

** The (**) indicates that the service specified constitutes only a part of the total range of activities covered by the CPC concordance (e.g. voice mail is only a component of CPC item 7523).

m.	store and forward, store and retrieve code and protocol conversion	n.a.
n.	on-line information and/or data processing (incl.transaction processing)	843**
o.	other	
D.	Audiovisual services	
a.	Motion picture and video tape production and distribution services	9611
b.	Motion picture projection service	9612
c.	Radio and television services	9613
d.	Radio and television transmission services	7524
e.	Sound recording	n.a.
f.	Other	
E.	Other	
3.	CONSTRUCTION AND RELATED ENGINEERING SERVICES	
A.	General construction work for buildings	512
B.	General construction work for civil engineering	513
C.	Installation and assembly work	514+516
D.	Building completion and finishing work	517
E.	Other	511+515+518
4.	DISTRIBUTION SERVICES	
A.	Commission agents' services	621
B.	Wholesale trade services	622
C.	Retailing services	631+632 6111+6113+6121
D.	Franchising	8929
E.	Other	
5.	EDUCATIONAL SERVICES	
A.	Primary education services	921
B.	Secondary education services	922
C.	Higher education services	923
D.	Adult education	924
E.	Other education services	929
6.	ENVIRONMENTAL SERVICES	
A.	Sewage services	9401
B.	Refuse disposal services	9402
C.	Sanitation and similar services	9403
D.	Other	

7.	FINANCIAL SERVICES	
A.	All insurance and insurance-related services	812**
a.	Life, accident and health insurance services	8121
b.	Non-life insurance services	8129
c.	Reinsurance and retrocession	81299*
d.	Services auxiliary to insurance (including broking and agency services)	8140
B.	Banking and other financial services (excl. insurance)	
a.	Acceptance of deposits and other repayable funds from the public	81115-81119
b.	Lending of all types, incl., inter alia, consumer credit, mortgage credit, factoring and financing of commercial transaction	8113
c.	Financial leasing	8112
d.	All payment and money transmission services	81339**
e.	Guarantees and commitments	81199**
f	Trading for own account or for account of customers, whether on an exchange, in an over-the-counter market or otherwise, the following:	
	– money market instruments (cheques, bills, certificate of deposits, etc.)	81339**
	– foreign exchange	81333
	– derivative products incl., but not limited to, futures and options	81339**
	– exchange rate and interest rate instruments, inclu. products such as swaps, forward rate agreements, etc.	81339**
	– transferable securities	81321*
	– other negotiable instruments and financial assets, incl. bullion	81339**
g.	Participation in issues of all kinds of securities, incl. under-writing and placement as agent (whether publicly or privately) and provision of service related to such issues	8132
h	Money broking	81339**
i.	Asset management, such as cash or portfolio management, all forms of collective investment management, pension fund management, custodial depository and trust services	8119+** 81323*

j.	Settlement and clearing services for financial assets, incl. securities, derivative products, and other negotiable instruments	81339** or 81319**
k.	Advisory and other auxiliary financial services on all the activities listed in Article 1B of MTN.TNC/W/50, incl. credit reference and analysis, investment and portfolio research and advice, advice on acquisitions and on corporate restructuring and strategy	8131 or 8133
l.	Provision and transfer of financial information, and financial data processing and related software by providers of other financial services	8131
C.	<u>Other</u>	
8.	<u>HEALTH RELATED AND SOCIAL SERVICES</u> (other than those listed under 1.A.h-j.)	
A.	<u>Hospital services</u>	9311
B.	<u>Other Human Health Services</u>	9319 (other than 93191)
C.	<u>Social Services</u>	933
D.	<u>Other</u>	
9.	<u>TOURISM AND TRAVEL RELATED SERVICES</u>	
A.	<u>Hotels and restaurants (incl. catering)</u>	641-643
B.	<u>Travel agencies and tour operators services</u>	7471
C.	<u>Tourist guides services</u>	7472
D.	<u>Other</u>	
10.	<u>RECREATIONAL, CULTURAL AND SPORTING SERVICES</u> (other than audiovisual services)	
A.	<u>Entertainment services</u> (including theatre, live bands and circus services)	9619
B.	<u>News agency services</u>	962
C.	<u>Libraries, archives, museums and other cultural services</u>	963
D.	<u>Sporting and other recreational services</u>	964
E.	<u>Other</u>	
11.	<u>TRANSPORT SERVICES</u>	
A.	<u>Maritime Transport Services</u>	
a.	Passenger transportation	7211
b.	Freight transportation	7212
c.	Rental of vessels with crew	7213

d.	Maintenance and repair of vessels	8868**
e.	Pushing and towing services	7214
f.	Supporting services for maritime transport	745**
B.	<u>Internal Waterways Transport</u>	
a.	Passenger transportation	7221
b.	Freight transportation	7222
c.	Rental of vessels with crew	7223
d.	Maintenance and repair of vessels	8868**
e.	Pushing and towing services	7224
f.	Supporting services for internal waterway transport	745**
C.	<u>Air Transport Services</u>	
a.	Passenger transportation	731
b.	Freight transportation	732
c.	Rental of aircraft with crew	734
d.	Maintenance and repair of aircraft	8868**
e.	Supporting services for air transport	746
D.	<u>Space Transport</u>	733
E.	<u>Rail Transport Services</u>	
a.	Passenger transportation	7111
b.	Freight transportation	7112
c.	Pushing and towing services	7113
d.	Maintenance and repair of rail transport equipment	8868**
e.	Supporting services for rail transport services	743
F.	<u>Road Transport Services</u>	
a.	Passenger transportation	7121+7122
b.	Freight transportation	7123
c.	Rental of commercial vehicles with operator	7124
d.	Maintenance and repair of road transport	6112+8867
e.	equipmentSupporting services for road transport services	744
G.	<u>Pipeline Transport</u>	
a.	Transportation of fuels	7131
b.	Transportation of other goods	7139
H.	<u>Services auxiliary to all modes of transport</u>	
a.	Cargo-handling services	741
b.	Storage and warehouse services	742
c.	Freight transport agency services	748
d.	Other	749
I.	<u>Other Transport Services</u>	
12.	<u>OTHER SERVICES NOT INCLUDED ELSEWHERE</u>	95+97+98+99

Annexure - 2

List of Foreign Banks – used in the analysis for DEA for calculating Efficiency

S.No.	Name of the Foreign Bank [DMUs]
1.	Bank Internasional Indonesia
2.	Krung Thai Bank Public Company Limited
3.	Mashreq Bank Psc
4.	United Overseas Bank Ltd.
5.	Sberbank
6.	National Australia Bank
7.	Westpac Banking Corporation
8.	Industrial And Commercial Bank of China
9.	Woori Bank
10.	Jsc Vtb Bank
11.	Antwerp Diamond Bank Nv
12.	Bank of Ceylon
13.	Commonwealth Bank of Australia
14.	Ab Bank Limited
15.	Oman International Bank S.A.O.G.
16.	Credit Suisse Ag
17.	Sonali Bank
18.	Chinatrust Commercial Bank
19.	State Bank of Mauritius Ltd.
20.	Abu Dhabi Commercial Bank Ltd.
21.	Rabobank International
22.	Ubs Ag
23.	Sumitomo Mitsui Banking Corporation
24.	Australia And New Zealand Banking Group Limited
25.	Firstrand Bank Ltd.

26.	Shinhan Bank
27.	Credit Agricole Corporate And InvestmentBank
28.	Bank Of Bahrain & Kuwait B.S.C.
29.	Societe Generale
30.	Bank of Nova Scotia
31.	Mizuho Corporate Bank Ltd.
32.	Jpmorgan Chase Bank National Association
33.	The Bank of Tokyo-Mitsubishi Ufj Ltd.
34.	Bnp Paribas
35.	Barclays Bank Plc
36.	Bank Of America N.T. And S.A.
37.	American Express Banking Corp.
38.	Dbs Bank Ltd.
39.	The Royal Bank of Scotland N.V.
40.	Deutsche Bank Ag
41.	Hongkong and Shanghai Banking Corpn. Ltd.
42.	Citibank N.A
43.	Standard Chartered Bank
44.	Ufj Bank Ltd.

S.No.	Name of the Domestic Bank [Dmus]
1.	Nainital Bank Ltd.
2.	Ratnakar Bank Ltd.
3.	Development Credit Bank Ltd.
4.	The Dhanalakshmi Bank Ltd.
5.	Catholic Syrian Bank Ltd.
6.	Lakshmi Vilas Bank Ltd.
7.	Tamilnad Mercantile Bank Ltd.
8.	City Union Bank Limited
9.	South Indian Bank Ltd.
10.	Karnataka Bank Ltd.
11.	Karur Vysya Bank Ltd.
12.	Yes Bank Ltd.
13.	Punjab and Sind Bank
14.	Ing Vysya Bank Ltd.
15.	Jammu & Kashmir Bank Ltd.
16.	Federal Bank Ltd
17.	State Bank of Mysore
18.	Dena Bank

19.	Indusind Bank Ltd.
20.	State Bank of Travancore
21.	Vijaya Bank
22.	State Bank of Bikaner and Jaipur
23.	Bank of Maharashtra
24.	Kotak Mahindra Bank Ltd.
25.	State Bank of Patiala
26.	Corporation Bank
27.	State Bank of Hyderabad
28.	Idbi Bank Limited
29.	United Bank of India
30.	Andhra Bank
31.	Indian Bank
32.	Oriental Bank of Commerce
33.	Allahabad Bank
34.	Uco Bank
35.	Syndicate Bank
36.	Indian Overseas Bank
37.	Union Bank of India
38.	Central Bank of India
39.	Axis Bank Limited
40.	Bank of India
41.	Canara Bank
42.	Bank of Baroda
43.	Icici Bank Limited
44.	Punjab National Bank
45.	Hdfc Bank Ltd.
46.	State Bank of India
47.	Bank of Punjab Limited
48.	Centurion Bank of Punjab Ltd.
49.	Bank of Rajasthan Ltd.
50.	Bharat Overseas Bank Ltd.
51.	Ganesh Bank of Kurundwad Ltd.
52.	Lord Krishna Bank Ltd.
53.	Sangli Bank Ltd.
54.	Sbi Commercial & International Bank Ltd.
55.	United Western Bank Ltd.
56.	State Bank of Indore
57.	State Bank of Saurashtra

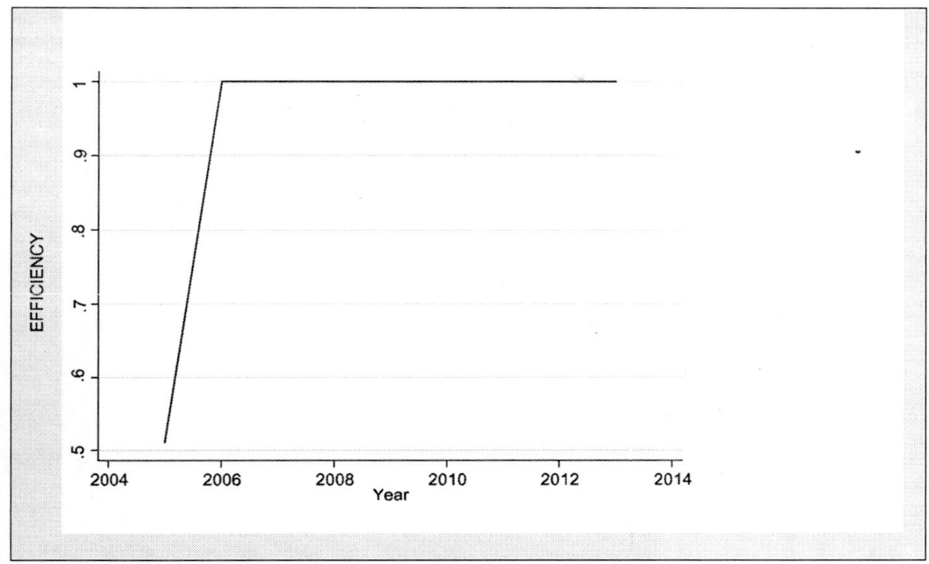

FIGURE 1: JP MORGAN CHASE BANK

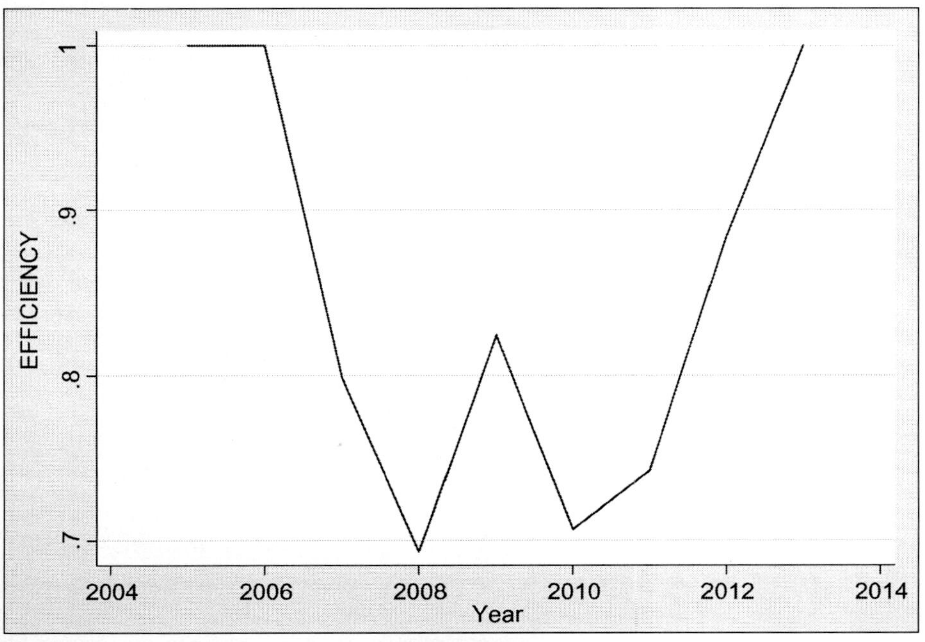

FIGURE 2

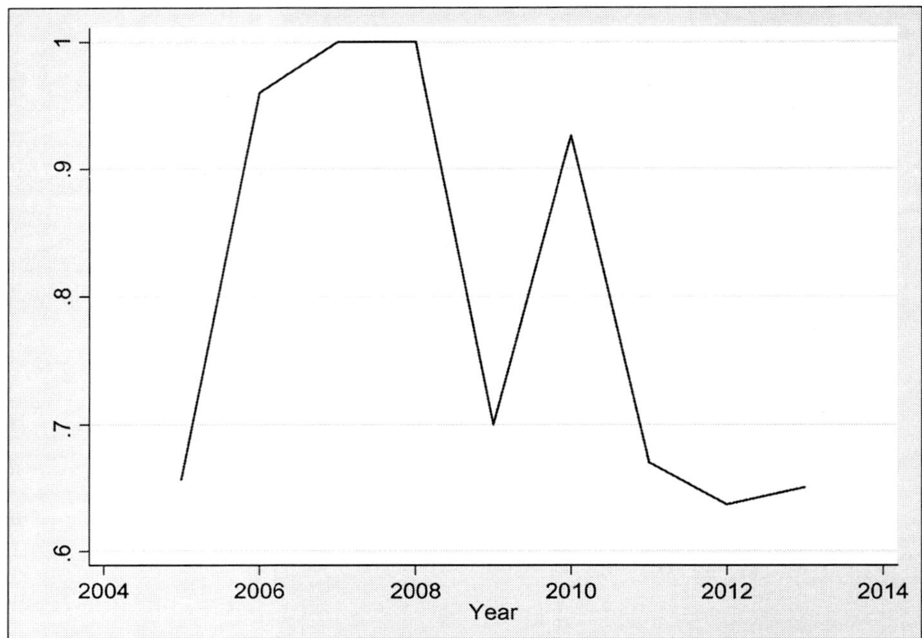

FIGURE 3

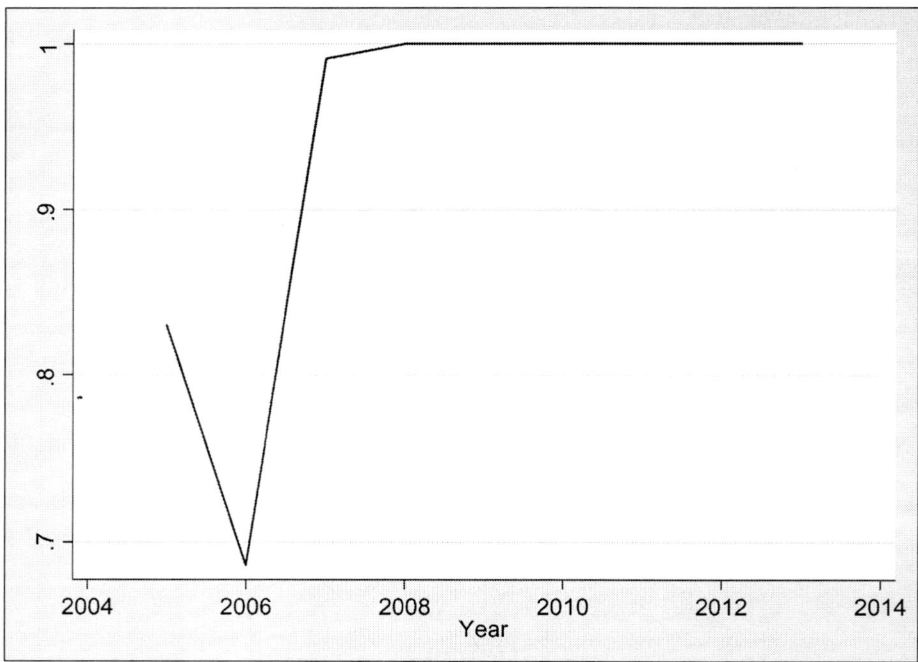

FIGURE 4

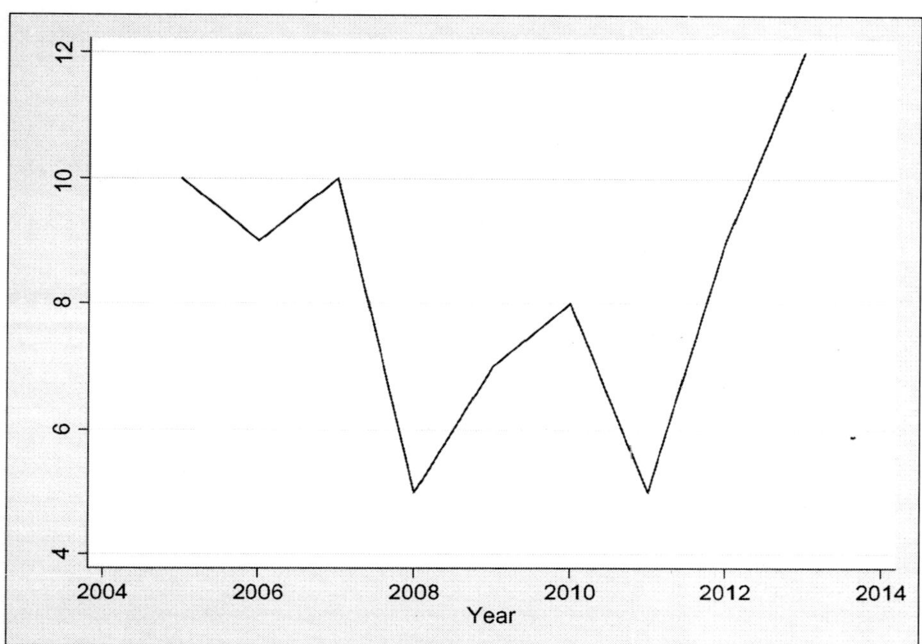

FIGURE 5

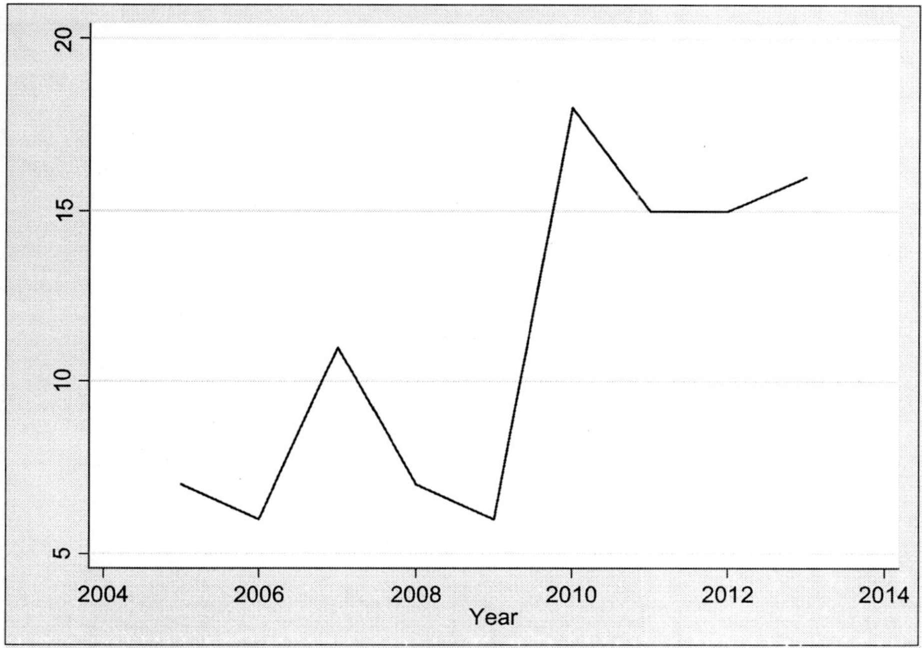

FIGURE 6

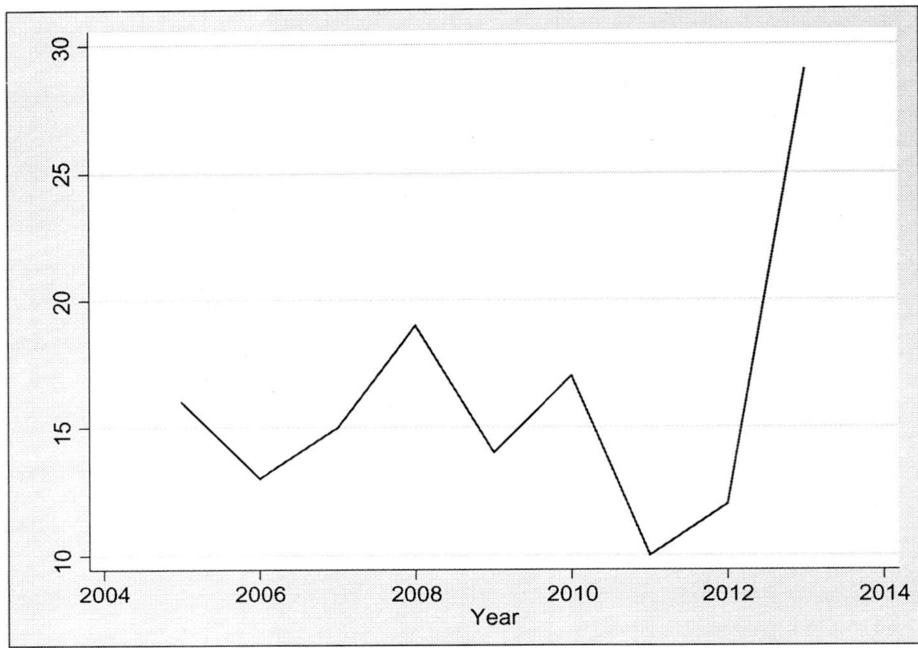

FIGURE 7

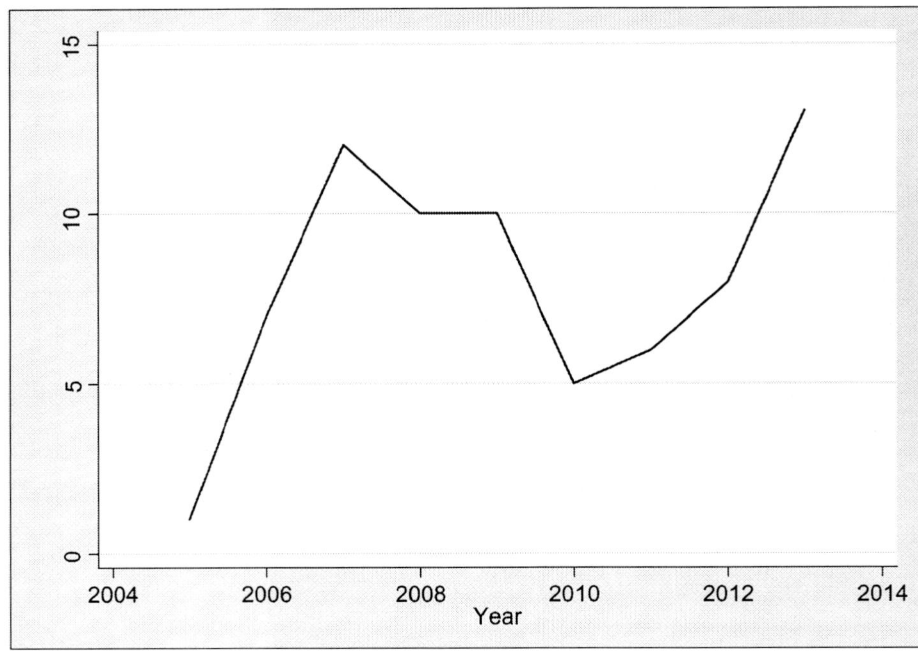

FIGURE 8

Annexure - 3A

COUNTRY-WISE BRANCHES OF INDIAN BANKS AT OVERSEAS CENTRES AS ON JANUARY 31, 2014

	Public Sector Banks												Private sector Banks			Total
Name of the Country	State Bank of India	Bank of India	Bank of Baroda	Union Bank of India	Punjab National Bank	Allahabad Bank	Indian Bank	Indian Overseas Bank	UCO Bank	Canara Bank	Syndicate Bank	IDBI Bank	ICICI Bank	AXIS Bank	HDFC Bank	
(1)	(2)	(3)	(4)	(5)	(6)	(7)	(8)	(9)	(10)	(11)	(12)	(13)	(14)	(15)	(16)	(17)
Afghanistan	-	-	-	-	1	-	-	-	-	-	-	-	-	-	-	1
Australia	1	-	1	-	-	-	-	-	-	-	-	-	-	-	-	2
Bahamas Island (Nassau)	1	-	1	-	-	-	-	-	-	-	-	-	-	-	-	2
Bahrain	2	-	1	-	-	-	-	-	-	1	-	-	1	-	1	6
Bangladesh	6	-	-	-	-	-	-	-	-	-	-	-	-	-	-	6
Belgium	1	1	1	-	-	-	-	-	-	-	-	-	-	-	-	3
Cambodia	-	1	-	-	-	-	-	-	-	-	-	-	-	-	-	1
Cayman Islands	-	1	-	-	-	-	-	-	-	-	-	-	-	-	-	1
Channel Islands	-	1	-	-	-	-	-	-	-	-	-	-	-	-	-	1
China	2	1	1	-	-	-	-	-	-	1	-	-	-	1	-	6
France	1	1	-	-	-	-	-	-	-	-	-	-	-	-	-	2
Fiji Islands	-	-	9	-	-	-	-	-	-	-	-	-	-	-	-	9
Germany	1	-	-	-	-	-	-	-	-	-	-	-	-	-	-	1
Hong Kong	2	2	2	1	2	1	-	2	2	1	-	-	2	1	1	19
Israel	1	-	-	-	-	-	-	-	-	-	-	-	-	-	-	1

(Contd…)

(1)	(2)	(3)	(4)	(5)	(6)	(7)	(8)	(9)	(10)	(11)	(12)	(13)	(14)	(15)	(16)	(17)
Japan	2	2	-	-	-	-	-	-	-	-	-	-	-	-	-	4
Kenya	-	4	-	-	-	-	-	-	-	-	-	-	-	-	-	4
Maldives Islands	3	-	-	-	-	-	-	-	-	-	-	-	-	-	-	3
Mauritius	-	-	9	-	-	-	-	-	-	-	-	-	-	-	-	9
Qatar	1(QFC)	-	-	-	-	-	-	-	-	-	-	-	1(QFC)	-	-	2
Saudi Arabia	1	-	-	-	-	-	-	-	-	-	-	-	-	-	-	**1**
Seychelles	-	-	1	-	-	-	-	-	-	-	-	-	-	-	-	**1**
Singapore	7	1	1	-	-	-	1	1	2	-	-	-	3	**1**	-	**17**
Sri Lanka	4	-	-	-	-	-	3	2	-	-	-	-	**1**	1	-	11
South Africa	1	1	2	-	-	-	-	-	-	-	-	-	-	-	-	4
South Korea	-	-	-	-	-	-	-	1	-	-	-	-	-	-	-	1
Sultanate of Oman	1	-	4	-	-	-	-	-	-	-	-	-	-	-	-	5
Thailand	-	-	-	-	-	-	-	1	-	-	-	-	-	-	-	1
United Kingdom	10	7	10	-	-	-	-	-	-	2	1	-	-	-	-	30
United State of America	4	2	1	-	-	-	-	-	-	-	-	-	1	-	-	8
United Arab Emirates	1(DIFC)	-	6 +1 (DIFC)	1 (DIFC)	1 (DIFC)	-	-	-	-	-	-	1 (DIFC)	1 (DIFC)	1 (DIFC)	-	**13**
Total	**53**	**25**	**51**	**2**	**4**	**1**	**4**	**7**	**4**	**5**	**1**	**1**	**10**	**5**	**2**	**175**

List of subsidiaries of Indian Banks abroad as on January 31, 2014

S. No.	Name of the Bank	Name of the Centre	Remarks
1.	SBI (Canada) Ltd.	Toronto Vancouver, Mississauga	100% by SBI
2.	SBI (California) Ltd.	Los Angeles, Artesia, San Jose (Silicon Valley)	100% by SBI
3.	Bank of Baroda (Uganda) Ltd.	Uganda	51% by BOB
4.	Bank of Baroda (Kenya) Ltd.	Kenya	86.71% by BOB
5.	Bank of Baroda (U.K.) Nominee Ltd.	London, UK	100% by BOB
6.	Bank of Baroda (Botswana) Ltd.	Gaborone, Botswana	100% by BOB
7.	Bank of Baroda (Guyana) Inc.	Georgetown Guyana (South America)	100% by BOB
8.	ICICI Bank UK Ltd.	London (UK)	100% by ICICI Bank
9.	ICICI Bank Canada Ltd.	Toronto (Canada)	100% by ICICI Bank
10.	Bank of Baroda (Tanzania)	Tanzania	100% by BOB
11.	ICICI Bank Eurasia LLC	Russia	100% by ICICI Bank
12.	Bank SBI Indonesia	Indonesia	76% by SBI
13.	SBI International (Mauritius) Ltd.	Mauritius, Port Louis	93.40% by SBI
14.	Punjab National Bank International Limited (PNBIL)	United Kingdom, London	100% by PNB
15.	Bank of Baroda (Trinidadand Tobago) Limited	Trinidad & Tobago	100% by BoB
16.	PT Bank of India Indonesia TBK	Indonesia	76% by BoI
17.	Bank of Baroda (Ghana) Ltd.	Ghana	100% by BoB
18.	Bank of India (Tanzania) Ltd.	Tanzania, Dar-Es Salaam	100% by BoI
19.	Druk PNB Bank Ltd.	Bhutan (Thimpu)	PNB
20.	Bank of Baroda (NewZealand) Ltd.	New Zealand (Auckland)	BoB
21.	JSC SB PNB Kazakhstan	Kazakhstan	63.64% by PNB

(Contd...)

22.	Bank of India (NewZealand) Ltd.	New Zealand (Auckland)	BoI
23.	Bank of India (Uganda) Ltd.	Uganda (Kampala)	BoI
24.	Axis Bank UK Limited	United Kingdom, London	100% by Axis Bank
25.	Bank of India (Botswana) Ltd.	Gaborone, Botswana	100% by BoI
26.	State Bank of India (Botswana) Ltd.	Gaborone, Botswana	100% by SBI

List of Joint Ventures of Indian Banks abroad as on January 31, 2014

Sr.No.	Name of the Bank	Name of the Centre	Remarks
1.	Bank of Bhutan	Bhutan	SBI 20%
2.	Indo Zambia Bank Ltd.	Zambia	BOB 20%BOI 20%CBI 20%
3.	Nepal SBI Bank Ltd.	Kathmandu (Nepal)	SBI 55.28%
4.	Everest Bank Ltd. Nepal	Nepal	PNB 20%
5.	Commercial Bank of India LLC	Moscow, Russia	SBI 60%Canara Bank40%
6.	Sterling Bank PLC	Nigeria (Lagos)	SBI 11.81%
7.	India International Bank (Malaysia) Bhd.	Malaysia (Kuala Lumpur)	BOB 40% IOB 35% Andhra Bank 25%

List of Representative offices of Indian Banks as on January 31, 2014

Sr. No.	Name of the Bank	Centre
1.	State Bank of India	Angola (Luanda)
2.	Punjab National Bank	Australia (Sydney)
3.	Union Bank of India	Australia (Sydney)
4.	ICICI Bank Ltd	Bangladesh (Dhaka)
5.	United Bank of India	Bangladesh (Dhaka)
6.	Bank of India	China (Beijing)
7.	Union Bank of India	China (Beijing)
8.	Indian Overseas Bank	China (Guang Zhou)
9.	ICICI Bank Ltd	China (Shanghai)
10.	AXIS Bank Ltd	China (Shanghai)
11.	Punjab National Bank	China (Shanghai)
12.	Allahabad Bank	China (Shenzen)
13.	Union Bank of India	China Shanghai
14.	State Bank of India	Egypt (Cairo)
15.	Corporation Bank	Hong Kong
16.	Bank of India	Indonesia (Jakarta)
17.	ICICI Bank Ltd	Indonesia (Jakarta)
18.	State Bank of India	Iran (Tehran)
19.	State Bank of India	Italy (Milan)
20.	Punjab National Bank	Kazakhstan (Almaty)
21.	HDFC Bank Ltd	Kenya (Nairobi)
22.	Central Bank of India	Kenya (Nairobi)
23.	ICICI Bank Ltd	Malaysia (Kuala Lumpur)
24.	United Bank of India	Myanmar (Yangon)
25.	Punjab National Bank	Norway (Oslo)
26.	State Bank of India	Philippines (Manila)
27.	ICICI Bank Ltd	South Africa (Johannesburg)
28.	State Bank of India	South Korea (Seoul)
29.	Bank of Baroda	Thailand (Bangkok)
30.	ICICI Bank Ltd	Thailand (Bangkok)
31.	State Bank of India	Turkey (Istanbul)
32.	Federal Bank Ltd	UAE (Abu Dhabi)
33.	ICICI Bank Ltd	UAE (Dubai)
34.	Punjab National Bank	UAE (Dubai)

(Contd…)

35.	AXIS Bank Ltd	UAE (Abu Dhabi)
36.	HDFC Bank	UAE (Abu Dhabi)
37.	ICICI Bank Ltd	UAE (Abu Dhabi)
38.	Union Bank of India	UAE (Abu Dhabi)
39.	Bank of India	UAE (Dubai)
40.	IndusInd Bank Ltd.	UAE (Dubai)
41.	Kotak Mahindra Bank	UAE (Dubai)
42.	Oriental Bank of Commerce	UAE (Dubai)
43.	Andhra Bank	UAE (Dubai)
44.	AXIS Bank Ltd	UAE (Dubai)
45.	Corporation Bank	UAE (Dubai)
46.	HDFC Bank	UAE (Dubai)
47.	Indian Overseas Bank	UAE (Dubai)
48.	State Bank of Travancore	UAE (Dubai)
49.	Canara Bank	UAE (Sharjah)
50.	IndusInd Bank	UK (London)
51.	Union Bank of India	UK (London)
52.	Dena Bank	UK (London)
53.	State Bank of India	USA (Washington)
54.	Andhra Bank	USA (New Jersey)
55.	Indian Overseas Bank	Vietnam (Ho Chi Minh City)
56.	Bank of India	Vietnam (Ho Chi Minh City)

Country-wise other banking offices of Indian Banks at Overseas Centres as on January 31, 2014

Name of the Country	State Bank of India	Bank of Baroda	Indian Overseas Bank	Total
Bahrain	SO – 1RC – 1	-	-	2
Bangladesh	IVCs – 2	-	-	2
Germany	MO – 1	-	-	1
Singapore	-	-	RC – 2	2
Sri Lanka	EC – 2	-	EC - 1	3
South Africa	MO – 2SO – 5	-	-	7
UAE	RHO – 1	EBSUs – 9	-	10
United Kingdom	EC – 1	-	-	1
Total	**16**	**9**	**3**	**28**

EBSU – Electronic Banking Service Unit; EC-Extension Counter; IVC – Indian Visa Centres; MO - Marketing office; SO-Sub office; RC – Remittance centre; RHO – Regional Head Office

Overseas offices of Indian Banks abroad as on January 31, 2014

Sr. No.	Name of the Bank	Branch	Subsidiary	Joint Venture Bank	Representative Office	Other Offices	Total
1.	Allahabad Bank	1	–	–	1	–	2
2.	Andhra Bank	–	–	–	2	–	2
3.	Bank of Baroda	51	9	2	1	9	72
4.	Bank of India	25	5	–	4	–	34
5.	Canara Bank	5	–	–	1	–	6
6.	Central Bank of India	–	–	–	1	–	1
7.	Corporation Bank	–	–	–	2	–	2
8.	Dena Bank	–	–	–	1	–	1
9.	Indian Bank	4	–	–	–	–	4
10.	Indian Overseas Bank	7	–	–	3	3	13
11.	IDBI Bank	1	–	–	–	–	1
12.	Punjab National Bank	4	3	1	5	–	13
13.	State Bank of India	53	5	4	8	16	86
14.	State Bank of Travancore	–	–	–	1	–	1
15.	Syndicate Bank	1	–	–	–	–	1
16.	UCO Bank	4	–	–	–	–	4
17.	Union Bank of India	2	–	–	5	–	7
18.	United Bank of India	–	–	–	2	–	2
19.	Oriental Bank of Commerce	–	–	–	1	–	1
20.	HDFC Bank Ltd.	2	–	–	3	–	5
21.	ICICI Bank Ltd.	10	3	–	8	–	21
22.	IndusInd Bank Ltd.	–	–	–	2	–	2
23.	Axis Bank Ltd	5	1	–	3	–	9
24.	Federal Bank	–	–	–	1	–	1
25.	Kotak Mahindra Bank	–	–	–	1	–	1
	Total	**175**	**26**	**7**	**56**	**28**	**292**

Annexure - 3B

Foreign Banks Branches in India as on January 31, 2014

Sl. No.	Name of Bank	Country of Incorporation	No of Branches in India
1.	AB Bank Ltd.	Bangladesh	1
2.	The Royal Bank of Scotland N.V.	Netherlands	10
3.	Abu Dhabi Commercial Bank Ltd.	UAE	2
4.	American Express Banking Corporation	USA	1
5.	Antwerp Diamond Bank N.V.	Belgium	1
6.	Bank Internasional Indonesia	Indonesia	1
7.	Bank of America	USA	5
8.	Bank of Bahrain & Kuwait BSC	Bahrain	3
9.	Bank of Ceylon	Sri Lanka	1
10.	Bank of Nova Scotia	Canada	5
11.	Barclays Bank Plc.	United Kingdom	7
12.	BNP Paribas	France	8
13.	Credit Agricole Corporate & Investment Bank	France	5
14.	Chinatrust Commercial Bank	Taiwan	2
15.	Citibank N.A.	USA	42
16.	DBS Bank Ltd.	Singapore	12
17.	Deutsche Bank	Germany	18
18.	HSBC Ltd	Hong Kong	50
19.	J.P. Morgan Chase Bank N.A.	USA	1
20.	JSC VTB Bank	Russia	1
21.	Krung Thai Bank Public Co. Ltd.	Thailand	1
22.	Mashreq Bank PSC	UAE	1
23.	Mizuho Corporate Bank Ltd.	Japan	4
24.	HSBC Bank Oman SAOG	Sultanate of Oman	2

(Contd...)

25.	Shinhan Bank	South Korea	3
26.	Societe Generale	France	3
27.	Sonali Bank Ltd.	Bangladesh	2
28.	Standard Chartered Bank	UnitedKingdom	101
29.	State Bank of Mauritius	Mauritius	4
30.	The Bank of Tokyo- Mitsubishi UFJ Ltd.	Japan	4
31.	UBS AG	Switzerland	1
32.	FirstRand Bank Ltd	South Africa	1
33.	United Overseas Bank Ltd	Singapore	1
34.	Commonwealth Bank of Australia	Australia	1
35.	Sberbank	Russia	1
36.	Credit Suisse A.G	Switzerland	1
37.	Australia and New Zealand Banking Group Ltd.	Australia	1
38.	Rabobank International	Netherlands	1
39.	Industrial & Commercial Bank of China Ltd.	China	1
40.	Woori Bank	South Korea	1
41.	National Australia Bank	Australia	1
42.	Westpac Banking Corporation	Australia	1
43.	Sumitomo Mitsui Banking Corporation	Japan	1
			314

List of Foreign Banks having Representative Offices in India as on January 31,2014

Sr. No.	Name of the representative office	Country of incorporation	Centre	Date of opening
1.	Raiffeisen Zentral Bank Osterreich AG	Austria	Mumbai	1.11.1992
2.	Fortis Bank	Belgium	Mumbai	6.10.1987
3.	K.B.C. Bank N.V.	Belgium	Mumbai	1.02.2003
4.	Royal Bank of Canada	Canada	Mumbai	1.2.2008
5.	Toronto Dominion Bank	Canada	Mumbai	16.11.2009
6.	Credit Industriel et Commercial	France	New Delhi	1.04.1997
7.	Natixis	France	Mumbai	4.01.1999
8.	Bayerische Hypo – und Vereinsbank	Germany	Mumbai	12.07.1995
9.	DZ Bank AG Deutsche Zentral – Genossenschafts Bank	Germany	Mumbai	22.02.1996
10.	Landesbank Baden – Wurttemberg	Germany	Mumbai	1.11.1999
11.	Commerzbank	Germany	Mumbai	23.12.2002
12.	BayernLB	Germany	Mumbai	15.4.2008

(Contd...)

13.	Norddeutsche Landesbank Girozentrale (NORD LB)	Germany	Mumbai	1.9.2008
14.	KfW IPEX Bank GmbH	Germany	Mumbai	1.4.2009
15.	DEPFA Bank	Ireland	Mumbai	9.3.2007
16.	Intesa Sanpaolo S.p.A	Italy	Mumbai	1.11.1988
17.	Uni Credito Italiano	Italy	Mumbai	1.08.1998
18.	Banca Populare Di Verona E Novara	Italy	Mumbai	18.06.2001
19.	BPU Banca –Banche Popolari Unite S.c.r.l	Italy	Mumbai	16.01.2006
20.	Monte Dei Paschi Di Sienna	Italy	Mumbai	07.04.2006
21.	Banca Popolare di Vicenza	Italy	Mumbai	29.04.2006
22.	CIMB Bank Berhad	Malaysia	Mumbai	23.11.2010
23.	Everest Bank Ltd.	Nepal	New Delhi	24.03.2004
24.	DNB Bank ASA	Norway	Mumbai	27.8.2008
25.	Caixa Geral de Depositos	Portugal	Mumbai Goa (EC)	8.11.1999
26.	Vnesheconombank (Bank for Foreign Economic Affairs)	Russia	New Delhi	1.3.1983
27.	Promsvyazbank	Russia	New Delhi	25.04.2006
28.	Gazprombank	Russia	New Delhi	12.7.2010
29.	Korea Exchange Bank	South Korea	New Delhi	27.8.2008
30.	Kookmin Bank	South Korea	Mumbai	1.06.2012
31.	Industrial Bank of Korea	South Korea	New Delhi	22.11.2012
32.	Banco de Sabadell SA	Spain	New Delhi	2.08.2004
33.	Banco Bilbao Vizcaya Argentaria	Spain	Mumbai	2.4.2007
34.	CaixaBank S.A.	Spain	New Delhi	1.2.2011
35.	Hatton National Bank	Sri Lanka	Chennai	1.01.1999
36.	Svenska Handlesbanken	Sweden	Mumbai	1.08.2006
37.	Skandinaviska Enskilda Banken AB	Sweden	New Delhi	1.02.2008
38.	Zurcher Kantonalbank	Switzerland	Mumbai	27.06.2006
39.	Mega International commercial Bank	Taiwan	Mumbai	2.12.2008
40.	Asya Katilim Bankasi AS	Turkey	Mumbai	1.9.2012
41.	Emirates Bank International	UAE	Mumbai	16.06.2000
42.	First Gulf Bank	UAE	Mumbai	26.10.2009
43.	Duncan Lawrie Ltd	United Kingdom	Kolkata	30.10.2009
44.	The Bank of New York Mellon	USA	Mumbai	27.10.1983
45.	Wells Fargo Bank N.A.	USA	Mumbai (Sub-office at Chennai and New Delhi)	1.11.1996

Annexure - 4

Ranks and Efficiency of the Foreign Banks (using DEA) from 2005 to 2013

	2005		2006		2007		2008		2009		2010		2011		2012		2013	
Decision Making Units	Rank	Efficiency (theta)	Rank	Efficiency (theta)	Rank	Efficiency (theta)	Rank	Efficiency (theta)	Rank	Efficiency (theta)	Rank	Efficiency (theta)	Rank	Efficiency (theta)	Rank	Efficiency (theta)	Rank	Efficiency (theta)
(1)	(2)	(3)	(4)	(5)	(6)	(7)	(8)	(9)	(10)	(11)	(12)	(13)	(14)	(15)	(16)	(17)	(18)	(19)
Bank Internasional Indonesia	31	0.16487	29	0.184554	1	1	1	1	1	1	1	1	1	1	1	1	41	0.0740367
Krung Thai Bank Public Company Limited	30	0.197439	1	1	17	0.488319	14	0.617772	11	0.709526	19	0.640284	1	1	1	1	1	1
Mashreq Bank Psc	1	1	1	1	1	1	8	0.84247	8	0.862447	1	1	1	1	1	1	1	1
Antwerp Diamond Bank Nv	13	0.662626	1	1	1	1	6	0.949575	1	1	21	0.565541	26	0.42303	14	0.822482	17	0.597929
Bank of Ceylon	12	0.679368	20	0.482796	11	0.625486	9	0.770246	1	1	1	1	1	1	1	1	1	1
Ab Bank Limited			9	0.951254	14	0.529522	11	0.738588	20	0.514368	1	1	10	0.900596	1	1	10	0.92593
Oman International Bank S.A.O.G.	19	0.513312	24	0.376137	25	0.392771	18	0.486104	27	0.287685	11	0.896819	16	0.618958	1	1	1	1
Sonali Bank	7	0.97561	25	0.314711	28	0.211999	29	0.228419	28	0.182163			34	0.0824042	21	0.578555	14	0.680808
Chinatrust Commercial Bank	28	0.276092	27	0.294048	24	0.402233	20	0.472302	23	0.412846	25	0.479818	25	0.427864	31	0.305419	36	0.209494
State Bank of Mauritius Ltd.	1	1	1	1	7	0.798701	12	0.693278	9	0.824356	15	0.70696	12	0.742531	13	0.883786	1	1
Abu Dhabi Commercial Bank Ltd	9	0.864148	1	1	12	0.561446	15	0.617015	18	0.553224	20	0.572691	23	0.457001	20	0.594064	18	0.586349
Ubs Ag									29	0.127175	18	0.662365	1	1	1	1	1	1
Firstrand Bank Ltd.											32	0.0595857	30	0.231044	36	0.177341	37	0.127503

(Contd…)

(1)	(2)	(3)	(4)	(5)	(6)	(7)	(8)	(9)	(10)	(11)	(12)	(13)	(14)	(15)	(16)	(17)	(18)	(19)
Shinhan Bank			10	0.886636	22	0.419641	17	0.54364	16	0.603039	1	1	15	0.644215	15	0.804108	13	0.707848
Credit Agricole Corporate and Investment Bank	18	0.517677	21	0.481939	10	0.669751	10	0.751711	7	0.973322	1	1	1	1	1	1	11	0.758489
Bank of Bahrain & Kuwait B.S.C.	21	0.446153	26	0.312741	26	0.390542	19	0.482726	26	0.347132	29	0.264951	22	0.4608	23	0.546932	19	0.758489
Societe Generale	23	0.444185	13	0.657579	9	0.710158	13	0.675898	21	0.465205	27	0.42737	13	0.731176	19	0.627899	24	0.440212
Bank of Nova Scotia	10	0.829788	12	0.685874	6	0.991047	1	1	1	1	1	1	1	1	1	1	1	1
Mizuho Corporate Bank Ltd.	26	0.387261	19	0.496931	23	0.407321	23	0.405369	19	0.544266	26	0.460583	17	0.611198	16	0.780875	12	0.737449
Jpmorgan Chase Bank National Association	20	0.510944	1	1	1	1	1	1	1	1	1	1	1	1	1	1	1	1
The Bank of Tokyo-Mitsubishi U Ltd.	27	0.376177	23	0.378058	13	0.529776	7	0.870217	1	1	12	0.832543	11	0.78918	17	0.710989	16	0.609179
Bnp Paribas	25	0.397939	22	0.383074	20	0.430631	21	0.461858	17	0.56702	16	0.686846	18	0.586708	25	0.487158	28	0.384519
Barclays Bank Plc	8	0.924256	1	1	27	0.346208	28	0.276446	10	0.793648	14	0.741457	19	0.550816	27	0.445036	21	0.556657
Bank of America N.T. and S.A.	11	0.730213	11	0.80476	8	0.727365	16	0.590304	13	0.682276	1	1	9	0.928381	22	0.576428	22	0.556657
American Express Banking Corp.	29	0.274513	28	0.278893	29	0.176407			31	0.075409	31	0.073703	31	0.178001	41	0.035034	43	0.0286713
Dbs Bank Ltd.	14	0.656733	8	0.960401	1	1	1	1	12	0.699706	10	0.926305	14	0.670216	18	0.636975	15	0.650479
The Royal Bank of Scotland N.V.	24	0.443573	17	0.564153	18	0.435499	25	0.337848	22	0.449249	23	0.498561	29	0.355557	32	0.279557	35	0.231265
Deutsche Bank Ag	22	0.444642	15	0.599861	19	0.434882	24	0.348107	24	0.406175	22	0.5211884	27	0.414946	30	0.390221	32	0.317131
Hongkong and Shanghai Banking Corpn. Ltd.	16	0.598384	16	0.575639	21	0.427171	26	0.331563	15	0.608643	17	0.673792	21	0.511725	29	0.401609	30	0.362086
Citibank N.A	17	0.531656	14	0.653997	16	0.509395	22	0.450569	14	0.609412	13	0.744959	20	0.54452	26	0.447419	26	0.402376
Standard Chartered Bank	15	0.626235	18	0.526448	15	0.516582	27	0.315801	25	0.38912	24	0.488652	24	0.45191	28	0.407765	29	0.369225
Ufj Bank Ltd	1	1																

Ranks and Efficiency of the Domestic Banks (using DEA) from 2005 to 2013

	2005		2006		2007		2008		2009		2010		2011		2012		2013	
Decision Making Units [Dmu's]	Rank	Efficiency (theta)	Rank	Efficiency (theta)	Rank	Efficiency (theta)	Rank	Efficiency (theta)	Rank	Efficiency (theta)	Rank	Efficiency (theta)	Rank	Efficiency (theta)	Rank	Efficiency (theta)	Rank	Efficiency (theta)
(1)	(2)	(3)	(4)	(5)	(6)	(7)	(8)	(9)	(10)	(11)	(12)	(13)	(14)	(15)	(16)	(17)	(18)	(19)
Ratnakar Bank Ltd.			29	0.483828	39	0.335386	34	0.520028	24	0.608626	9	0.729549	43	0.214366	5	0.871684	8	0.879328
Development Credit Bank Ltd.	47	0.344104	45	0.294892	40	0.329785	50	0.324174	49	0.308962	49	0.274309	47	0.20129	37	0.558206	7	0.904712
The Dhanalakshmi Bank Ltd.			38	0.416443	38	0.370757	47	0.401939	46	0.44151	46	0.350544	45	0.212514	46	0.318001	46	0.482084
Catholic Syrian Bank Ltd.	26	0.564635	40	0.389482	37	0.376271	48	0.388064	47	0.35221	45	0.366799	44	0.212996	44	0.414913	42	0.513212
Lakshmi Vilas Bank Ltd.	27	0.564543	25	0.520556	23	0.515166	33	0.525013	40	0.512109	27	0.601821	21	0.387781	31	0.62241	31	0.686381
Tamilnad Mercantile Bank Ltd.	8	0.815509	8	0.697085	16	0.578465	29	0.557222	30	0.569901	21	0.64809	13	0.40569	13	0.726358	9	0.876292
City Union Bank Limited	1	1	7	0.778414	12	0.6237	10	0.675954	10	0.691153	5	0.785735	6	0.50353	8	0.7925	13	0.828976
South Indian Bank Ltd.	18	0.647812	22	0.541241	4	1	17	0.628124	26	0.601765	16	0.662996			19	0.682953	22	0.757452
Karnataka Bank Ltd.	9	0.781515	5	0.257944	9	0.668907	22	0.61731	15	0.65902	23	0.630609	29	0.348803	30	0.63037	28	0.735052
Karur Vysya Bank Ltd.	16	0.669693	13	0.610307	15	0.587592	19	0.624984	14	0.662583	17	0.656018	10	0.422527	12	0.729896	29	0.7348
Yes Bank Ltd.	48	0.247212	1	1	1	1	4	0.890674	5	0.75572	7	0.755618	7	0.48022	1	1	1	1
Punjab and Sind Bank	46	0.373821	33	0.431543	32	0.412387	40	0.476713	34	0.54262	13	0.670684	14	0.404883	26	0.632407	15	0.825
Ing Vysya Bank Ltd.	43	0.44553	41	0.376375	41	0.311515	49	0.330792	48	0.337661	47	0.340942	46	0.212092	45	0.404478	43	0.512637
Jammu & Kashmir Bank Ltd.	7	0.820929	6	0.791668	11	0.635213	7	0.723731	6	0.735649	18	0.655204	15	0.395193	15	0.706752	16	0.813019
Federal Bank Ltd.			11	0.634678	18	0.447884	14	0.645081	12	0.677274	14	0.66701	20	0.395193	21	0.659468	34	0.677821

(Contd...)

(1)	(2)	(3)	(4)	(5)	(6)	(7)	(8)	(9)	(10)	(11)	(12)	(13)	(14)	(15)	(16)	(17)	(18)	(19)
State Bank of Mysore	45	0.438461	36	0.425921	34	0.395232	38	0.485078	31	0.568226	26	0.602665	28	0.359139	38	0.553497	32	0.685882
Dena Bank	40	0.479091	26	0.501111	30	0.428742	35	0.493256	37	0.522449	32	0.578194	26	0.378762	20	0.671884	10	0.867464
Indusind Bank Ltd.	1	1	15	0.599935	8	0.6801	11	0.674416	36	0.522465	35	0.550147	37	0.287477	16	0.695448	27	0.736379
State Bank of Travancore	13	0.688671	18	0.582193	22	0.515781	26	0.587958	27	0.60068	34	0.561745	22	0.38349	27	0.632079	19	0.76194
Vijaya Bank	14	0.681392	16	0.592719	19	0.536733	12	0.662414	16	0.657141	30	0.588043	33	0.329335	10	0.748018	11	0.836328
State Bank of Bikaner and Jaipur	38	0.48431	39	0.413937	35	0.391566	37	0.487259	33	0.562771	36	0.545264	36	0.305247	39	0.538795	39	0.60511
Bank of Maharashtra	28	0.561862	14	0.600053	27	0.450548	36	0.4917	38	0.517555	39	0.534893	39	0.273287	41	0.493563	35	0.67536
Kotak Mahindra Bank Ltd.	1	1	44	0.319178	6	0.835679	23	0.61415	25	0.604491	25	0.603	42	0.217869	4	0.93732	4	0.979952
State Bank of Patiala	11	0.767465	10	0.64421	17	0.574061	6	0.728328	4	0.848651	4	0.802692	17	0.393476	17	0.694213	21	0.758224
Corporation Bank	24	0.583765	20	0.563946	21	0.517774	25	0.605896	13	0.67373	12	0.674162	8	0.44945	6	0.823044	5	0.965628
State Bank of Hyderabad	21	0.594206	23	0.539744	24	0.514766	13	0.658849	9	0.710501	6	0.781238	12	0.419196	18	0.693096	24	0.746691
Idbi Bank Limited	1	1	1	1	1	1	1	1	1	1	1	1	4	0.664212	1	1	1	1
United Bank of India	35	0.523924	31	0.464134	28	0.4478	43	0.470517	39	0.512687	29	0.589036	16	0.394191	22	0.64806	18	0.77112
Andhra Bank	39	0.481797	27	0.500239	29	0.440647	31	0.553993	32	0.565601	33	0.575761	18	0.392809	14	0.709782	17	0.799776
Indian Bank	32	0.539382	28	0.498921	31	0.416638	46	0.445693	43	0.500144	37	0.543529	19	0.392514	28	0.631878	38	0.636978
Oriental Bank of Commerce	10	0.779929	9	0.682761	10	0.6381	5	0.754923	7	0.734884	8	0.733495	5	0.515904	9	0.762979	12	0.832548
Allahabad Bank	36	0.512734	17	0.582575	5	1	15	0.63712	23	0.610664	24	0.626419	24	0.380478	23	0.646959	26	0.738229
Uco Bank	29	0.55898	19	0.748455	16	0.844066	27	0.594294	19	0.643529	10	0.725084	9	0.442534	7	0.795623	6	0.962452
Syndicate Bank	37	0.508126	28	0.617718	19	0.741988	16	0.631121	21	0.616696	28	0.59428	27	0.362978	32	0.60724	33	0.677904
Indian Overseas Bank	23	0.584096	21	0.558973	20	0.518077	20	0.62219	29	0.576156	42	0.499229	25	0.379963	29	0.63102	20	0.758763
Union Bank of India	15	0.675628	31	0.464134	28	0.4478	9	0.69038	20	0.62291	22	0.639845	32	0.33643	33	0.588616	30	0.696688
Central Bank of India	34	0.527785	26	0.635049	27	0.71509	32	0.538508	17	0.650802	19	0.652687	35	0.307424	35	0.569914	36	0.645931

(Contd…)

(1)	(2)	(3)	(4)	(5)	(6)	(7)	(8)	(9)	(10)	(11)	(12)	(13)	(14)	(15)	(16)	(17)	(18)	(19)
Axis Bank Limited	12	0.705881	19	0.568591	14	0.611883	28	0.579022	28	0.577539	41	0.525222	40	0.256115	36	0.565099	40	0.603991
Bank of India	33	0.533615	21	0.680144	26	0.717613	30	0.557163	22	0.61272	31	0.585157	30	0.346654	24	0.643176	23	0.748447
Federal Bank Ltd.	19	0.613777	11	0.634678	18	0.557884	24	0.606634	18	0.647315	20	0.649034	11	0.419275	11	0.736496	14	0.828781
Bank of Baroda	30	0.555343	23	0.665478	23	0.735517	44	0.464241	44	0.48922	40	0.52759	23	0.381821	25	0.642508	25	0.740159
Icici Bank Limited	6	0.890292	2	1	1	1	1	1	3	0.959687	11	0.694262	34	0.317047	40	0.506481	41	0.562432
Punjab National Bank	44	0.441198	24	0.652533	28	0.669154	39	0.482475	35	0.527161	38	0.541379	31	0.3425	34	0.581171	37	0.641626
Hdfc Bank Ltd.	22	0.591927	2	1	7	0.69535	18	0.626039	42	0.508473	43	0.434093	41	0.225031	42	0.470078	45	0.510977
State Bank of India	31	0.550283	18	0.755881	25	0.72014	45	0.462926	45	0.472378	44	0.419292	38	0.285649	43	0.455911	44	0.510977
Bank of Punjab Limited																		
Centurion Bank of Punjab Ltd.			46	0.257944	42	0.306966	51	0.31021										
Bank of Rajasthan Ltd.	42	0.470749	43	0.339166	36	0.390943												
Bharat Overseas Bank Ltd.			30	0.466881														
Ganesh Bank of Kurundwad Ltd.			1	1														
Lord Krishna Bank Ltd.			35	0.428713	33	0.406093												
Sangli Bank Ltd.			42	0.353473	25	0.157862												
Sbi Commercial & International Bank Ltd.	25	0.572804	1	1	1	1	1	1	1	1	1	1	1	1				
United Western Bank Ltd.			34	0.430362														
State Bank of Indore	20	0.596476	24	0.534573	25	0.504323												
State Bank of Saurashtra			12	0.610454	26	0.492126	41	0.472515										

Standard Deviation and Co-oefficient of Variation of Foreign banks efficiency for the period 2005-2013

	2005	2006	2007	2008	2009	2010	2011	2012	2013		
Decision Making Units [DMU's]	Efficiency (theta)	Efficiency (theta)	Efficiency (theta)	Efficiency (theta)	Efficiency (theta)	Efficiency (theta)	Efficiency (theta)	Efficiency (theta)	Efficiency (theta)	Standard Deviation	Coefficient of Variation
(1)	(2)	(3)	(4)	(5)	(6)	(7)	(8)	(9)	(10)	(11)	(12)
Bank Internasional Indonesia	0.16487	0.184554	1	1	1	1	1	1	0.074037	0.405817	0.689754
Krung Thai Bank Public Company Limited	0.197439	1	0.48832	0.617772	0.709526	0.640284	1	1	1	0.269552	0.458149
Mashreq Bank Psc	1	1	1	0.84247	0.862447	1	1	1	1	0.061519	0.104562
Antwerp Diamond Bank Nv	0.662626	1	1	0.949575	1	0.565541	0.42303	0.822482	0.597929	0.20979	0.356574
Bank of Ceylon	0.679368	0.482796	0.62549	0.770246	1	1	1	1	1	0.192145	0.326584
Ab Bank Limited		0.951254	0.52952	0.738588	0.514368	1	0.900596	1	0.92593	0.188468	0.320333
Oman International Bank S.A.O.G.	0.513312	0.376137	0.39277	0.486104	0.287685	0.896819	0.618958	1	1	0.261676	0.444762
Sonali Bank	0.97561	0.314711	0.212	0.228419	0.182163		0.082404	0.578555	0.680808	0.287678	0.488957
Chinatrust Commercial Bank	0.276092	0.294048	0.40223	0.472302	0.412846	0.479818	0.427864	0.305419	0.209494	0.090057	0.153067
State Bank of Mauritius Ltd.	1	1	0.7987	0.693278	0.824356	0.70696	0.742531	0.883786	1	0.119491	0.203095
Abu Dhabi Commercial Bank Ltd.	0.864148	1	0.56145	0.617015	0.553224	0.572691	0.457001	0.594064	0.586349	0.162222	0.275724
Ubs Ag					0.127175	0.662365	1	1	1	0.341402	0.580271
Firstrand Bank Ltd.						0.059586	0.231044	0.177341	0.127503	0.063229	0.107468
Shinhan Bank		0.886636	0.41964	0.54364	0.603039	1	0.644215	0.804108	0.707848	0.177231	0.301234
Credit Agricole Corporate and Investment Bank	0.517677	0.481939	0.66975	0.751711	0.973322	1	1	1	0.758489	0.197676	0.335984
Bank of Bahrain & Kuwait B.S.C.	0.446153	0.312741	0.39054	0.482726	0.347132	0.264951	0.4608	0.546932	0.758489	0.13856	0.235506
Societe Generale	0.444185	0.657579	0.71016	0.675898	0.465205	0.42737	0.731176	0.627899	0.440212	0.120915	0.205516
Bank of Nova Scotia	0.829788	0.685874	0.99105	1	1	1	1	1	1	0.105772	0.179778

(Contd...)

(1)	(2)	(3)	(4)	(5)	(6)	(7)	(8)	(9)	(10)	(11)	(12)
Mizuho Corporate Bank Ltd.	0.387261	0.496931	0.40732	0.405369	0.544266	0.460583	0.611198	0.780875	0.737449	0.137122	0.233063
Jpmorgan Chase Bank National Association	0.510944	1	1	1	1	1	1	1	1	0.153695	0.261231
The Bank of Tokyo-Mitsubishi Ufj Ltd.	0.376177	0.378058	0.52978	0.870217	1	0.832543	0.78918	0.710989	0.609179	0.207024	0.351872
Bnp Paribas	0.397939	0.383074	0.43063	0.461858	0.56702	0.686846	0.586708	0.487158	0.384519	0.099625	0.16933
Barclays Bank Plc	0.924256	1	0.34621	0.276446	0.793648	0.741457	0.550816	0.445036	0.556657	0.238968	0.406166
Bank of America N.T. and S.A.	0.730213	0.80476	0.72737	0.590304	0.682276	1	0.928381	0.576428	0.556657	0.146514	0.249026
American Express Banking Corp.	0.274513	0.278893	0.17641		0.075409	0.073703	0.178001	0.035034	0.028671	0.094956	0.161394
Dbs Bank Ltd.	0.656733	0.960401	1	1	0.699706	0.926305	0.670216	0.636975	0.650479	0.15565	0.264554
The Royal Bank of Scotl and N.V.	0.443573	0.564153	0.4355	0.337848	0.449249	0.498561	0.355557	0.279557	0.231265	0.100586	0.170963
Deutsche Bank Ag	0.444642	0.599861	0.43488	0.348107	0.406175	0.521188	0.414946	0.390221	0.317131	0.081119	0.137876
Hongkong and Shanghai Banking Corpn. Ltd.	0.598384	0.575639	0.42717	0.331563	0.608643	0.673792	0.511725	0.401609	0.362086	0.115427	0.196188
Citibank N.A	0.531656	0.653997	0.5094	0.450569	0.609412	0.744959	0.54452	0.447419	0.402376	0.103402	0.175749
Standard Chartered Bank	0.626235	0.526418	0.51658	0.315801	0.38912	0.488652	0.45191	0.407765	0.369225	0.089854	0.152723
Ufj Bank Ltd.	1									0	0

Standard Deviation and Co-oefficient of Variation of Foreign banks efficiency for the period 2005-2013

Decision Making Units [DMUs]	2005 Efficiency (theta)	2006 Efficiency (theta)	2007 Efficiency (theta)	2008 Efficiency (theta)	2009 Efficiency (theta)	2010 Efficiency (theta)	2011 Efficiency (theta)	2012 Efficiency (theta)	2013 Efficiency (theta)	Standard Deviation	Coefficient of Variation
(1)	(2)	(3)	(4)	(5)	(6)	(7)	(8)	(9)	(10)	(11)	(12)
Ratnakar Bank Ltd.		0.483828	0.33539	0.520028	0.608626	0.729549	0.214366	0.871684	0.879328	0.224786039	0.387329
Development Credit Bank Ltd.	0.344104	0.294892	0.32979	0.324174	0.308962	0.274309	0.20129	0.558206	0.904712	0.20215305	0.513885
The Dhanalakshmi Bank Ltd.		0.416443	0.37076	0.401939	0.44151	0.350544	0.212514	0.318001	0.482084	0.077938808	0.208268
Catholic Syrian Bank Ltd.	0.564635	0.389482	0.37627	0.388064	0.35221	0.366799	0.212996	0.414913	0.513212	0.093847344	0.236023
Lakshmi Vilas Bank Ltd.	0.564543	0.520556	0.51517	0.525013	0.512109	0.601821	0.387781	0.62241	0.686381	0.079702831	0.145332
Tamilnad Mercantile Bank Ltd.	0.815509	0.697085	0.57847	0.557222	0.569901	0.64809	0.40569	0.726358	0.876292	0.135979337	0.208323
City Union Bank Limited	1	0.778414	0.6237	0.675954	0.691153	0.785735	0.50353	0.7925	0.828976	0.132383156	0.178362
South Indian Bank Ltd.	0.647812	0.541241	1	0.628124	0.601765	0.662996		0.682953	0.757452	0.130839159	0.189542
Karnataka Bank Ltd	0.781515	0.257944	0.66891	0.61731	0.65902	0.630609	0.348803	0.63037	0.735052	0.16368249	0.276411
Karur Vysya Bank Ltd.	0.669693	0.610307	0.58759	0.624984	0.662583	0.656018	0.422527	0.729896	0.7348	0.087840268	0.138734
Yes Bank Ltd.	0.247212	1	1	0.890674	0.75572	0.755618	0.48022	1	1	0.253734977	0.320308
Punjab And Sind Bank	0.373821	0.431543	0.41239	0.476713	0.54262	0.670684	0.404883	0.632407	0.825	0.142935763	0.269687
Ing Vysya Bank Ltd.	0.44553	0.376375	0.31152	0.330792	0.337661	0.340942	0.212092	0.404478	0.512637	0.080752606	0.222118
Jammu & Kashmir Bank Ltd.	0.820929	0.791668	0.63521	0.723731	0.735649	0.655204	0.395193	0.706752	0.813019	0.123258591	0.176719
Federal Bank Ltd.		0.634678	0.44788	0.645081	0.677274	0.66701	0.395193	0.659468	0.677821	0.105102199	0.17501
State Bank of Mysore	0.438461	0.425921	0.39523	0.485078	0.568226	0.602665	0.359139	0.553497	0.685882	0.101599656	0.202565
Dena Bank	0.479091	0.501111	0.42874	0.493256	0.522449	0.578194	0.378762	0.671884	0.867464	0.138147815	0.25266
Indusind Bank Ltd.	1	0.599935	0.6801	0.674416	0.522465	0.550147	0.287477	0.695448	0.736379	0.180277847	0.282352
State Bank of Travancore	0.688671	0.582193	0.51578	0.587958	0.60068	0.561745	0.38349	0.632079	0.76194	0.100111078	0.169535
Vijaya Bank	0.681392	0.592719	0.53673	0.662414	0.657141	0.588043	0.329335	0.748018	0.836328	0.13458453	0.215063

(Contd…)

(1)	(2)	(3)	(4)	(5)	(6)	(7)	(8)	(9)	(10)	(11)	(12)
State Bank of Bikaner and Jaipur	0.48431	0.413937	0.39157	0.487259	0.562771	0.545264	0.305247	0.538795	0.60511	0.090056756	0.187001
Bank of Maharashtra	0.561862	0.600053	0.45055	0.4917	0.517555	0.534893	0.273287	0.493563	0.67536	0.104872347	0.205238
Kotak Mahindra Bank Ltd.	1	0.319178	0.83568	0.61415	0.604491	0.603	0.217869	0.93732	0.979952	0.267194764	0.393471
State Bank of Patiala	0.767465	0.64421	0.57406	0.728328	0.848651	0.802692	0.393476	0.694213	0.758224	0.130586973	0.189216
Corporation Bank	0.583765	0.563946	0.51777	0.605896	0.67373	0.674162	0.44945	0.823044	0.965628	0.149869442	0.230277
State Bank of Hyderabad	0.594206	0.539744	0.51477	0.658849	0.710501	0.781238	0.419196	0.693096	0.746691	0.112995977	0.17973
Idbi Bank Limited	1	1	1	1	1	1	0.664212	1	1	0.105527987	0.109618
United Bank of India	0.523924	0.464134	0.4478	0.470517	0.512687	0.589036	0.394191	0.64806	0.77112	0.109889878	0.205126
Andhra Bank	0.481797	0.500239	0.44065	0.553993	0.565601	0.575761	0.392809	0.709782	0.799776	0.1211452	0.217175
Indian Bank	0.539382	0.498921	0.41664	0.445693	0.500144	0.543529	0.392514	0.631878	0.636978	0.081522012	0.159303
Oriental Bank of Commerce	0.779929	0.682761	0.6381	0.754923	0.734884	0.733495	0.515904	0.762979	0.832548	0.087723509	0.12268
Allahabad Bank	0.512734	0.582575	1	0.63712	0.610664	0.626419	0.380478	0.646959	0.738229	0.158859889	0.249293
UCO Bank	0.55898	0.748455	0.84407	0.594294	0.643529	0.725084	0.442534	0.795623	0.962452	0.149914781	0.213655
Syndicate Bank	0.508126	0.617718	0.74199	0.631121	0.616696	0.59428	0.362978	0.60724	0.677904	0.1012701	0.170105
Indian Overseas Bank	0.584096	0.558973	0.51808	0.62219	0.576156	0.499229	0.379963	0.63102	0.758763	0.097897468	0.171801
Union Bank of India	0.675628	0.464134	0.4478	0.69038	0.62291	0.639845	0.33643	0.588616	0.696688	0.12032426	0.209769
Central Bank of India	0.527785	0.635049	0.71509	0.538508	0.650802	0.652687	0.307424	0.569914	0.645931	0.112896493	0.193788
Axis Bank Limited	0.705881	0.568591	0.61188	0.579022	0.577539	0.525222	0.256115	0.565099	0.603991	0.115465871	0.208116
Bank of India	0.533615	0.660144	0.71761	0.557163	0.61272	0.585157	0.346654	0.643176	0.748447	0.112988257	0.187457
Federal Bank Ltd.	0.613777	0.634678	0.55788	0.606634	0.647315	0.649034	0.419275	0.736496	0.828781	0.106401148	0.168183
Bank of Baroda	0.555343	0.665478	0.73552	0.464241	0.48922	0.52759	0.381821	0.642508	0.740159	0.117985184	0.204131
ICICI Bank Limited	0.890292	1	1	1	0.959687	0.694262	0.317047	0.506481	0.562432	0.243260428	0.315913
Punjab National Bank	0.441198	0.652533	0.66915	0.482475	0.527161	0.541379	0.3425	0.581171	0.641626	0.101964227	0.18808
HDFC Bank Ltd.	0.591927	1	0.69535	0.626039	0.508473	0.434093	0.225031	0.470078	0.510977	0.199568295	0.354825

(Contd...)

(1)	(2)	(3)	(4)	(5)	(6)	(7)	(8)	(9)	(10)	(11)	(12)
State Bank of India	0.550283	0.755881	0.72014	0.462926	0.472378	0.419292	0.285649	0.455911	0.510977	0.137900378	0.267858
Bank of Punjab Limited											
Centurion Bank of Punjab Ltd.		0.257944	0.30697	0.31021						0.023910516	0.081968
Bank of Rajasthan Ltd.	0.470749	0.339166	0.39094							0.054123256	0.135211
Bharat Overseas Bank Ltd.		0.466881								0	0
Ganesh Bank of Kurundwad Ltd.		1								0	0
Lord Krishna Bank Ltd.		0.428713	0.40609							0.01131	0.027096
Sangli Bank Ltd.		0.353473	0.15786							0.0978055	0.38255
Sbi Commercial & International Bank Ltd.	0.572804	1	1	1	1	1	1			0.14948746	0.159203
United Western Bank Ltd.		0.430362								0	0
State Bank of Indore	0.596476	0.534573	0.50432							0.038353936	0.070358
State Bank of Saurashtra		0.610454	0.49213	0.472515						0.060930994	0.116052
Mean	0.617094	0.58435	0.580963	0.589981	0.610304	0.612464	0.371941	0.653874	0.744745		

Annexure - 5

Insurance Companies Operating in India Life Insurers*

Public Sector	Private Sector
1. Life Insurance Corporation of India	1. Aegon Religare Life Insurance Co. Ltd.
	2. Aviva Life Insurance Co. Ltd.
	3. Bajaj Allianz Life Insurance Co. Ltd.
	4. Bharti AXA Life Insurance Co. Ltd.
	5. Birla Sun Life Insurance Co. Ltd.
	6. Canara HSBC OBC Life Insurance Co.Ltd.
	7. DHFL Pramerica Life Insurance Co. Ltd.
	8. Edelweiss Tokio Life Insurance CompanyLtd.
	9. Exide Life Insurance Co. Ltd.
	10. Future Generali Life Insurance Co. Ltd.
	11. HDFC Standard Life Insurance Co. Ltd.
	12. ICICI Prudential Life Insurance Co. Ltd.
	13. IDBI Federal Life Insurance Co. Ltd.
	14. IndiaFirst Life Insurance Co. Ltd.
	15. Kotak Mahindra Old Mutual Life Insurance Co. Ltd.
	16. Max Life Insurance Co. Ltd.
	17. PNB MetLife India Insurance Co. Ltd.
	18. Reliance Life Insurance Co. Ltd..
	19. Sahara India Life Insurance Co. Ltd.
	20. SBI Life Insurance Co. Ltd.
	21. Shriram Life Insurance Co. Ltd.
	22. Star Union Dai-ichi Life Insurance Co. Ltd
	23. TATA AIA Life Insurance Co. Ltd.

Non-Life Insurers*

Public Sector	Private Sector
1. National Insurance Company Ltd.	1. Bajaj Allianz General Insurance Co. Ltd.
2. The New India Assurance Company Ltd.	2. Bharti AXA General Insurance Co. Ltd.
3. Oriental Insurance Company Ltd.,	3. Cholamandalam MS General Insurance Co.Ltd.
4. United India Insurance Company Ltd.	4. Future Generali India Insurance Co. Ltd.
	5. HDFC ERGO General Insurance Co. Ltd.
Specialised Insurers	6. ICICI Lombard General Insurance Co. Ltd.
5. Agriculture Insurance Co Ltd.	7. IFFCO Tokio General Insurance Co. Ltd.
6. Export Credit Guarantee Corporation Ltd.	8. L & T General Insurance Co. Ltd.
	9. Liberty Videocon General Insurance Co. Ltd.
	10. Magma HDI General Insurance Co. Ltd.
	11. Raheja QBE General Insurance Co. Ltd.
	12. Reliance General Insurance Co. Ltd.
	13. Royal Sundaram Alliance Insurance Co.Ltd.
	14. SBI General Insurance Co. Ltd.
	15. Shriram General Insurance Co. Ltd.
	16. TATA AIG General Insurance Co. Ltd.
	17. Universal Sompo General Insurance Co.Ltd.
	Standalone Health Insurers
	18. Apollo Munich Health Insurance Co. Ltd.
	19. Cigna TTK Health Insurance Co. Ltd.
	20. Max Bupa Health Insurance Co. Ltd.
	21. Religare Health Insurance Co. Ltd.
	22. Star Health and Allied Insurance Co. Ltd.

Re-Insurer*

General Insurance Corporation of India

*As on 31st March, 2014

Annexure - 6

Panel Unit Root Tests Notes Levin, Lin and Chu (2002)

Levin, Lin and Chu (2002) staretd panel unit root test by considering the following basic ADF specification:

$DY_{it} = \alpha Y_{it-1} + \Sigma^{pi}_{j=1}\ ß_{it} DY_{it-j} + X^{*}_{it}\ \delta + \varepsilon_{it}$ (1I)

where

DY_{it} = difference term of Y_{it}

$Y_{i\ t1}$ = Panel data

$\alpha = \rho - 1$

pi = the number of lag order for difference terms

X^{*}_{it} = exogenous variable in model

ε_{it}= the error term of equation

Define DY^{*}_{it} by taking DY_{it} and removing the autocorrelations and deterministic components from equation 1I as well as can be rewritten and give by equation 2I (equation 2I has been called that first set equation).

$DY^{*}_{it} = DY_{it-1} + \Sigma^{pi}_{j=1}\ ß^{*}_{it} DY_{it\,j} + X^{*}_{it}\ \delta^{*} + \varepsilon_{it}$ (2I)

And define the analogous $\acute{y}_{it-1}$ using the second set of coefficients and it has been presented give by equation 3I.

$\acute{y}_{it-1} = Y_{it-1} + \Sigma^{pi}_{j=1}\ ß^{*}_{it}\ DY_{it.j} - X^{*}_{it}$ (3I)

After that take both $DY^{*}_{i\ t}$ and $\acute{y}_{i\ t-1}$ dividing by the regression standard error (S_i) also can express more detail of these variable following that : (see both equation 4I and 5I).

$D\acute{Y}_{it} = (DY^{*}_{it}/S_i)$ (4I)

$\acute{Y}_{it} = (\acute{y}_{it-1}/S_i\ )$ (5I)

Where S_i are estimated standard error from each ADF in equation 1I and lastly an estimate of the coefficient may be obtained from equation 6I.

$D\acute{Y}_{it} = \alpha\acute{Y}_{it} + \eta_{it}$ (6I)

LLC(2002) showed that under the null hypothesis, a modified t-statistics for the resulting $\alpha^{\wedge}$ is asymptotical normally distributed as well as it has been presented give by equation 7I.

$$t^* = [t\text{-}(N\check{T})S_N\sigma^{\wedge\text{-}2}\ Se(\alpha^{\wedge})\mu mT^*]/[\sigma mT^*] \rightarrow N(0,1) \quad (7I)$$

where

t^* = the standard t-statistic for $\alpha^{\wedge} = 0$

$\sigma^{\wedge 2}$ = the estimated variance of the error term η

$Se(\alpha^{\wedge})$ = the standard error of $\alpha^{\wedge}$

$\check{T} = T\text{-}(\Sigma_i pi/N)\text{-}1$

LLC (2002) panel unit root test has null hypothesis and alternate hypothesis can be stated as below

H_0: panel data has unit root (assumes common unit root process)

H_1: panel data has not unit root

Im, Pesaran and Shin (2003)

Let Y_{it} be the observation on the ith cross-section unit at time t and suppose that it is generated according to following simple dynamic linear heterogeneous panel data model and can be written in equation 10I.

$$Y_{it} = (1\text{-}\ \phi_i) + \phi_i\ Y_{it\text{-}1} + \varepsilon_{it} \quad (10I)$$

where

i = 1,….,N are cross-section unit or series

t = 1,….,t are observed over periods

ε_{it} = error term of equation 10I

Y_{it} = panel data

And $\varepsilon_{it} = \gamma_i\ f_t + \varepsilon_{it}$ in which f_t is the unobserved common effect as well as ε_{it} is the individual-specific error. It is convenient to rewrite equation 10I to be equation 11I follow up:

$$DY_{it} = \alpha_i + \beta_i Y_{i,t\text{-}1} + \gamma_i\ f_t + \varepsilon_{it} \quad (11I)$$

where

DY_{it} = differential into Y_i

$\alpha_i = (1\text{-}\phi_i)$

$\beta_i = \text{-}\ (1\text{-}\phi_i)$

γ_i = coefficient of f_t

ε_{it} = error term of equation 11I

The null hypothesis or unit root hypothesis of interest, $\phi_i = 1$, can now be expressed as $H_0 : \beta_i = 0$ for all i and against the null hypothesis as $H_1 : \beta_i < 0$, $i=1,2,\ldots,N_1, \beta_i = 0$, $i= N_1+1, N_2+2,\ldots, N$. The average of the t-statistics for α_i received from equation 11I by estimated also this t-statistics can show below that: (see equation 12I).

$t^*_{NT} = \Sigma^N_{t=1} t_i \times_i (pi))/N$ (12I)

The properly standardized t^*_{NT} has an asymptotic standard normal distribution and also it was rewritten to be new t-statistics as well as can show below that : (see equation 131).

$W_{t^*NT} = \sqrt{n}\ [(t_{NT}\text{-}N^{-1}\Sigma^n_{t=1}\ E(t_{iT}(p_i)))]/\sqrt{(N^{-1}\Sigma^n_{i=1}\ var(t_{i\ x}(p_i)))}$ (131)

Where W_{t^*NT} is W-statistics has been used to test panel data based on Im, Pesaran and Shin (2003) techniques. IPS technique hypothesis can be stated as below

H_0: panel data has unit root (assumes individual unit root process)

H_1: panel data has no unit root

Fisher-Type Test using ADF and PP-Test (Maddala and Wu (1999) and Choi (2001))

Madala and Wu (1999) proposed the use of the Fisher (P_λ) test which is based on combining the P-values of the test-statistics for unit root in each cross-sectional unit. Let p_i are U[0,1] and independent, and $-2\log_e p_i$ has a X^2 distribution with 2N degree of freedom and can be written in equation 14I.

$P_\lambda = -2\ \Sigma^N_{\ i=1} \log_e p_i$ (14I)

where

P_λ = Fisher (P_λ) panel unit root test

N = all N cross-section

$-2\ \Sigma^N_{i=1}\ \log_e\ p_i$ = it has a X^2 distribution with 2N degree of freedom

In addition, Choi (2001) demonstrates that: (see more detail of Choi (2001) demonstrates that in equation 15I).

i=1

$Z = (1/\sqrt{N_{i=1}})[\Sigma^N_{i=1}\ \phi_i^{\ -1}(p_i)] \rightarrow N(0,1)$ (15I)

where

Z = Z-statistic panel data unit root test

N = all N cross-section in panel data

ϕ_i^{-1}= the inverse of the standard normal cumulative distribution funciton

p_i = it is the P-value from the ith test

Both Fisher (P_λ) Chi-quare panel unit root test and Choi Z-statistics panel data unit root test have non-stationary as null hypothesis as well as to show below that:

H_0: panel data has unit root (assumes individual unit root process)

H_1: panel data has no unit root

Panel co-integration

Pedroni's cointegration test

Pedroni cointegration test is an estimation of the following panel cointegration regression:

$y_{i,1} = \alpha_i + \rho_i t + \beta_{li} \times l_{i,1} + \ldots + \beta_{Mi} \times M_{i,t} + \varepsilon_{i,1}$

for t = 1..., T: i = 1 ...N; m = 1 ..., where

T refers to the number of observations over time which in this research is observations from the year 2005 till 2012.

N refers to the number of individual members in the panel which in this reserch is 8 countries

M refers to the number of regression variables which in this research are 4 BIPER, M2GDP.GDPP AND DOMCREDIT

The following steps are followed. First, after estimation the residuals $\hat{\varepsilon}_{i,t}$ are stored. Than the difference is taken for the original data series for each member, and the residuals are computed for the differenced regression $\Delta y_{i,t}=\sigma_{1i}\Delta x_{1i,t}+\sigma_{2i}\Delta x_{2i,t}+ \ldots + \sigma_{Mi}\Delta ix_{M,ti}+ \eta_{i,t}$. Third, we calculate$L^{\wedge 2}_{11i}$ as the long run variance of $\eta\hat{}_{i,t}$ using any kernel estimator. Fourth, using the residual $\varepsilon_{i,t}$ of the original cointegrating equation,the appropriate autoregressive model is estimated. For instance for the non-parametric statistics the follwoing is estimated $\hat{\varepsilon}_{i,t}=\psi\hat{}_i\hat{\varepsilon}_{i,t-1}+\hat{\kappa}_{i,t}$ and the residuals are used to compute the long run variance of $\hat{\kappa}_{i,t}$, denoted $\sigma^{\wedge 2}_i$. The term λ_i is computed as $\lambda\hat{}_i =1/2(\sigma^{\wedge 2}_i-\hat{s}^2_i)$, where s^2_i is just the simple variance of $\hat{\kappa}_{i,t}$. On the other hand, for the parametric statistics,$\hat{\varepsilon}_{i,t}=\psi_i\varepsilon_{i,t-1}+\Sigma^{Ki}_{k=1}\psi_{i,k}\Delta\hat{\varepsilon}_{i,t-k}+\mu^{\wedge *}_{i,t}$is estimated the residuals are used to compute the variance of $m^{\wedge *}_{i,t}$, denoted $\hat{s}^{*2}_i$. Using each of these steps, the following statistics are computed and then applied to the appropriate mean and variance adjustment terms reported in Pedroni (1999: 666).

Panel t-statistic (non parametric):

$$Z_{tN,T} = \left(\sigma^2_{N,T} \sum_{t=1}^{N}\sum_{t=1}^{T} L^{-2}_{11,} \bar{\varepsilon}^2_{i,t-1}\right)^{-1/2} \sum_{t=1}^{N}\sum_{t=1}^{T} L^{-2}_{11i} \left(\bar{\varepsilon}_{i-t-1}, \Delta\bar{\varepsilon}_{i,t} - \bar{\lambda}_i\right) \qquad (19)$$

Group t-statistic (parametric)

$$N^{-1/2}\, \bar{Z}^*_{tN,T} = N^{-1/2} \sum_{i=1}^{N}\left(\sum_{t=1}^{N} \bar{s}_i^{*2}\varepsilon_{i,t-1}^{*2}\right)^{-1/2} \sum_{t=1}^{T} \bar{\varepsilon}^*_{i,t-1}\, \Delta\bar{\varepsilon}^*_{i,t}$$

(One Way) Fixed Effects Model

In one way fixed effects using Dummy regression each country will be allowed to have its own intercept and will be included regressors in the equation

Consequently, this form of estimation is also known as *Least Squares Dummy Variables (LSDV).*

$$y_{it} = \sum_{i=1}^{N} a_{oi} D_{it} + a_1 x_{it} + u_{it}$$

Bibliography

Adams, M., J. Andersson, L. F. Andersson, and M. Lindmark, 2005, The Historical Relation between Banking, Insurance and Economic Growth in Sweden: 1830 to 1998,Working Paper SBE 2006/2, University of Wales Swansea.

Aliber, Robert Z. 1976,"Towards a Theory of International Banking. Federal Reserve Bank of San Fransisco", Economic Review Spring, 5-8.

Andrew Cornford (2006), "Statistics for International Trade in Banking Services: Requirements, Availability and Prospects" A Study of Financial Markets Center.

Anastasios D. Varias and Stella Sofianopoulou,"4th International Conference on Applied Operational Research, Proceedings", (2012) Vol. 4: 254-261.

Apostolos Gkoutzinis (2005), "International Trade in Banking Services and the Role of the WTO: Discussing the Legal Framework and Policy Objectives of the General Agreement on Trade in Services and the Current State of Play in the Doha Round of Trade Negotiations" International Lawyer, Volume 39. No. 4, Winter 2005.

Arena, M., 2008, Does Insurance Market Activity Promote Economic Growth? A Cross-Country Study for Industrialized and Developing Countries, Journal of Risk & Insurance, 75(4): 921-946.

Ball, Clifford A., and Adrian E. Tschoegl. 1982. The Decision to Establish a Foreign Bank Branch or subsidiary: An Application of Binary Classification Procedures. Journal of Financial and Quantitative Analysis 17 (3), 411-424.

Bank for International Settlements (2009), '79th Annual Report', 1 April 2008 to 31 March 2009.

Banker, R.D., Charnes, A., and Cooper, W.W. (1984), "Some Models for Estimating Technical and Scale Efficiencies in Data Envelopment Analysis", Management Science, Vol. 30, No. 9, pp. 1078-1092.

Barth, J., G. Caprio and R. Levine (2001): The Regulation and Supervision of Banks around the World: A New Database, World Bank Policy Research Working Paper No. 2588, Washington DC.

Berger A.N. (2007). International Comparisons of Banking Efficiency. Financial Markets, Institutions and Instruments, Vol. 16 (3), pp. 119-144.

Boussofiane, A., Dyson, R.G., and Thanassoulis, E. (1991), "Applied Data Envelopment Analysis", European Journal of Operational Research, Vol. 52, pp. 1-15.

Brealey, R.A., Kaplanis, E.C., 1996. The Determination of Foreign Banking Location. Journal of International Money and Finance 15(4), 577-597.

Carter, R L and Dickinson, G M (1992): Obstacles to the Liberalization of Trade in Insurance, Thames Essay No.58, Hemel Hempstead: Harverster Wheatsheaf, See Appendix IV, 175-188.

Charnes, W.W. Cooper, B. Golany, L.Seiford and J.Stutz (1985): Foundation of Data Envelopment Analysis for Pareto-Koopmans Efficient Empirical Production. Journal of Econometrics (Netherlands), 30, 91-107.

Charnes, W.W.Cooper and E. Rhodes (1978): Measuring the Efficiency of Decision making Units. European Journal of Operational Research, 12, 429-444.

Charnes, W.W. Cooper and Q.L.Wei (1986): A Semi-infinite Multicriteria Programming Approach to Data Envelopment Analysis with Infinitely many Decision-making Units. The University of Texas at Austin, Center for Cybernetic Studies, Report CCS 551 (1986).

Charnes, W.W.Cooper, Q.L.Wei and Z.M. Huang (1989): Cone Ratio Data Envelopment Analysis and Multi-objective Programming. International Journal of Systems Science, 20, 1099-1118.

Chen, S-H., Liao, C.C.,: Are Foreign Banks more Profitable than Domestic Banks? Home- and Host-country Effects of Banking Market Structure, Governance, and Supervision. Journal of Banking and Finance 35(4) (2011), 819-839.

Claessens, Stijn, and Neeltje Van Horen, (2013), "Impact of Foreign Banks," The Journal of Financial Perspectives, Vol. 1, No. 1, 1-14.

Contador, C.R. and Ferraz, C.B. (2007). Insurance and Economic Growth: Some International Evidences. RBRSi, Rio de Janeiro, Brazil, 1:1, 41-78.

Cull, Robert, and Maria Soledad Martinez Peria, (2010), "Foreign Bank Participation in Developing Countries: What Do We Know about the Drivers and Consequences of This Phenomenon?" World Bank Policy Research Working Paper WPS 5398 (Washington).

Das, U.S. (2007) Insurance Services: Development and Liberalization – Some Observations, Monetary and Financial Systems Department, Washington D.C.: IMF.

Devarakonda S. (2016). Insurance Penetration and Economic Growth in India. FIIB Business Review. 2016; 5(3): 3-12. doi:10.1177/2455265820160301

Devarakonda, Srijanani & Munipalle, Usha. (2017). Relationship between Economic Growth and the Banking and Insurance Trade Performance for Select Asian Countries – Panel Co-Integration Model. AIMS International Journal of Management. 11. 117. 10.26573/2017.11.2.3.

Drogendijk, R. and Hadjikhani, A. (2008), "Internationalisation of Bank Enterprises in New Emerging Markets: The Case of Penetration and Expansion into Eastern European Countries", International Journal Business and Emerging Markets, 1(1), pp. 80-104.

Dekker D and Post T (2001), "A Quasi-concave DEA model with an Application for Bank Branch Performance Evaluation". European Journal of Operational Research 132: 296-311. Engwall, L. 1994.

Dwivedi A.K. & Charyulu D.K., (2011). Efficiency of Indian Banking Industry in the Post Reform Era. Indian Instute of Management, Ahmedabad, India. W.P. No. 2011-03-01

Enz, R (2000): The S-curve Relation between per-capita Income and Insurance Penetration, Geneva Papers on Risk and Insurance, 25 (3): 396-406.

Fre, R., and Primont, D. (1993), "Measuring the Efficiency of Multi-Unit Banking", Journal of Banking and Finance, Vol. 17, pp. 539-544.

FICCI Survey on the Status of the Indian Banking Industry – Progress and Agenda Ahead.

Focarelli, D., Pozzolo, A.F., 2005. Where do Banks expand abroad? An Empirical Analysis. Journal of Business 78(6), 2435-2464.

Goldberg, L.G., and Denise Johnson. 1990. "The Determinants of US Banking Activity Abroad". Journal of International Money and Finance 9, 123-137.

Gootilz, B and Mattoo, A. (2009) Services in Doha: whats on the Table?, Policy Research Working Paper 4903 (April), World Bank.

Grigorian A David and Manole Vlad," Determinants of Commercial Bank Performance in Transition: An Application of Data Envelopment Analysis", IMF Working paper –WP/02/126.

Han.L., Li.D., Moshirian, F and Tian.Y. (2010) "Insurance Development and Economic Growth", The Geneva Papers on Risk and Insurance – Issues and Practice, 35(2): 183-199.

Handbook on Indian Insurance Statistics 2010-11, IRDA.

Haiss, P., and K. Sümegi, 2008, The Relationship of Insurance and Economic Growth in Europe: A Theoretical and Empirical Analysis, Emprica, 35(4): 405-431.

International Monetary Fund (IMF), 2012, "The IMF's Financial Surveillance Strategy; Foreign Bank Participation in Developing Countries: What Do We Know about the Drivers and Consequences of This Phenomenon? IMF Policy Paper (Washington).

III (2011) Insurance Industry Employment Trends: 1990-2011 (October). Available at http://www.iii.org/presentations/ insurance-industry-employment-trends-1990-2011.html

Jean Grey (1981). The Multinational Bank: A Financial MNC? Journal of Banking and Finance, Vol. 5, issue 1, March 1981, Pages 33-63.

Jones, G. (Ed.). (1992). Multinational and International Banking. Edward Elgar Publishing Ltd.

Kapopoulos, P. and Lazaretou, S. (1997) Monetary Relations, International Banking and finance, eds. Papazizi, Athens.

Khoury, S.J., 1979. International Banking: A Special Look at Foreign Banks in the US. Journal of International Business Studies 10(3), 36-52.

King, R.G. and R. Levine (1993): Finance and Growth: Schumpeter might be Right, Quarterly Journal of Economics 108, 717-37.

Kugler, M., and R. Ofoghi, (2005), Does Insurance Promote Economic Growth? Evidence from the UK, Working paper, University of Southampton.

Lambkin, M. and Muzellec, L. (2008) Rebranding in the Banking Industry following Mergers and Acquisitions, International Journal of Bank Marketing, 26(5), pp. 328-352.

Lang, G., & Welzel, P. (1996). Efficiency and Technical Progress in Banking: Empirical Results for a Panel of German Cooperative Banks. *Journal of Banking and Finance,* 20: 1003-23.

Levine, R. and S. Zervos (1998): Stock Markets, Banks and Economic Growth, American Economic Review 88, pages 537-58.

Liadaki A and Gaganis C (2010). Efficiency and Stock Performance of EU Banks: Is There a Relationship? The International Journal of Management Science 38: 254-259.

Maria Borga (2006), "Improving Insurance, Wholesale, Retail and Financial Services Measures in FATS and Cross-border Trade" 7th OECD International Trade Statistics Expert Meeting 11-14 September 2006.

Marin Opriescu & Alina Manta (2011), Annals of University of Craiova - Economic Sciences Series, 2011, Vol. 4, issue 39, pages 229-242.

McCauley, R., & Zukunft, J. (2008). Asian Banks and the International Interbank Market. BIS Quarterly Review, 67-79.

McKinsey & Co (2004), "Mergers & Acquisitions in the Indian Banking Sector". McKinsey & Co (2005), " Indian Banking 2010: Towards a High Performing Sector".

Michael Francis (2002), "Trade in Banking Services and the Implementation of Monetary Policy". A Paper Presented at the New Zealand Economics Association, 26-28 June 2002.

Mitra, Arup (2008), Tertiary Sector Growth: Issues and Facts", *Artha Beekshan,* Vol. 16, No. 4, March.

Mohan, Rakesh (2007), India's Financial Sector Reforms – Fostering Growth while Containing Risk, Address at Yale University, New Haven, 3rd December 2007.

MSITS (2002), "Manual on Statistics on International Trade in Services" United Nations.

Qian, L., Delios, A., 2008. Internalization and Experience: Japanese Banks' International Expansion, 1980-1998. Journal of International Business Studies 39(2), 231-248.

Rajan, R.G. and L. Zingales (2003), 'Saving Capitalism from Capitalists, Crown Business', New York.

Ram, R., 1999, Financial Development and Economic Growth: Additional Evidence, Journal of Development Studies, 35(4), pages 164-174.

Rangan, Nanda, Richard Grabowski, Hassan Y. Aly, and Carl Pasurka (1988)," The Technical Efficiency of U.S Banks," Economics Letters Vol. 28, No. 2, pp. 169-75.

Reddy, Y. V (2008), 'Global Financial Turbulence and Financial Sector in India: A Practitioner's Perspective', Address at the Meeting of the Task Force on Financial Markets Regulation Organized by the Initiative for Policy Dialogue at Manchester, United Kingdom, on July 1, 2008.

Robert, McCauley, McGuire, Partick & Von Peter, Goetz, (2012) :After the Global Financial Crisis: From International to Multinational Banking? 2012. Journal of Economics and Business, Vol. 64, No. 1.

Robert Z Aliber, International Banking – a Survey (1984), Journal of Money, Credit and Banking Vol. 16, No. 4, Part 2: Bank Market Studies (Nov., 1984), pp. 661-678.

Sandeep Joshi and Manmeet Singh Rai, "Redefining the 'Doctrine of Insurable Interest' for Life Insurance – The New Dimensions!", Executive Chartered Secretary, October, 2006, p. 965.

Sastry, D V S (2011): Life Insurance Penetration in India, Journal of Social and Economic Policy, Vol. 8, No. 2, 207-215.

Seema Joshi (2008), Growth and Structure of Tertiary Sector in Developing Economies", Academic Foundation, Delhi, 2008.

Seth, R., Nolle, D.E., Mohanty, S.K., 1998. Do Banks Follow their Customers abroad? Financial Markets, Institutions and Instruments 7(4), 1-25.

Sherman, H.David, and Franklin gold, "Bank Branch Operating Efficiency: Evaluation with Data Envelopment Analysis," Journal of Banking and Finance (June 1985). pp. 297-315.

Sinha, R K, Nizamuddin M M and Alam, I (2012), An Investigation of Insurance Penetration and Density of India by Geography, 16th Annual Conference of Asia-Pacific Risk and Insurance Association (APRIA), July 2012, Seoul, South Korea.

Siriopoulos, C., Tziogkidis, P. (2009). How do Greek Banking Institutions React after Significant events? – A DEA Approach (Forthcoming in Omega).

Subhass, C. Ray & Abhiman Das (2010): Distribution of Cost and Profit efficiency: Evidence from Indian Banking, European Journal of Operational Research, 201, pp. 297-307.

Sufian, F. (2010). Modelling Banking Sector Efficiency: A DEA and Time Series Approach. ISSN 1392-1258. Ekonomika 2010 Vol. 89(2).

Sufian, F. (2007). Mergers and Acquisitions in the Malaysian Banking Industry: Technical and Scale Efficiency Effects. International Journal Financial Services Management, Vol. 2 (4), pp. 305-326.

Sufian, F. & Abdul Majid, M.Z. (2007). "Singapore Banking Efficiency and its relation to Stock Returns": A DEA Window Analysis Approach. *International Journal of Business Studies*, 15(1): 83-106.

Sümegi, K., and P. Haiss, 2008, The Relationship between Insurance and Economic Growth: Review and Agenda. The Icfai Journal of Risk and Insurance, 1 (2): 32-56.

Thrall, R.M, "Overview and Recent Developments in DEA: The Mathematical Programming Approach," IC Institute, Conference Proceedings, University of Texas, Austin, 1989.

Tschoegl, Adrian E. 1987. International Retail Banking as a Strategy: An Assessment. Journal of International Business Studies 19 (2), 67-88.

Ursacki, T., Vertinsky, I., (1992). Choice of Entry, Timing and Scale by Foreign Banks in Japan and Korea. Journal of Banking and Finance 16(2), 405-421.

Usha, M, "Growth of Services Sector in India: Some issues for Consideration", SEDME, pp. 85-98.

United Nations Conference on Trade and Development, 1964, Proceedings of the United Nations Conference on Trade and Development, First Session, Volume 1, Final Act and Report (Geneva: United Nations), pp. 55.

United Nations Conference on Trade and Development, 1972, Handbook of International Trade and Development Statistics (New York: United Nations).

United Nations Conference on Trade and Development, 1988, Trade and Development Report 1988: Services in the World Economy (Geneva: United Nations), pp. 245-256.

United Nations Conference on Trade and Development, 1990, Handbook of International Trade and Development Statistics (New York: United Nations).

United Nations Conference on Trade and Development, 1991, Handbook of International Trade and Development Statistics (New York: United Nations).

United Nations Conference on Trade and Development, 1984, Insurance in the Context of Services and the Development Process, TD/B/1014 (Geneva: United Nations).

Venkatesh. M (2013), "A Study of Trend Analysis in the Insurance Sector in India", The International Journal of Engineering and Science (IJES), Volume 2, Issue 6, Pages 01-05.

Varma, J.R. (1996), "Financial Sector Reforms: The Unfinished Agenda", Paper Presented at the Seminar on Economic Reforms: The Next Step at Rajiv Gandhi Institute for Contemporary Studies, New Delhi, October 2-4, 1996.

Ward, D., and R. Zurbruegg, 2000, Does Insurance Promote Economic Growth? Evidence from OECD Countries, The Journal of Risk and Insurance, 67(4), pages 489-506.

Williams, B., (1997), "Positive theories of Multinational Banking: Eclectic Theory versus Internalization Theory". Journal of Economic Surveys 11(1), pages 71-100.

Zheng W, Liu, Y and Yiting, D: "New Paradigm for International Insurance Comparison: with an Application to Comparison of Seven Insurance Markets.

Index

❐ ❐ ❐ ❐ ❐